THE NEW SUPERPOWERS

THE NEW

Germany, Japan, the U.S

St. Martin's Press
NEW YORK

SUPERPOWERS
and the New World Order

Jeffrey T. Bergner

Design by Glen M. Edelstein

Library of Congress Cataloging-in-Publication Data

Bergner, Jeffrey T.
    The new superpowers : Germany, Japan, the U.S., and the new world order.
       p. cm.
    "A Thomas Dunne book."
    Includes index.
    ISBN 0-312-06425-X
    1. World politics—1989–   2. Germany—Foreign relations. 3. Japan—Foreign relations. 4. United States—Foreign relations. 5. Security, International. I. Title.
    D860.B47 1991   327'.09'049—dc20   91-18236

First Edition: September 1991
10 9 8 7 6 5 4 3 2 1

For Susan

Whoever thinks the future is going to be easier than the past is certainly mad.

George Kennan

CONTENTS

PART 1
THE REUNIFICATION OF GERMANY

PART 2
JAPAN—THE SUN RISES AGAIN

CONCLUSION.   THE YEAR 2000: GERMANY,
                         JAPAN, AND AMERICA

Foreword
By
Senator Richard G. Lugar

AS DR. JEFFREY BERGNER POINTS OUT in his book, *The New Superpowers*, the twentieth century began with three emerging powers: the United States, Germany, and Japan. The twenty-first will open with much the same situation.

Yet the much-heralded permanent five nations of the United Nations Security Council, revived during the Gulf War, do not include Germany *or* Japan. Indeed, they include the major nations which defeated Germany and Japan and demanded their unconditional surrender midway through the twentieth century.

The past decade has witnessed alarmist publications warning that Germany and Japan were already economic superpowers in a world in which economic competition was king. The United States and the Soviet Union were described as cold warriors who were rapidly exhausting themselves and their physical resources while Germany and Japan, having discovered where real strength resides, had sprinted past the muscle-bound entries.

Suddenly, Desert Storm appeared to reshuffle the deck. The

United States seemed to be a superpower all by itself. The Soviet Union was collapsing economically and disintegrating politically, while Germany and Japan remained preoccupied with internal debates on their respective roles in the world.

In the wake of Iraq's invasion of Kuwait on August 2, 1990, President Bush was able to draw upon his vast contacts and experiences as a vice-presidential visitor to eighty countries, as former ambassador to the United Nations, as former U.S. envoy to China, and as former director of the Central Intelligence Agency, to organize a multinational coalition to reverse Iraq's aggression. Great Britain rallied to assist the United States immediately. Prime Minister Thatcher even counseled President Bush not "to go wobbly" when he described the problems the coalition was encountering. France sent troops to the region. The Soviet Union supported U.S. diplomatic initiatives to an unprecedented extent. Even China, long an advocate of third-world nations' prerogatives against the West, abstained from negative votes in the U.N. Security Council and thus allowed that body to act decisively for the first time in four decades.

But the responses from Germany and Japan were disappointing. Ultimately the two countries paid roughly $9 billion and $13 billion respectively, to fulfill their pledges of support for the coalition. The money came only after heavy solicitation by President Bush and members of his cabinet.

For both countries, Desert Storm came at an inconvenient moment. The Germans asked for understanding that the monumental task of unification had taxed their political and financial powers fully. The Germans were trying to arrange the departure of 380,000 Soviet troops, to integrate the former German Democratic Republic's armed forces into the new Bundeswehr, and to cope with massive economic dislocation in eastern Germany. Though the time in which Germans will seriously debate sending military forces beyond their borders will come, that time was clearly not at hand during Desert Storm.

For its part, the Japanese debate on the use of military force is even further in the future. Prime Minister Kaifu led a courageous debate in the Japanese diet to provide $13 billion for a cause that many Japanese did not understand. Although the need for Japan to play a clearer role in the world is apparent, Desert Storm left a sense of disquiet both in Japan and among Japan's friends. Japan's long-time protector, the United States, itself seemed to be urging Japan to venture back into the world and to make the difficult choices that are required of a world power.

The timeliness and importance of Jeff Bergner's examination of the superpowers is obvious. The maintenance of world peace will depend upon the solidarity of U.S.-German and U.S.-Japanese friendship, partnership, cooperation, and alliance. For every sudden critic who discovers the many ways that Germany and Japan are allegedly unfaithful in trade practices or in fulfilling international political and military obligations, there must be even more well-informed observers who view clearly the century ahead. Positive relationships between the major powers will be essential to preserve a world which is hospitable to the growth of democratic institutions and liberal economic systems.

Jeff Bergner served as chief of staff of the Senate Committee on Foreign Relations during the first year of my chairmanship in 1985. Even then, I was deeply impressed with his scholarship and with his legion of friends in the countries in which we traveled. In both public and private life, he has demonstrated an ability to seize the future and persuade a large number of his countrymen to understand our opportunities, risks, and obligations.

I am deeply pleased that he has chosen to share some of his best insights and conclusions in this book. His boldness and wisdom are combined in equal measure here. He illustrates why we must act upon the possibilities to maintain strong friendships with Germany and Japan. He also offers a host of warnings about the dangers if we do not succeed. He has made a remarkable contribution to the future of sound American foreign policy.

Preface

AS THE TWENTIETH CENTURY DAWNED, three energetic, newly industrialized nations rose to contest the dominance of the British Empire. These nations, whose peculiar virtues were well suited to the industrial age, were Germany, Japan, and the United States. After two world wars, global colonization and decolonization, and a protracted Russian experiment with Marxism, the twentieth century will end much as it began. Once again, relations between Germany, Japan, and the United States will be decisive for the entire world.

This is not easy to comprehend. For Americans coming of age during the last forty years, the bipolar world of U.S.–Soviet conflict seemed to have the permanence of a law of nature. Geopolitically, other nations counted only as objects of competition between the two great superpowers; none by itself could tip the balance of power. Old habits of thought die hard. Some Americans still express concern, for example, that Germany might become "neutral." Neutral as between what and what? The phrase "neutral Germany" conveys the image of a Germany shuttling between East and West, between the free, democratic West and the not yet free, not democratic East—caught, as it were, between the conflicting values, policies, and interests of two larger powers. Yet Germany will itself soon be a stronger power than the Soviet Union. Germany may shuttle between East and West, as has been its historical tendency, but it will not do so as a ''neutral'' between two permanent antagonists.[1] It will do so as a power whose own dominant interests drive the Soviet response, not vice versa.

So, too, with Japan. Politicians and observers debate whether Japan should take further steps to bring its successful economy into line with the norms of balanced trade and open markets. Is Japan's economic strength a threat to the United States? What is missed here is that we are soon to confront a Japan that is not only economically dominant, but also politically and militarily dominant in its region. The implications of Japan for America in the 1990s do not center around whether Japan owns more or less Iowa farmland but whether, and in what degree, the United States will be able to exercise its influence for democracy and universality in the Western Pacific. Japan's economy is already larger than the Soviet Union's; a decade from now it will dwarf the Soviet economy.

To date, both Germany and Japan have appeared reluctant, even diffident, about exercising their growing power. They have seemed self-absorbed, unable to muster even a small contingent of men and arms to join the United Nations coalition against Iraq. But is this really so strange? Neither nation had an active geopolitical interest in the Persian Gulf. Had the coalition been formed, say, to deal with aggression in Poland or the Balkans, or in Korea or on the Chinese mainland, one might have predicted a greater level of interest.

Further, in fairness it should be recalled that despite their economic strength and their forty years of democracy, neither Germany nor Japan is a member of the United Nations Security Council. Perhaps, too, it should be recalled that the permanent members of the U.N. Security Council were drawn precisely from the allies who defeated Germany and Japan. The anomaly of the second and third strongest economic powers in the world being absent from the Security Council will have to be addressed before one can expect full enthusiasm from these nations to enforce the decisions of the U.N.

At the present time, both Germany and Japan *are* self-absorbed. Neither yet knows how to express its growing strength in world affairs. But unless one postulates the emergence of something totally new in world history—nations that make no effort to translate their economic success into the service of political ideals—there is no reason to doubt the growth of German and Japanese political influence. In Europe, Germany's growing strength means that it will inevitably play a larger role, if only because its neighbors will demand to know its deepest intentions with great exactitude. In the Pacific, Japan's power will also assume new dimensions, especially as long as the United States continues to press Japan to rearm for reasons that are now inexplicable.

We are sleepwalking if we think that the Soviet military threat can recede and that no further consequences will follow. Those who argue the exclusive preeminence of economic power are like citizens who are daily protected by unseen police forces, and who thereby see no role for force in life. Yet economies exist within the context of security systems and in the service of political ideals. Economies can propel these systems to success or doom them to failure; they are also shaped by them in very fundamental ways.

The view that the world is heading toward multipolar mercantilism with regional economic power centers including not only the United States, the Soviet Union, Germany, and Japan, but also China, India, and perhaps Brazil, is misleading. China will not become a major world power in the foreseeable future, nor will India, Brazil, or a host of the other candidates for newly emerging world powers play much of a role. By the year 2000 there will be three great powers. These three will account for one-half of all the economic activity in the entire world. Because of its nuclear capability, the Soviet Union will also count as half of a superpower. And unlike the past forty years, when the American share of the world economy gradually declined from its artificial postwar high, the combined portion that these three nations produce will not shrink over the coming decade; if anything, it will grow.

The world is *not* becoming more and more equal in all of its component parts. The rich and strong are getting richer and stronger. There is even some evidence that the poorest countries are getting poorer, and that the gap between rich and poor is growing.[2] What is occurring is a growing equality at the the top, and it is yet to be seen how this shift will translate itself into relations with the third world, the one area where even end-of-history devotees acknowledge there is still plenty of history to be made.

What will relations among the three great powers be like a decade hence? Are we really to suppose—or worse yet, to assume—that Germany and Japan will share every single ideal that their dominant political parties have espoused during the forty-five years of their reemergence as great powers? Is the end of history at hand, in which it remains but to bring the democratic ideal to the backward, developing nations still outside its sway? It would be comforting to think so.

But we will have to look again at actively managing the political and security relations—as well as the economic relations—among the leading nations of what we now call the alliance of the West. Indeed, it is no longer clear what "the West" means. In the absence of an aggressive Soviet military and ideological threat, "the West" has ceased to be a meaningful term. Today's geopolitical fault lines require a new language.

Once again, the great initiatives to influence the world for good or ill are shifting. No one can reasonably fault how the Federal Republic of Germany and Japan have functioned during the forty-five years of their tutelage. How they will function on their own, as it were, remains to be seen. Even in America, which has the most stable history of all the leading powers, a relative change in economic strength has not fully played itself out in our own politics. Intense foreign competition and the decline of significant American industries has prompted considerable national soul-searching and occasional bursts of demagoguery. We are likely to see more of this in the future.

America's tendency is to savor victory and to demobilize the forces that brought it about. Americans do not wish to be reminded that new problems arise out of the solutions to yesterday's problems. This has happened before. Great differences between the United States and the Soviet Union were muted and subsumed in the face of the common threat presented by Hitler's Germany. When that threat was overcome, the same differences surfaced with a vengeance.

There are no fundamental ideological differences that now divide the governments of the three powers. Yet we are on the verge of a new world in which a common enemy has left the field. Intrinsic differences of tradition and location are already arising in places where they have been long suppressed. History is full of surprises. In 1904–1905, Japan defeated Russia militarily. The surprise of a similar contemporary event could not be greater now than it was then for an entire continent of Europeans. Yet it happened. We are in the midst of a period of radical transformation. It is difficult to anticipate the full consequences of the changes that are now occurring as a result of the decline of the Soviet Union, the reunification of Germany, and the growth of German and Japanese power.

There is very little guidance to be gained from the years of the bipolar conflict between the United States and the Soviet Union. More and more, this period appears as a unique interlude in the history of world affairs. It is striking how dated even the most thoughtful political treatises written prior to the opening of the Berlin Wall in November 1989 now seem. Under these circumstances, there is no choice but to set aside the conventional wisdom by which we have oriented ourselves for four decades and to think anew.

Acknowledgments

I AM GRATEFUL TO MANY PEOPLE for their assistance in completing this book. Michael Kilian and Gerry Warburg were early sources of inspiration for this project and I benefited from their insights. Maura Pierce provided many useful suggestions as to substance and style, as well as considerable help in compiling the manuscript. Douglas Bergner offered helpful criticisms and suggestions along the way. My son Jason Bergner prepared many of the charts and the bibliography.

I am especially grateful to my family—my wife Susan, Amanda, Jason, Jessica, and Jonathan—for their patience, understanding, and encouragement throughout the process of writing this book. The same is true for my business partners Van Boyette and David Bockorny, who were unfailingly generous with the author's preoccupation during the past twelve months. I would also like to express my appreciation for the confidence and the assistance provided by St. Martin's Press, particularly Tom Dunne and David Meskill.

I am painfully aware of the book's many omissions and of the topics that are treated far too briefly to be fully persuasive. Some of the trees in the forest through which I have roamed have not been adequately identified and described. My intention, however, was not to write a political, economic, or military history of modern Germany or Japan; many valuable works already exist on each of the specific subjects touched upon in this book. My intention was to integrate a great deal of material in an attempt at reorientation in a time of rapid and fundamental change.

Finally, I should say that the reflections in this book have benefited from many off-the-record conversations with U.S. government officials and with German and Japanese friends alike. I hope that the views expressed here cause no pain to the latter; those who know me well will be aware of the positive spirit in which they are intended.

Introduction

The Transitory Bipolar World of 1945-1985

We have reason to be confident that the "correlation of forces" is shifting back in our favor.

—*George Shultz, 1985*

Initiatives in World History

AT ANY GIVEN TIME in a nation's history, only so many reasonable options are available. At times, these may be fundamental in nature; at other times, they may be so limited and constrained that policy seems almost foreordained.

So, too, at any given time, it is not open to every nation to affect world history in profound ways. For some nations, perhaps there is never a time to do so. For the others, at one moment or another the capacity to undertake decisive action may rest in the hands of just several, or even only one nation. Opportunities are not doled out democratically. Anyone who witnessed the 1988 presidential campaign in America must have realized that this was not a contest of bold and imaginative ideas. That was not the candidates' fault alone; opportunities to reshape the world were not readily available. Such an opportunity did not present itself until August of 1990, when Iraq invaded Kuwait—and then it was seized with full force.

It is of course possible for leaders to undertake irrational, spasmodic, or even suicidal policies. But outside the context of such actions, nations must play the roles—with as much vigor and creativity as possible—that both the accidents and the dynamics of history have assigned to them. And so there are great moments at which the initiative to act, or not to act, comes upon nations. How their leaders respond to the possibilities before them is the true test of leadership. There have undoubtedly been many potentially extraordinary leaders in world history who have simply not had ample scope to display their talents to the fullest. If it seems remarkable that great crises often produce great leaders, perhaps it is because there are usually leaders waiting "in reserve" to rise to such occasions.

The Post-World War II World

Looked at in this way, there have been a number of initiative points since World War II. Many of these moments, not surprisingly, fell to the United States to decide whether to act, and if so, how. The very manner by which the war came to an end provided the first such occasion. The U.S. decision to drop atomic weapons on Japan in 1945 was of great consequence, for it affected events and places far beyond Japan. The American decision to use atomic bombs not only avoided a major invasion and guaranteed a speedy end to the war; it also guaranteed that the Soviet Union would not occupy any significant portion of Japan in the postwar period.[1] It is easy to forget now the possibility that Japan could have shared the fate of Germany and Korea to be divided between Communist and noncommunist sectors. Soviet invasion plans for the island of Hokkaido were well underway when the blasts of Hiroshima and Nagasaki brought the war to a prompt conclusion. Who can contemplate the subsequent history of the region, including the Korean War, had Japan been divided in two?

The Truman administration's attitudes about Japan were shaped in part by its early and unhappy experience in dealing with the Soviet Union in Europe after Germany's surrender in May 1945.

Yet it took several more years before this experience reached its final postwar form in Europe itself. Repeated attempts were made to work with the Soviet Union in the cooperative way that had been sketched out by the allied powers as early as 1943.

It was not until 1948 that the fundamental outlines of postwar Europe as they would remain for the following forty years became clearly drawn. In the immediate postwar years, the United States had a variety of options available. These ranged from assertive nuclear blackmail to roll back Soviet forces behind the borders of the Soviet Union, to nonchalance and withdrawal in the face of yet another internal European wrangle. The middle course of "containment" arose out of a decision about Germany—namely, the American response to the Berlin blockade of 1948. In retrospect, this action set the terms for what would be the prevailing American doctrine over the following four decades, and thus it stands as a fundamental point in postwar history.

The world became accustomed after 1948 to a two-power confrontation in which the United States and the Soviet Union stared hostilely at one another across heavily defended borders. This world offered danger and challenge, but it was conceptually simple to understand. No third country could, by itself, tip the balance against either belligerent: the combination of self-sufficiency in vital resources, relative geographic insularity, political stability, and overwhelming nuclear power provided for each of the superpowers a degree of protection against the shifting alliances that have marked so much of world history.

It is instructive to remember that this world was the deliberate creation of no one. Rather, it emerged out of the ashes of World War II *despite* the conscious intentions of Western officials and as a result of the happenstance balance of conventional forces in Europe at the end of the war. It was the desire of the West to create, to a far fuller extent than emerged, a world peace order in which the kind of aggression that triggered World War II would no longer be possible. This was particularly so with regard to Germany, which had twice in thirty years taken steps that led to war. But it was true in a more general way, as an entire generation of Western leaders sought to step beyond the limited utility of the League of Nations to create a more effective world order. The institutions of this order were to be three—the United Nations, the International Monetary Fund, and the World Bank. Of these, the United Nations would be charged with the task of insuring peaceful conflict resolution through its mechanism, above all, of the Security Council. On this council served the victors of the second war, the nations in whose hands world politics lay in the immediate postwar years.

But the Soviet Union soon showed itself to be different than the other victorious allies; it pressed forward aggressively with actions that served both a narrow national self-interest and a militant world-wide ideology. This behavior, which was rooted intrinsically in the nature of the Soviet regime, prevented the emergence of a harmonious postwar political order in which the powers of Germany and Japan had been wholly and presumably permanently defanged.

Indeed, the Soviet Union emerged as a world leader precisely because two of its principal competitors had been temporarily removed from the world scene. With its troops massed in East Europe, and with its ideological energy directed outward in many locations, the Soviet Union was a significant power. But it was never the equal of the United States. Indeed, had Germany and Japan set upon a more pacific course of economic growth in the 1930s, they undoubtedly would have been advantaged in the long term vis-a-vis the Soviet Union which, though finally achieving economic growth in the 1930s, was saddled with a fundamentally irrational economic and political system. It was not organic Soviet growth in the 1930s that alarmed Germany and Japan. As the historian Paul Kennedy has said, "Russia was much weaker at the end of the 1930s than it had been five or ten years earlier—and in the meantime both Germany and Japan had greatly increased their arms output and were becoming more aggressive."[2]

It was the intrinsic power of the United States that concerned Germany and Japan in the 1930s. Both the German and Japanese economies—indeed, those of all other countries—were but a small fraction of the American economy in the 1930s. It was the growing American conversion of its economic strength into military production that jeopardized the success of Germany and Japan. Hence, both prewar Germany and prewar Japan calculated that time was not on their side.[3]

Thus, it could be said that the Soviet Union emerged as one of only two great powers after World War II almost by default. It did not possess state-of-the-art industrial capabilities; it did not possess a broad and highly educated middle class; and it did not possess a leadership elite with cosmopolitan experience. What it *did* have was an army, ruthlessly aggressive rulers, and the absence of its usual competitors.

But the army and all the discipline in the world would have existed in vain because of a new factor that promised to change the rules of war: atomic weapons. To be sure, the United States did not utilize its atomic monopoly in 1948 when the Soviet Union blockaded Berlin. But unless the U.S.S.R. could obtain atomic weapons, the American monopoly would forever constrain Soviet influence and expansion. That limit would be more or less direct, more or less subtle; but it would be real. America had shown no apparent reluctance to employ atomic weapons on Japan. To a Soviet leadership which itself would have had no scruples about using atomic weapons, it was clear that the Soviet Union would be condemned to an inferior status so long as it did not possess these weapons.

For that reason, there was no higher priority in the mind of Stalin and his colleagues than to acquire the capability to produce atomic weapons. That capability was not long in coming. In 1949, the Soviet Union successfully tested its first atomic weapon. Work on the far more powerful thermonuclear weapon was underway in both the United States and the Soviet Union. The United States tested its first hydrogen bomb in 1952; the first Soviet test occurred in 1953, a mere nine months later.

This ended the Western monopoly on weapons of mass destruction. As the Soviet Union developed the capability to deliver these weapons, it guaranteed its status as one of the world's two military superpowers. As it did, an inverse development of course occurred on the American side: the United States went from being *unwilling* to use its nuclear superiority to being *unable* to use it. The logic of nuclear deterrence resulted in two powers with the capacity to destroy one another, but with no meaningful way to employ that capacity.

Ironically, the very nuclear weapons which gave the Soviet Union such enormous power also constrained that power, for they were counterbalanced by the American nuclear umbrella that extended over Europe and Japan. What is more, that power was contained without resort to warfare. In this way, mankind's most horrible creations have played—to date, at least—a profoundly stabilizing and positive role. The American nuclear umbrella over Europe and Japan permitted the development of these regions to the level they have now achieved, a level that brings them far closer to the United States than they were on the eve of World War II. Those who argue the priority of economic power should understand that the growth of the Japanese and German economies has taken place within a framework of military stability that has permitted this very occurrence.

There is another side to this. Nuclear weapons were required by the Soviet Union to attain superpower status; they will be required all the more fully in order for it to *retain* that status. Imagine a Soviet Union today without nuclear weapons. This Soviet Union would possess a large population and a large land mass, but by no other criterion would it be a superpower. This Soviet Union would, by virtue of its size and population, be able to defend itself against a nonnuclear attack, but its influence would scarcely extend beyond its own borders. Its nuclear capability is the one thing that does and will continue to make the Soviet Union a world power.

This suggests that there will be hard and fast limits beyond which the Soviet Union cannot plausibly be expected to reduce its nuclear weapons. As additional nations acquire the ability to produce and deliver nuclear weapons, that will place a premium on the Soviet Union's strategic nuclear capabilities. For this reason, the idea that the total elimination of nuclear weapons is "an ultimate objective to which we, the Soviet Union, and all other nations can agree"[4] does not seem persuasive. It seems unlikely that the proposed agreement for nuclear disarmament discussed at the Reykjavik summit could or would have been implemented.

Without nuclear weapons, the Soviet Union would become a second-rate power overnight. Soviet defense spending priorities seem to reflect this line of thought. Even as the Soviet Union has cut overall defense spending, reduced troop levels, and drawn down its forces in Eastern Europe, it has continued full-scale modernization of its strategic forces.[5] The Soviet Union played to its strength in the decades after World War II. That strength was military power.

The same motives that impelled the Soviet Union to acquire a nuclear arsenal will now require it to hold onto that arsenal ever more tightly.

The Great Gamble

By the early 1960s, the Soviet Union had acquired a significant, if still slightly inferior, strategic force. As illustrated in the Cuban missile crisis, each side displayed a keen appreciation for the capacities of the other. For more than a decade a stalemate ensued in which all conflicts occurred at the margins of the U.S.–Soviet contest. Each side sought its advantage in many small ways, but neither was able to alter in any appreciable way the military balance that existed between them.

It was not until about a decade after the Cuban missile crisis that the Soviet leadership genuinely flirted with the belief that it might prevail in the superpower conflict. By the middle of the 1960s, the United States was fully engaged in Vietnam, which was the preeminent symbol of the policy of containment in that decade. Unlike the prior massive military effort at containment, the Korean War, this struggle did not end in stalemate but with an American withdrawal and the subsequent military and political collapse of the forces the United States supported. The consequences of this outcome were profound both in the eyes of the Soviet leadership and for America's policy of containment. For the first time since 1948, it was doubtful whether the United States was prepared to contain communist expansion. To be sure, American forces in Europe offered no opportunity for direct Soviet aggression there. But on the fringes of the U.S.–Soviet conflict there were many opportunities at hand.

It is difficult to draw any other conclusion than that the Soviet leadership was emboldened by the U.S. failure in Vietnam and the subsequent internal divisions in America. It is from the 1970s that one sees a major effort by the Soviet Union, well beyond anything hitherto attempted, to expand its influence in far-flung parts of the world. The Soviets strongly supported revolution in the Western Hemisphere, particularly in Central America; significant increases in their support for the guerilla war in El Salvador dated from this time. Then, Nicaragua offered an easier opportunity for success, and by 1979 the Soviet Union had a friendly regime in Managua. In Africa, the Soviet Union became deeply involved in Ethiopia, and offered substantial assistance to one warring faction in Angola. This assistance included as many as 50,000 Cuban troops as well as logistical support and weapons. The Soviet Union also moved briskly to develop and deepen relationships with radical Arab states. The failure of the Arabs in the 1973 war against Israel offered a fertile field of resentment for such Soviet efforts.

At last, the Soviet Union was emboldened to do what it had never done since it moved into Eastern Europe at the end of World War II: commit its own forces to the invasion of another country. In December 1979, the Soviet Union invaded Afghanistan and installed a new government there.

All of these actions occurred in the context of growing capabilities in both strategic and conventional forces. The Soviet Union substantially increased the size and quality of its Far East fleet in the 1970s. In addition, it developed a new class of intermediate-range nuclear missiles, the SS20, which it targeted on both Western Europe and the Far East. Soviet military spending grew steadily throughout the 1970s.[6]

The American response to these actions remained very much in doubt throughout most of the 1970s. On the positive side of the ledger stood two developments. First, it became obvious that there was no way for the gradual erosion of the close and cooperative relationship between the Soviet Union and China to be repaired. The national interests of these two large countries reasserted themselves above ideological considerations. At the beginning of the 1970s China was at worst a neutral factor for the Soviet Union; by the end of the decade it was decidedly another problem for Soviet military planners. The second development occurred in the Middle East. Egypt decided that its alignment with the Soviet Union was not productive, and forged a closer relationship with the West, a decidedly positive accomplishment of American diplomacy.

But these two developments stand alone as instances of American success in the 1970s. In virtually every other sphere, it appeared that the West lost ground in that decade. The American position in

Central America was weaker than it had been. American legislators openly debated whether containment made sense in Latin America. Containment came face to face with a new doctrine in foreign policy—the doctrine of human rights. To be sure, supporting human rights was always presented as a more nuanced, more intelligent *means* of containment. But the difficulty arose that specific cases never permitted the luxury of taking a long-term, human rights approach. Thus, much of U.S. policy toward the third world resulted in deep internal political disagreements over widely divergent means to a common end.

In response to Soviet efforts in Angola, the American administration proposed assistance to the opposing faction. The Congress, however, passed an amendment prohibiting such assistance. The administration had argued that assistance was a way to prevent direct U.S. involvement. The Congress saw it more as a pathway into direct military involvement. In this way, the experience of Vietnam hung over the debate over U.S. military assistance for fifteen years.

It is worth recalling a phenomenon in Europe that now appears thoroughly bizarre, the phenomenon of Eurocommunism. Communist parties in several Western European nations, including France, Italy, and Portugal were alive and well, and it was not possible to predict what would be the limit of their attractiveness. Over and above this, relations between the United States government and the governments of Western Europe were often confused and unsatisfactory. The inability to deploy neutron weapons in Europe stood as a signal example of these difficulties. There was an inescapable sense in the late 1970s that the West had lost its moorings, with Soviet intrusions into new areas met with rhetoric rather than response. Nowhere was this more true than with regard to the invasion of Afghanistan, the response to which ranged between fatalism and domestic political controversy over a proposed grain embargo against the Soviet Union.

On the surface, it was difficult to conclude anything but that trends were moving favorably in the Soviet Union's direction. But what was occurring beneath the surface? Many Western observers and analysts pointed to the large share of the Soviet economy that was directed toward the military. Estimates ranged in the neighborhood of 15 percent of the Soviet economy, about two and one-half times the American military's share. At the time, official American estimates suggested that the Soviet economy was about half the size of the American, and therefore concluded that Soviet military spending was exceeding that of the United States each year. Some observers suggested that this was the source of potential trouble for the Soviet Union, because Soviet consumers would not be prepared to suppress their consumption forever. Given the high levels of military spending, however, it was difficult to know how much would be too much. At all events, Western analyses suggested that the Soviet economy was still continuing to grow by 3 to 4 percent a year,[7] and that Soviet military spending was therefore merely increasing in tandem with the growth of the Soviet economy.

But as we now know, the Soviet economy's growth had slowed substantially by the late 1970s. In fact, it appears that there must have been virtually no growth in Soviet productivity throughout the 1970s.[8] This can mean but one thing: throughout the late 1970s and early 1980s the Soviet military was taking a far greater portion of the economy than official Western estimates had supposed.[9] In other words, the share of military spending, high to begin with, grew increasingly higher throughout the 1970s and early 1980s.[10] Consumption's share of the Soviet economy must have been forced downward throughout this period, a theoretical deduction wholly in keeping with common sense and anecdotal impressions.

In short, it seems now that the Soviet leadership under Brezhnev must have undertaken a great gamble. By further emphasizing the military component of Soviet power, could the Soviet Union secure such gains as to improve its position in the world and more securely guarantee its power? For those who argue the thesis that economic strength alone is true power, the Soviet empire served for nearly forty years as living proof of what determined military power can achieve even if undertaken by leaders who care little about the underlying health of their economy.

The Western Response

Would the Soviet gamble succeed? From our present vantage point this gamble looks to have been the last gasp of an empire trying to strengthen its hand by further growth. But it is easy now to forget that the West's response to the military challenge of the Brezhnev years was by no means foreordained. In opposition to the comfortable, almost Marxian, belief that the West would inevitably succeed because of its stronger economic base, it is well to remember that the West of the late 1970s had several possible responses to the Soviet challenge.

The initiative lay with the West, and above all with the United States. How would the West respond? Would the United States attempt to reduce its role overseas and purchase peace in little increments, such as President Carter's proposed troop withdrawal from South Korea? This withdrawal had been planned during the middle of the continuing Soviet military buildup, and well after Soviet efforts to strengthen their forces in the Far East were underway. As such, its timing was almost incredible, and it caused deep concern in many Asian capitals about long-term American intentions for East Asia. Would the United States turn inward upon itself, as so much in its long insular history suggested was possible? Or would the United States step up to the challenge directly?

The answer began to emerge as early as 1979. At that time, an extraordinary situation developed. For the first time since the end of World War II, and probably since the mid-nineteenth century, Congress adopted a more aggressively internationalist position than the president. It was Congress that compelled President Carter to drop his proposed plan to reduce U.S. forces in Korea. It was Congress that pressed the president to accept the Taiwan Relations Act, and thus to maintain, as much as was practicable, a relationship with both mainland China and Taiwan. It was Congress that strengthened the agreement to give the Panama Canal to Panama.

It was Congress that forced the first significant increase in the defense budget in the late 1970s. When President Carter sent the Strategic Arms Limitation Treaty (SALT) to the Senate in June 1979, he did so without reference to the level of defense spending he had proposed earlier in the year. Indeed, he was pointed in saying that the treaty should be considered on its own merits, without "linkage" to other issues of Soviet behavior at all. As the Senate debated SALT in 1979, it became clear that the price of passage would be for President Carter to submit an expanded defense budget the following year with real growth of at least 3 to 5 percent. Senator Henry Jackson pressed the case that an arms limitation treaty must be accompanied by a vigorous modernization of U.S. strategic forces.

The Soviet invasion of Afghanistan ended discussion of SALT, which was already floundering badly in the Senate. Despite the fact that the treaty did not go forward, defense spending began its upward ascent at that time, and President Carter proposed major increases in defense spending in fiscal years 1980 and 1981.

Soviet actions were of concern not only to Americans. In each of the leading nations of West Europe and in Japan those actions were triggering deeper and deeper concern. The tangible effects of this began to be felt in national elections. The first reaction was seen in England, where Margaret Thatcher became prime minister in 1978. She had campaigned on a platform that sharpened as much as possible the differences between socialism and a market-oriented economic system, arguing explicitly for greater defense expenditures to counter growing Soviet capabilities.

In Germany, the Social Democratic Party came to the end of its decade-long dominance. The Free Democratic Party (FDP) left the ruling coalition and joined together with the Christian Democratic Union and Christian Social Union (CDU/CSU) alliance to elect Helmut Kohl chancellor in 1982. Kohl's government undertook immediate economic reforms. In the election of 1983 he campaigned on the basis of his economic reforms and on firmness in countering Soviet military power.

In Japan, the United States was pressing for greater defense expenditures. Beginning in 1980 these entreaties fell on more receptive ears in Tokyo. Tokyo began what was to be a decade of 6 to 7 percent yearly increases in defense spending and agreed to take on new roles and assignments in Pacific defense.

But perhaps nothing indicated a change in Western attitudes so clearly as the election of Ronald Reagan. He had campaigned on the need to rebuild America's strength and prestige in the world, and by November 1980 it was clear that an overwhelming majority of voters responded to that theme. Reagan acted on the premise for which he was elected. He submitted a series of defense budgets in the early 1980s that within five years propelled U.S. defense spending to nearly twice its earlier levels. None of these increases was accompanied by commensurate reductions in domestic spending or by increased tax revenues. Reagan made clear the priority of defense spending increases at every juncture. The federal deficit—that traditional bogeyman of Republicans—was relegated to the back burner. Congress and the president reached an unspoken agreement that both domestic spending and defense spending would grow, and that taxes would not be raised to pay for these increases. This was the course of least political resistance, and, whatever its merits, it could be said to have fairly reflected the mood of the public at that time. Even as late as 1987, President Reagan was still reluctant to endorse any reduction in the levels of defense spending he proposed. In the fall of 1987, senior administration officials met with congressional leaders in a "budget summit" to respond to the stock market crash. At that time, Senator Packwood of Oregon, the ranking Republican on the Senate Finance Committee, proposed an agreement that would have resulted in significant reductions in both domestic spending and defense spending. Congressional Democrats opposed the cuts in domestic spending; the president fought any reduction in defense spending. Despite much self-generated publicity, the summit produced nothing of substance. It did, however, set the tone for subsequent budget summits, no one of which has produced meaningful reductions in the deficit. In the end, because of changes in Gorbachev's policies, Republicans will discover that they will have cuts in defense spending and continued increases in domestic spending.

The only military action aimed at the Soviet Union or its proxies during the Reagan years was the invasion of Grenada. Despite the fact that the capture of this small island within a matter of hours was the only direct Western application of force, the policies of the West were too much for the Soviet Union. There are signs that as early as 1982 the Soviet leadership began to understand that it could not count on acts of stupidity and fear in the West to offset the Soviet Union's growing gap in productive capacity. In objective analyses put before the Soviet leadership around that time, it was obvious that after all its efforts, the Soviet Union was relatively worse off vis-a-vis the West than it had been a decade before. In short, the gamble had failed.

By the early 1980s, the Soviet Union found that its policy of squeezing ever more for the military out of its economy had not achieved positive results. Quite to the contrary. Internally, the Soviet Union had made none of the reforms that would have been necessary to increase its productive capacity. As a result, increases directed toward the military simply were transferred from consumption. Had the Soviet Union adopted certain internal reforms along with its military buildup, it might in time have been able to have its cake and eat it, too. But that was not what happened.

Externally, the Soviet Union found that it stimulated a hostile alliance of nations ringing its borders. NATO unity in the early 1980s remained unshaken in the face of Soviet threats. Japan persisted in its slow but steady defense buildup. And China entered onto a far more independent course that betrayed quite clearly the Chinese judgment that the Soviet Union was its principal threat. Above all, the United States, with its massive economy and superior technological base, appeared galvanized to compete directly with the Soviet Union in military spending. No program so fully reflected this will as the Strategic Defense Initiative, a program which at least hinted at the possibility of changing the rules of nuclear stalemate for the first time in the nuclear age.

The Soviet Union found that it could not use its strategic power. Nuclear deterrence limited the possibility of direct Soviet military applications of force. The Soviet military buildup had not succeeded in producing political and economic advantages; it succeeded only in producing neighbors who ringed the Soviet Union with suspicion and with growing military arsenals. In this regard, the Soviet leadership had only itself to thank for the feeling of encirclement and hostility about which it so frequently complained. Its economic problems were magnified throughout the 1970s and 1980s by acts of omission—specifically, a failure to reform the domestic system. Soviet external problems were the result of acts of commission. In a very real way, the external problems that General Secretary Gorbachev inherited when he took office in 1985 were brought about by the policies of the Soviet Union itself.

The Decline of the Soviet Union

Faced with Western resolve, the initiative passed to the Soviet Union in the mid-1980s. How did the Soviet Union propose to resolve its own pressing problems created by an ever stronger and more successful ring of nations which surrounded it? Would it redouble its efforts to play to its strength, namely, further expansion of its military might, support for insurgencies, and the threat of force? Was there a way for the Soviet leadership to regenerate the sagging ideology that seemed to promise little and offer even less? Could the steady decline in economic growth be reversed?

Successive ailing leaders—Brezhnev at the end, Andropov, and Chernenko—were unwilling or unable to address these problems directly. Andropov undertook to instill greater discipline in the Soviet people with his campaign against alcoholism and laziness. This, however, was a variant on a standard theme; insofar as it urged people to work harder to make an irrational system succeed, its effect was bound to be marginal. For a time, the Soviet Union was able to move neither forward nor backward.

All this changed with the accession of Gorbachev in early 1985. In a series of steps that can only be described as breathtaking, he moved to shift the orthodox view of Marxism; he reinterpreted Soviet history; he withdrew Soviet forces from Afghanistan; and he signaled the loosening of the Soviet hold over Eastern Europe. These were radical steps. They were possible only because it was apparent to a significant portion of the Soviet elite that the previous course of Soviet leadership was a recipe for disaster. There were but two alternatives: to move forward with Gorbachev toward an uncertain goal or to continue further down a path toward inevitable failure. The relative decline of the Soviet Union was simply too obvious to ignore.

Gorbachev was able to see clearly the external dilemma of his country. Like a dog in a choke collar, the more the Soviet Union struggled to expand its influence, the tighter became the ring that gripped it in place. This dictated a policy of relaxation. Internally, the problem was more difficult to assess, and so too were the solutions. It appears now that Gorbachev believed that the Soviet

Union required only a "breathing space" to regain its momentum.[11] In this regard, Gorbachev continued Andropov's policies of exhortation. To them he proposed to add an additional layer of political reforms and some economic incentives. The political reforms had the added virtue of securing Gorbachev's position more firmly against his competitors.

But as Gorbachev discovered, the internal problems of the Soviet Union went far too deep to allow for ministrations at the margin. By about 1987 it was clear that the economy was on a downward spiral that could easily become a free fall. Economic growth continued to slow to the point that by 1989 the Soviet economy actually declined—a decline which continued throughout 1990.[12] Predictions for 1991 are for further stagnation, and possibly significant reductions in the size of the economy.[13]

These problems are the result of the fundamental structure of the Soviet economy. But that structure had been flawed since the end of the world war. Why should growth have ceased in the late 1980s?

GNP Growth Rates in Eastern Europe, 1950–1988
(Percent Increase)

YEAR	BULGARIA	CZECHO-SLOVAKIA	GDR	HUNGARY	POLAND	ROMANIA
1950–55	5.0	3.0	6.4	4.7	4.6	7.2
1955–60	7.8	6.3	5.0	4.6	4.5	4.4
1960–65	6.5	2.0	2.9	4.3	4.1	5.2
1965–70	4.7	3.5	3.2	3.1	3.8	4.6
1970–75	4.5	3.4	3.5	3.4	6.6	6.2
1975–80	1.2	2.2	2.4	2.3	0.9	3.9
1980–85	0.9	1.4	1.8	0.9	1.2	2.0
1986	4.8	2.1	1.5	2.2	2.7	5.8
1987	−0.8	1.0	1.8	1.0	−1.7	1.1
1988[1]	1.8	1.4	1.8	1.1	1.9	2.1

[1]**Preliminary**

Source: Thad P. Alton, "East European GNP's Domestic Final Uses of Gross Product, Rates of Growth, and International Comparison," in U.S. Congress, Joint Economic Committee, *Pressures for Reform in the East European Economies*, vol. 1, 101st Congress, 1st sess. Washington, D.C., 20 Oct. 1989: 80–81.

Some of the reasons appear to be systemic. Without attributing too much precision to the specific figures, it appears that economic growth was slowing to a crawl throughout the Soviet empire.

A second reason relates to the liberalization that Gorbachev had set into motion. Gorbachev raised expectations that improvements would occur in the consumer goods sector. As it was then configured, however, the Soviet economy had no hope of providing more and better consumer goods in the near term. This meant that additional consumer goods had to be imported. In 1989 hard currency imports grew by 20 percent to $34.2 billion.[14] At the same time, the Soviet Union experienced what was for it a severe misfortune —the worldwide decline in oil prices in the latter half of the 1980s.[15] Fully 60 percent of all Soviet hard currency exports had come from the sale of oil and natural gas. Beyond that, much of its economic influence over its satellites came from their reliance on Soviet oil and natural gas. The world price decline coincided with the depletion of the Soviet Union's most readily available fuel reserves.

It has sometimes been said that the Soviet Union is in reality a third world economy with a large and well-developed military. Perhaps the better comparison is that it is essentially an oil-exporting nation with a large and well-developed military. Indeed, the period of relative Soviet ascendancy in the late 1970s coincided precisely with the ascendancy of all the oil-exporting nations, and the time of greatest difficulty for the industrialized nations of the West. As oil prices declined in the 1980s, so too did the salience of the oil-exporting nations. Over the past fifteen years there has been an inverse relationship between what has been good for the industrialized economies and what has been good, at least in principle, for the Soviet economy.

The Soviet Union made poor use of its oil revenues. Some were directed toward third world adventures that prompted responses from the West. The remainder were simply wasted. At this time, the Soviets are beginning to pay the long and painful price for these mistakes. In 1989 oil exports declined 200,000 barrels a day.[16] The increases in imports and the decline in oil exports produced a $1.8 billion hard currency deficit. This has continued to the present time, and there are no signs that this will be reversed in the near future. The Soviet Union will require substantial new Western imports in order to expand its oil production, and these requirements will compete with consumer goods for hard currency imports. Soviet debt to Western nations is rising rapidly; from 1984 to 1989 net Soviet hard currency debt nearly tripled.[17] Whether the West will risk massive new lending to a Soviet economy that has not demonstrated it can productively utilize such funds is an open question. Having been burned by experience in making risky international loans, Western banks will be very cautious. The negative lending experiences in East Europe and Latin America in the 1970s and early 1980s will have to be weighed by Western governments against the short-term stability that known risky loans could bring to the Soviet Union.

Although rising expectations and declining oil exports have exacerbated its problems, the structure of the Soviet economy itself remains the principal barrier to economic success. And Gorbachev has only begun to address this problem. Political constraints make it difficult to take decisive action; yet decisive action is the most needed thing. Gorbachev could take to heart Churchill's dictum: ''Lack of decision is the worst fault from which a policy can suffer.'' Without fundamental economic restructuring, the Soviet economy is likely to decline further and further in a morass of half-measures and uncertainties.

What makes decisiveness so difficult in the final analysis, however, is this: Even with decisive restructuring, the Soviet economy will continue to face insuperable difficulties.[18] This has provided a disincentive to radical reform. The fact is that there is no known course by which the Soviet Union will be able to reverse its economic decline in the near term.

What are the consequences of this dilemma? First, it appears that the Soviet military will undergo a period of reductions. This did not occur in the first years of Gorbachev's rule; to the contrary, Soviet military spending actually grew approximately 3 percent in 1986 and in 1987. In the early years under Gorbachev the military continued to increase its share of the Soviet economy. By 1989, however, this process had reversed itself. Defense spending in 1989 is estimated to have been somewhere between flat and a 4 percent reduction.[19] Limitations on defense spending are likely to be severe over the next decade. This is true not so much because of an unwillingness to reduce consumption as for two other reasons. First, the rationale for much of the Soviet Union's military spending has been called into doubt. If Soviet troops leave East Europe on their announced schedules, there will simply be no need for the current size of standing forces. Shortages of military housing and other problems will exacerbate this situation; but the fundamental reality will be the absence of any overriding purpose to retain the Soviet military in its current configuration. For reasons already discussed, reductions in strategic forces will be slow in coming; but reductions in procurement of conventional weapons and in force levels are predictable.

For the sake of argument, let us suppose that the Soviet GNP currently stands at $1.6 trillion.[20] Let us further suppose that Soviet military spending is approximately equal to U.S. military spending. At the equivalent of $300 billion, this would mean that the Soviet Union currently spends about 18.75 percent of its GNP on the military, or more than three times the comparable U.S. share. These figures are in line with most estimates of Soviet military spending. If the military share declines over the next decade to 12 percent of a stagnant Soviet economy, U.S. defense spending at even 4 percent of the U.S. economy (assuming 3 percent growth) would double Soviet spending by the end of the decade. It will be very difficult for the Soviet military to remain untouched in a no-growth economy. In this circumstance, it is likely that the military will husband its resources carefully to protect its core missions at home and will be disinclined to expend resources on risky ventures abroad.

This is the best case scenario for the Soviet Union. Worse cases are not difficult to envision. Whenever an economy is in transition away from subsidies toward market prices, political instability is a possibility. This is as true for the Soviet Union as for any other nation. But it is not only—indeed, it is not mainly—the unhappiness of disorganized citizens that is a threat to stability. The Soviet leaders' dilemma is exacerbated by the fact that their country is an agglomeration of deeply divided ethnic nationalities. There are preexisting fault lines around which instability has and will organize itself. This is not the place for an extended discussion of the "nationalities problem" in the Soviet Union.[21] Suffice it to say that a downward spiraling economy could at best result in generalized discontent with the central government; at worst it could split apart the country into Russia and a host of smaller national states.

The decline of the Soviet Union's long-term capacity to affect world events can be dated from General Secretary Gorbachev's accession to power in 1985. This is emphatically *not* to say that Gorbachev caused the decline, through willfulness or mismanagement. He is not so much the cause of the Soviet Union's dilemma since 1985 as its symptom. That a man committed to loosening the Soviet grip on Eastern Europe, reducing defense spending, and withdrawing from Afghanistan should come to power so soon after Brezhnev, Chernenko, and Andropov is a sign of the ferment that must have occurred within the Kremlin in the years from 1982 to 1984.

At all events, Gorbachev has set the Soviet Union on a course from which it cannot fully return. We should be clear: it is distinctly possible that the Soviet Union could revert to repression, especially in light of the long pattern of subservience that has marked the history of the Russian people. What is meant here is that the course of repression can no longer guarantee a world leadership role for the Soviet Union. The future of a Soviet Union that reverts to repression and breaks off its political and economic relationships with the world's leading powers will be more akin to that of a large Albania than to a world power.

In America there is great concern about the decline of the competitive position of U.S. industries. It seems as if the defeated nations of World War II are arising again to challenge the United States in terms of productivity, technology, and the will to succeed. This feeling is very real. But America still competes. One can only imagine the force of a similar feeling in the Soviet Union, where it is obvious that other nations actually *are* surpassing them.

Gorbachev's course has not been taken because of its intrinsic attraction, or even because it offers so high a probability of success; to the contrary, it is a testimonial to the fact that no other course for the Soviet Union offers even the slim hope that is held out by dismantling its empire. The task facing Gorbachev is to make the best of a very bad situation. But steps such as the withdrawal from Afghanistan, the removal of SS20 missiles from the Western part of the Soviet Union, and the breakup of the East European satellite system are not purely military matters. When a nation loses the will to impose its system on others—which the Soviet Union had been doing for forty years—that is profoundly disorienting.

Consider the Vietnam experience for the United States. The United States has been a militant democracy-spreading nation for the entirety of the twentieth century, and, if one counts westward expansion across the American continent, for its entire 200-year history. The defeat in Vietnam was a serious, disorienting experience for Americans. Only a few years ago an intense debate ensued over whether the President could exceed fifty-five military training personnel in El Salvador, a nation in the Western Hemisphere under attack from guerrillas advocating a retrograde ideology of force that has now been nearly universally discredited. That was a full decade after the end of the Vietnam War. Americans are not exactly shrinking violets, and still the effect of Vietnam was so severe and long-lasting that commentators could still be discussing in 1991 whether the victory over Iraq meant that the "Vietnam syndrome" had been finally overcome. Yet Americans never doubted that the professed goal of democratization was in error in Vietnam, but only the means to implement it. Americans of all stripes, from the left to the right, have all along supported a militant ideology of democratization, sometimes under the title of human rights and other times more directly through the use of military force.

It is not simply the *means* which the Soviet Union employed in Afghanistan or East Europe that have been discredited; it is the entire ideology of communism on which these conquests rested that is now disbelieved. Expansion has not been incidental to Soviet ideology in the past four decades; it has been fueled by that ideology. And now it is over. This surely prefigures a deep period of national soul searching. The Soviet Union must now begin to find anew the proper way to express its character. This will be a period in which the country turns inward in order to try to "perfect" itself, that is, to find its own way to accommodate its tradition of centralization with both the challenge of international competition and demands of resurgent ethnic groups. This may be the picture of a nation which, from time to time, might still look for inexpensive ways to reach beyond its own borders to guarantee itself a role; but it is not the picture of a militant, expansionary nation that will seek a leadership role in world politics.

General Secretary Gorbachev held in his hands the future of Eastern Europe. But now that he has permitted Eastern Europe to slip free, his capacity to influence events in Europe will decline. For a brief time he possessed the initiative; now that initiative will pass to Germany, whose decisions above all others will shape the face of Europe.

PART ONE
The Reunification of Germany

The future is in the laps of the gods. It will probably be decided, once again, by Germany's decisions. And Germany is, as it always was, a mutable, Proteuslike, unpredictable country, particularly dangerous when it is unhappy.

—*Luigi Barzini*

CHAPTER ONE

East, West, and the Dissolution of the Soviet Empire

The Constraint of German Options

ALTHOUGH GENERAL SECRETARY GORBACHEV is admired in many lands, nowhere has he been so fully appreciated as in the Federal Republic of Germany. There, the homeland of "Gorbymania," he reached a favorable approval rating at one point in early 1989 of no less than 90 percent. This was far higher than that of any other world leader, and certainly far in excess of the approval rating of the chancellor of the Federal Republic itself. It was at that time twice the favorable approval rating of the American president whose troops ultimately maintained the security of the Federal Republic. Gorbachev's approval rating in West Germany far exceeded his approval rating among his own people.

What have successful West Germans found in this man from a more backward country whose only modern product—missiles— are pointed at their own homes and cities? The answer, of course, is that General Secretary Gorbachev was the one man in the world who was capable of ending the division of Germany and the alliance system which grew up around that division. No one else could offer this. And it was a gift which the General Secretary could offer to no one but the Germans.

It was a gift that was a long time in coming. Germany was a divided, occupied power for forty-five years. During those four and one-half decades, neither East nor West Germany had much latitude for independent action. This was manifestly true in the East. On only one occasion did the East German people act in defiance of the Soviet-controlled regime. On June 16, 1953, workers in East Berlin who were concerned about scheduled increases in production quotas, refused to work. This demonstration, which grew quickly to include both political and economic demands, was suppressed by Soviet force the following day.

The government of East Germany could not be said to have exercised even that much independence in its entire history. To be sure, differences of opinion between the East German government and Moscow arose from time to time. Such disputes probably resulted in Walter Ulbricht's fall from power in 1971. But, it should be noted, virtually every instance of disagreement was resolved firmly and wholly to the satisfaction of Moscow. Further, as was frequently the case, Ulbricht's problem arose from attempting to be a better Communist than the Russians themselves. Soviet domination of East Germany throughout the postwar period was thorough, complete, and total.

In West Germany, the Federal Republic's latitude for action was somewhat greater. But on the whole, its policies were also highly constrained by its context. Once the initial decision was made by Konrad Adenauer and his party to firmly align the noncommunist portion of Germany with the values and the defense system of the West, the fundamental decision was made. To be sure, this option was revisited on several occasions. In 1952 Stalin offered German unity in exchange for German neutrality. Later in that decade, Adenauer and Franz Josef Strauss considered briefly the possibility of an ''Austrian'' solution, again a variant of German neutrality. But given the nature of Soviet totalitarian rule, these efforts were simply never feasible. As one commentator has observed, ''The Soviet Union failed to make the West Germans feel that unity, the key to which lies in Moscow, was more important than freedom, the key to which lies in Washington.''[1] The simple fact recognized by successive governments of West Germany was that if the Federal Republic were not closely aligned with the West, and with the United States in particular, it would have purchased unity at the cost of obliterating German freedom for the foreseeable future. Breaking away from the West would have been somewhat akin to committing suicide—a grand act which can be exercised but one time. This was not a serious option.

Within the context of the Western alliance, the Federal Republic occasionally undertook different policies than the United States. Differences relating to the opening toward the East, or *Ostpolitik*, short-range missile modernization, trade policy, and the export of high technology to Middle East nations are examples. But these were tactical differences, usually resolved expeditiously. Compared with a unified Germany with its own independent ideas and the capability to put its ideas into practice, these differences will seem in retrospect to have been inconsequential.

This is to say, in other words, that the options of both Germanies were severely constrained for the past forty-five years. Only now will Germany be in a position to pursue its ''own'' policies. For the past two generations, German leaders have borne witness to the wisdom of Bismarck's words:

> We can put the clock forward but that doesn't make time pass any faster, and the ability to wait as the situation develops is a *sine qua non* of practical politics.[2]

This mindset was fixed in place in West Germany by Adenauer, a man whose patience caused many to suspect that perhaps he did not deeply favor German unification after all. As late as 1966, however, Adenauer could say:

> I shall not give up the hope that one day Soviet Russia will see that a divided Germany, and so a divided Europe, is not to its advantage. . . . We must keep on as we have been doing, steadily pursuing the same goal, without wavering and with a great deal of patience.

> For patience is and remains the strongest weapon of the conquered
> —and, after all, we are still a conquered people.[3]

The Germans waited, patiently, for forty-five years, the entire life-
time of a majority of Germans in both the East and the West. They
at last found in General Secretary Gorbachev the man who could
deliver Germany from the constraints under which it labored for so
long.

And Gorbachev will continue to be revered in Germany in exact
proportion to his capacity to take back what he has offered. As
Soviet troops depart from the eastern portion of Germany, the general secretary can expect to return to more human proportions. Very
soon the Soviet Union will be more in need of what Germany can
give than vice versa. And Germany will once again look upon the
Soviet Union not as an oppressor or a deliverer, but as its too-large
Russian neighbor to the east.

The Division of Germany

In assessing the meaning of reunification, it is well to recall the
origin of Germany's division. Germany was divided for so long
following World War II that it must almost have seemed that division
was the natural, intended result of the war. But the postwar division
of Germany was by no means a foregone conclusion; to the contrary,
it was a result actually intended by none of the leading allied powers.
Indeed, it took a series of steps over nearly a quarter-century before
the two portions of Germany were fully consolidated as states.

This is not to say that formal partition of Germany had not been
considered by the allies. At the Teheran Conference in 1943, various
partition schemes were discussed.[4] One point of view argued that
the Germans were by nature so aggressive that there would be no
peace in Europe unless their nation were partitioned. Although the
concept of a partitioned Germany was discussed, no specific agreements were struck as to the roles and powers of each of the allied
governments. The exception was in the east. There it was agreed
that the German border on the east ought to be established along

the Oder and Neisse rivers, and that the lands to the east ought to revert to Poland. Throughout these discussions, it remained an unstated goal of President Roosevelt to insure that the ultimate resolution of Germany's fate would be secured jointly by the United States, Britain, and the Soviet Union. Roosevelt did not want to offer any temptations to either Germany or the Soviets to contemplate a separate peace.

The first specific plans for the future of postwar Germany were agreed to in 1944. The European Advisory Commission plan for the occupation of postwar Germany was agreed to in the London Protocol of September 12 and subsequently amended several months later. It created three zones and a special Berlin area within the German borders of 1937 (again, with the exception of the east). The three zones were to be occupied by the forces of each of the three allied powers, with the Soviet zone in the east, the British zone in the northwest, and the American zone in the southwest. The Berlin area was in turn divided into three parts, each under separate military occupation, with the whole of the Berlin area to be "jointly" administered. As a practical matter, this agreement guaranteed a leading role for each power in controlling its own zone. However, there is ample evidence that no permanent occupation along these lines was contemplated, and that further arrangements would obviously be required.

These further arrangements were spelled out on August 2, 1945. The Potsdam Agreement, which had accepted France as a fourth occupying power, created a hybrid arrangement in which each occupying power was given great latitude in its own zone, but also clearly specified a common, or joint occupation of Germany:

> In accordance with the Agreement on Control Machinery in Germany, supreme authority in Germany is exercised, on instructions from their respective Governments, by the Commanders-in-Chief of the armed forces of the United States of America, the United Kingdom, the Union of Soviet Socialist Republics, and the French Republic, each in his own zone of occupation, and also jointly, in matters affecting Germany as a whole, in their capacity as members of the Control Council.[5]

In addition to a jointly administered occupation of Germany in regard to matters affecting "Germany as a whole," the Potsdam Agreement called for "uniformity of treatment of the German population throughout Germany" and a Germany that "shall be treated as a single economic unit."[6] Although the agreement specifically declined to create a new central German government, it called for the creation of "certain essential central German administrative departments, headed by State Secretaries" who were to work under the direction of the Control Council.[7] All of this was to remain in force "for the time being" in "the initial control period."

To what end were these practical arrangements put in place? What was to be the ultimate goal of occupation, and how much time would be necessary to achieve it? Surely a relatively permanent allied occupation of Germany was not in the cards, at least not in the view of the Americans. America's first thought was to redeploy U.S. forces to the ongoing war in the Asian theater. When Japan surrendered suddenly in August 1945, that plan gave way to wholesale demobilization. Meanwhile, another practical political problem had arisen. The state of the German economy in late 1945 and 1946 was dismal. Hunger was prevalent and rationing was the order of the day. This problem was exacerbated by the forced removal of ethnic Germans from Poland, Czechoslovakia, and Hungary. Despite Soviet assurances to the contrary, food from the agricultural east was not forthcoming into the French, British, and American zones. As the Germans were in no position to provide for themselves, food was being shipped to Germany from America at considerable cost. The idea that the Nazi war machine had been defeated in order that the German people should become permanent wards of the American people was not politically salable in America on a long-term basis. The Potsdam Agreement had envisioned the rebuilding of Germany's capacity to feed itself and to produce sufficient goods for basic subsistence, as well as for reparations to the Soviet Union. The question of how to bring Germany to self-sufficiency in at least food production assumed a new urgency.

As the allies contemplated the long-term future of Germany, there were several areas of agreement, several areas of disagreement, and many unresolved issues. It was uniformly accepted that Germany should be thoroughly denazified, demilitarized, decentralized, and decartelized. In addition, although Stalin must have entertained a different private view, all the allies publicly subscribed to the democratization of Germany to the point where it might one day be possible for the German people "to take their place among the free and peaceful peoples of the world."[8]

Beyond this there was little agreement, even at a conceptual level. The French, newly brought into the four-power arrangement, sought a Germany that was permanently divided. France argued for the incorporation of the Saar into France, and for a final severing of the Ruhr and the Rhineland from any subsequent German state. Such provisions were necessary, it was argued, to insure protection against a unified Germany.

The British basically supported the United States, attempting where possible to accommodate France's concerns. But even among American leaders, there was no unanimity. Some, like Treasury Secretary Henry Morgenthau, Jr., took a strong position against allowing any reindustrialization in Germany. In his so-called pastoral letter, he argued for an agrarian Germany in which the industries of the Saar and the Ruhr would be "put out of action and closed down."[9] In this he was opposed by Assistant Secretary of War John McCloy, who saw positive benefits in allowing Germany to get back on its feet—in a controlled, democratic way, of course.

It was, however, the Soviet Union which interposed conditions that caused the most discord. Two issues emerged: reparations and the status of the eastern territories. The Soviet Union essentially dictated the fate of the territory of Germany to the east of the Oder-Neisse line. It annexed the area around Königsberg, which it renamed Kaliningrad, and moved the Polish border west to the Oder-Neisse line. In doing this it moved both its own borders and Poland's westward into territory that had been unambiguously German long before the Nazi aggression of the late 1930s. Presented with these steps, the United States and Britain acceded to the Soviet position, though with a caveat that the final disposition of these territories would await a formal peace settlement.

The issue of reparations proved more troublesome, freighted as it was with the idea that World War I reparations had been a causal factor in bringing Hitler to power. The Soviet Union took the position that because of its tremendous suffering and losses from the

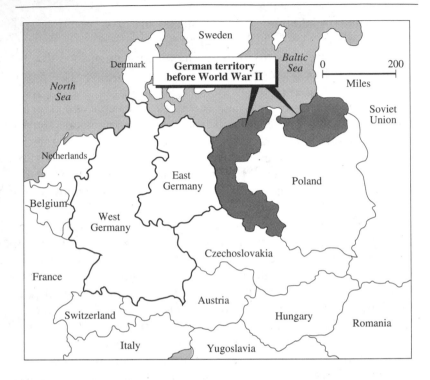

Nazi invasion, it was entitled to reparations. The United States accepted this view in principle. Further, it was understood that reparations should not be paid in money, as that had bred considerable resentment among the German populace after World War I. The Potsdam Agreement provided that each allied power could take from its own zone what reparations it pleased. Further, it stated that the Soviet Union was also to receive from the Western zones "15 percent of . . . industrial capital equipment . . . as is unnecessary for the German peace economy" in exchange for an equivalent value of food and other commodities from its zone, and an additional 10 percent of industrial capital equipment "without payment or exchange of any kind in return."[10]

This was a formula for disaster. Under the stated terms, the Soviet Union dismantled and removed factories, rail and rolling stock, vehicles, timber, and livestock. It has been estimated that between one-fourth and one-half of East Germany's industrial capital was taken.[11] At the same time, the Soviet Union also expected the Western powers to comply with the Potsdam Agreement, although it was not sending food westward. After fruitless efforts to come to a reasonable understanding, the deputy chief of the American military government in Germany, General Lucius Clay, ceased reparations payments in May 1946. The Soviet Union continued to extract reparations from its zone until the mid-1950s.

In the end, however, it was not the issue of reparations or any other single issue that led to the semipermanent division of Germany. The Soviet Union simply did not share the same suppositions as the other allies. The British, and especially the French, shared the Soviet Union's visceral suspicions about a unified Germany; they were also skeptical of the abstract idealism of the Americans.[12] Each of the allied powers pursued its interests as it saw them. But Soviet intentions diverged radically from those of the three Western powers. From the first days after the capture of Berlin, the U.S.S.R. tried to create a German Marxist regime under its domination. The old differences that had been temporarily subsumed in the face of Hitler's threat rose again to the surface and prevented the joint administration of occupied Germany.

The division of Germany was not the conscious intent of any party, but the result of the balance of the forces that were required to defeat Germany, and the fact that no one force was willing or able to work its will on the other. That the result of this balance was the division of Germany into two semipermanent states was regrettable for the Germans. But in the eyes of those leaders who had just concluded a long and difficult struggle against Germany, it was not a sufficient pretext to embark on yet another war.

The Creation of Two German States

The realities of Soviet and American military force, rather than the collective intent of the victors of World War II, created the initial division of Germany. That division became ever more fully institutionalized as the Cold War wore on. On the surface, the reunification of Germany appeared ever less imminent. On the surface, the course appeared to run in the opposite direction: toward the consolidation of Germany as two separate states. The steps in this process were not the product of a far-sighted intelligence seeking to impose an intelligible outcome on Central Europe. In reality, the stages in the evolution of the two German states can be understood only as practical responses to immediate problems that were presented to decision makers.

The very first of these problems arose out of the occupation dilemma of the Western powers. Faced with the urgent need to feed the people of the Western-governed sectors, and faced with continuing difficulties in securing Soviet cooperation toward that end, the West sought a way to restore at least a minimal level of self-sufficiency and productivity to the German economy. The requisite step—which succeeded beyond all imagination—was the introduction of currency reform in the Western sectors. The creation of a common currency (a step whose importance was reconfirmed in Germany in 1990) created a de facto unity in the territory it covered. This was well understood by the French, who at first opposed currency reform and the introduction of the common currency into its sector. The French believed, rightly, that this would have the practical effect of unifying the Western sectors. This was also well understood by the Soviet Union, which had been freely printing money in the East in order to secure its own advantage. The Soviets realized that a new and stable currency in the West offered but one possible outcome: it would drive the economies of all the Western sectors closer. This was also true for the Western sectors of Berlin, which lay fully within the Soviet zone.

The Soviet response to currency reform was not long in coming. Four days after the change, on June 24, 1948, they blockaded Berlin. It is instructive to consider this response. On one hand, it betrayed the inability of the Soviet Union to affect the decision in the Western zones. In that sense, it clearly represented the effective boundary between East and West along the sector lines which had been drawn. On the other hand, the Soviet blockade was more than just an effort to bring the Western sectors of Berlin into its orbit. For the four-power control of Berlin was clearly spelled out in the London Agreement and well understood by all parties. Although there had never existed a formal detailing of access rights, a failure to respond to the Soviet blockade would have had ramifications well beyond the Western sectors of Berlin. Berlin was always understood by the allies as a "special place," somehow symbolic of the German nation. Failure to defend Berlin would have been a message that the West was unprepared to defend the rights it had won fairly in the war. The Western powers, after all, had exchanged with the Soviet Union 16,000 square miles of German territory they had conquered for 185 square miles of Berlin. This step, despite well-founded reservations by Churchill, was undertaken as a good-faith implementation of the London Agreement. To have allowed the Soviet Union to take control of these 185 square miles would have been a disquieting indication of American lack of resolve to defend its right in Germany.

What might have been the consequences had the United States acquiesced in the blockade of Berlin? Would the Cold War in Europe have unfolded differently had the West ceded all of Berlin to the Soviet Union? It is hard to say. Much, of course, would have depended upon whether and where the United States subsequently drew the line against Soviet intrusions. But it seems fair to say that the loss of Berlin would have made it far more difficult for West German leaders to align themselves fully with the West. It would no doubt have made the temptations to a neutral unity far more attractive.[13] It is interesting to speculate upon where such a unified, neutral Germany would be today, and how significantly the prospects for European integration would have been retarded.

At all events, the decision to defend Berlin guaranteed the creation of the new Federal Republic of Germany in the West. By the time the blockade ended in 1949, the outlines of that new government had already taken shape. Without a clear Western commitment to defend its prerogatives, the Federal Republic would have clearly been in doubt. As it was, many thoughtful Germans were concerned that the creation of a government in the West could be a decisive step against a unified Germany. They were uncertain that such a step should be taken, particularly in light of the fact that the new government's powers would still be closely constrained by the occupying powers. To provide assurances for these concerns, the occupying powers agreed to the creation of a provisional "Basic Law" in lieu of a constitution, as well as specific procedures for the integration of Germans in the Soviet sector into this new entity under article 23 of the law.

The founding of the German Democratic Republic in the East was a clear-cut response to the Western determination to create the Federal Republic. The constitution of the German Democratic Republic also stressed the importance of German unity and presented itself as a provisional arrangement until such time as unity could be achieved.

The Western powers found in the first chancellor of the Federal Republic all for which they could have hoped. Konrad Adenauer took a firm position in favor of a market economy and a strong Western orientation. He was frequently attacked by political opponents for preferring a Western alignment to the unification of the German nation. Adenauer followed the logic of his position to the end; he agreed to the creation of West German armed forces which would be directed against the forces of the East. Armed Germans in the West would confront armed Germans in the East. This was of course a complex step for a nation that had come into existence in the manner of the Federal Republic. As in the case of Japan, American objectives were apparently contradictory: to found a pacific, democratic nation and also to create a strong ally against the Soviet Union. Growing armaments of the East German government helped tip the balance in favor of a West German army.

From the beginning, it was clear that the only way to create a large West German military force was to tie it into a multilateral structure. This was the intent of the original French plan for a European Defense Community. When that scheme collapsed, the principle of multlateralism was retained, albeit in a different way. West Germany was to be allowed to create a national defense force of 500,000 men, but this force would be wholly in the service of the North Atlantic Treaty Organization (NATO). It would possess no forces independent of NATO. In addition, West Germany agreed that it would not produce or possess nuclear weapons.[14] In exchange for these assurances, Adenauer insisted on sovereignty for West Germany. This was ratified in the Paris Agreement of 1954, which went into effect in the following year. That agreement contained a provision in article 7 that the signatory states, including France, Britain, and the United States would pursue "their common aim of a reunified Germany enjoying a liberal democratic constitution, like that of the Federal Republic, and integrated within the European Community.'' Despite this provision, it was apparent that another step had been taken toward the consolidation of two Germanies.

Beneath the surface, the Federal Republic worked carefully to retain ties to the people of East Germany. This possibility, however, was dealt a fateful blow with the construction of the Berlin Wall in 1961. Although the West was always prepared to consider reunification on a free, democratic basis, it was also true that the West initiated many steps to build up its sector as a free, powerful force. Given the realities of Soviet obstructionism and the Soviet vision of society, this policy made good sense. But in fairness it should be said that the West had not hesitated to undertake steps to consolidate the Western sectors of Germany to the exclusion of the East. Now the East had taken just such a step in an effort to isolate itself from the West. This was a dynamic beyond the control of the West. Indeed, it soon became painfully clear that the West had no more leverage to stop the construction of the Berlin Wall than the Soviet Union had had to prevent currency reform in 1948. In short, the West was not able to prevent a deep wedge from being placed between East and West Germany. This had a profound impact not only upon the lives of East Germans, but also upon the calculation of West German leaders, who had cause to wonder whether reunification was receding into the mists of improbability.

The Federal Republic retained its fundamental tie to the West; it had no desire or incentive to change that. Yet there was a growing realization that the German Democratic Republic was a reality that would not disappear soon, if ever. Both the United States and the Soviet Union, prodded by their respective German counterparts, were prepared to accept a more normal relationship between East and West, and particularly in Berlin. This resulted in the Quadripartite Agreement of 1971 and the Basic Treaty between the two Germanies in 1972. The Basic Treaty created the mutual recognition of sovereignty for the two German states, specifying respect for ''each other's territorial integrity'' and ''each other's independence and autonomy in their internal and external affairs.'' The two German states agreed to exchange diplomatic missions to be located at each respective government's seat. Following the diplomatic recognition of the G.D.R. by the Federal Republic, more than 100 nations recognized the government of East Germany. The United States did so on September 4, 1974. The Basic Treaty reversed the Hallstein Doctrine, according to which the Federal Republic would maintain diplomatic relations with no nation that recognized East Germany except the Soviet Union.

Throughout this period, then, an observer of the political life in the region would have concluded that Germany was moving inescapably in the direction of a permanent, or at least semipermanent, division into two states. To be sure, the Federal Republic never entered into any agreement or policy without one eye on the people of East Germany. In that regard, for example, in 1957 the Federal Republic reserved a right to reexamine its participation in the Treaty of Rome in the light of German reunification. Despite these and other reservations, however, the goal of reunification appeared to be ever further away. As scholars frequently noted, division was not an exception in German history, it was rather the norm. Germany had been a unified nation only from 1871 to 1945, a total of seventy-five years of its history. For part of those seventy-five years, Germany's eastern territory was split by the Polish Corridor created after World War I. Also, during those seventy-five years Germany's boundaries shifted frequently, and by no means only as a result of Nazi conquests. This experience can be contrasted to that of Britain, Japan, France, or even the United States.

The realities of division produced a legion of observers who found evidence that East and West Germany were growing apart culturally as well as politically. One observer could write in December 1987:

> Honecker, in fact, has dismissed unity as a "fireside dream." Time and history seem to be with Honecker. A woman in West Berlin spoke of the widening gulf of mutual incomprehension that her mother, who lives in Kiel in the West, is finding when she visits siblings in Leipzig in the East. After four decades of separate economic and political development, Germans, East and West, are learning that they may have little more in common with one another than they do with German-speaking Austrians.[15]

This theme recurred right up until the East German elections of March 1990 put it to rest. Throughout the 1980s, there was a tendency for scholars to take the relatively bland unification statements of the Federal Republic (prior to November 1989), the vehement objections of the G.D.R. in the East, and the studied indifference of the West German populace as the whole truth about reunification.

But reunification was always a goal of the German people. What prevented this goal from appearing in its full scope was the unlikelihood of its immediate realization. As late as 1987—two years into Gorbachev's rule—only 3 percent of West Germans thought unification was achievable within the next decade.[16] At a political level, it was clear that excessive attention to this issue would have made its realization less likely. Impatience for unity would have offered leverage to the Soviet Union over the terms of reunification.

Patience was not indifference, however, as the world learned when the Berlin Wall opened on November 9, 1989. Germany was not split for four and a half decades because of a lack of interest on the part of the German people; the division was there because of the policy of the Soviet Union and the conditions it would have placed on reunification anytime prior to 1990.

In the end, West German leaders knew that if they hewed to the values and the policies of the West, they could count on American support for article 7 of the Basic Treaty to bring about reunification. They knew, too, that American support would be sufficient to bring along the somewhat less enthusiastic British and French. The Soviet Union was the obstacle. Until the U.S.S.R. allowed East Germany to break free of its stranglehold, there would be no unified Germany. But what could impel the Soviet Union to allow this to happen—an outcome so fully at odds with all that it stood for throughout the postwar period?

The Dissolution of the Soviet Empire

The answer lay not at all in developments in East Germany but within the Soviet Union itself. For essentially nothing had changed within East Germany up until 1989; the government there lumbered on without significant threat. Despite reforms taking place in Poland throughout the 1980s, the East German regime remained on a steady course, apparently untouched by the developments in neighboring Poland. Deep popular dissatisfaction existed in East Germany, but there was little or no way in which it could be expressed until Hungary opened its borders with Austria and allowed East Germans free passage out of the East bloc. This was a decision which set into motion the chain of events that led inexorably to the collapse of the Berlin Wall. When Hungary decided to turn aside the 1968 East German–Hungarian treaty preventing emigration through each other's territory without specific permission, East Germans at last found a way to express their pent-up frustration: they left East Germany by the thousands.

But however liberal Hungary had become in prior months, one fact must be borne in mind: Hungary checked in advance to see how the Soviet Union would react to a decision to allow East Germans free access to Austria.[17] The Soviet leadership had just recently offered pointed criticism of the policies of Erich Honecker's government. They interposed no objection to the Hungarian decision, thus offering a green light to proceed.

These developments were neither contrived by nor even anticipated by the peoples of East or West Germany. The centrality of East Germany to the maintenance of the Soviet Union's European empire seemed to deprive Germany of any meaningful hope of unification. Reflecting on the postwar division, one West German observer wrote in 1987:

> We should realize today that peace in Europe develops on the basis of the division of Germany rather than on the basis of its reunification.
>
> It now looks as if the time has come to lay down priorities and choose between the dream of a united Germany and the reality of an evolving European Community.
>
> Since 1969 we have been pursuing a policy of nonreunification for the sake of human beings on both sides. Isn't it time to give this policy the mark of finality?[18]

This theme was to find many variants in the late 1980s as Germans and non-Germans alike speculated on how the future of Europe could evolve with two, rather than one, German states.

It would be romantic to believe that the peoples of Eastern Europe rose up and took their fates into their own hands and, against all odds, broke free from the overwhelming power of the Soviet Union. It would even be pleasant to think that a series of carefully calculated steps in Eastern Europe brought about this result. But this is not what happened. The Soviet leadership's own example encouraged the loosening of the ossified structures of Eastern Europe. Even more, rapid change was brought about by the consistent and unambiguous statements of the Soviet leadership that it would not intervene militarily to shore up local communist governments.

Thus, the forces against which the people of Eastern Europe revolted were their own Communist governments. This required considerable personal courage in many instances. But the end could not be in doubt. Suddenly deprived of their trump card—the armed forces of the Soviet Union—successive East European governments collapsed quickly. This was a new reality in East Europe. In every previous instance—in East Berlin in 1953, in Budapest in 1956, and in Prague in 1968—it was Soviet military power that restored Communist power in East Europe. The decision to withhold Soviet military force was profoundly disorienting to the Communist officials of the East European governments who depended upon it. None survived for even six months.

It was a change in Soviet policy, not the actions of East Europeans themselves, that was decisive. This is proved above all by one consideration: each East European nation experienced its transformation at approximately the same time. The reformers of Hungary and Poland were no more, or less, successful than those nations whose regimes resisted reform to the bitter end.

These developments suggested nothing less than a sea change in one of the core components of the Soviet Union's security policy. The engaging countenance of General Secretary Gorbachev seen so frequently in the late 1980s exuded great confidence about Soviet governance and power. This confidence was founded upon absolutely nothing. Soviet problems had by 1989 become so severe that the long-term maintenance of Russian power in East Europe was possible only at prohibitive cost. And the Soviet leadership could no longer understand the reasons to pay these costs. As early as its departure from Afghanistan, the U.S.S.R. had lost its will to impose on a small, backward neighbor a system that it did not find satisfactory itself. At a time of deep reassessment of what could be retained from Leninism and what is intrinsically Russian, the Soviet leadership could not find it within itself to be a militant force beyond its own borders.

Having come to this pass, the Soviet Union found little to stop its free fall from Eastern Europe. Soviet troops will be gone from Czechoslovakia and Hungary by mid-1991, and they will be cut in half in Poland by 1991. All 380,000 Soviet troops stationed in East Germany are due to return home over the next three years. When these withdrawals are completed, the Soviet Union will possess not one single military base or facility anywhere in Europe outside its own boundaries. The most heavily defended border in the world will soon be totally undefended. This will create a power vacuum in the middle of Europe that will be filled up in one way or another.

It will also produce for Germany many new options, for it will be above all Germany's decision as to how this vacuum is filled. In this regard, we might say that the Soviet people have something to gain from the policies of glasnost and perestroika; the Americans more yet; the Europeans a great deal; and Germany absolutely everything. Why, then, should the Soviet Union have undertaken this course? It could only have come from utter exhaustion. The question several years ago was: could the Soviet Union save East Europe for communism? The question now is: can it save itself from communism? The liberalization of Eastern Europe is the siren song of the Soviet empire. The principal beneficiary of the dissolution of the Soviet Union will be a strong and increasingly powerful Germany.

CHAPTER TWO

The Continuing German Economic Miracle

The Economy of West Germany

IN 1989 AND THE FIRST HALF of 1990, the West German economy grew at a real rate of 4 percent. Among the leading industrialized nations, only Japan exceeded this rate of growth. West Germany's inflation rate continued its steady decline from an already low 4 percent in the beginning of the 1980s, dipping below 3 percent. Unemployment continued to decline, despite the large influx of refugees from East Germany and Eastern Europe. In 1989 more than 330,000 new jobs were created, and over 400,000 new jobs were created in 1990. Estimates of German economic growth for 1990 continued to rise throughout the year, from 3 to 3.5 and finally to nearly 4 percent. All underestimated the final figure of 4.6 percent. This places West German economic growth well above that of the other leading European nations, and second only to Spain in the European Community. In short, on the eve of unification the dynamic West German economy was humming like a finely tuned Mercedes.

This should have been no surprise. The West German economy experienced almost uninterrupted strong growth throughout its forty-five-year history. The 1948 currency reform set this process in motion; almost from the day on which the new currency was introduced in the Western sectors of occupied Germany, productivity sprang back to life. Within a year of the currency reform, caloric intake of Germans had risen substantially, surpassing the level of the victorious, but impoverished, British. It has been estimated that by 1949, overall West German production reached 89 percent of its 1936 prewar level.[1] By the early 1950s the West German economy surpassed its highest prewar level of industrial production. So much for the agrarian Germany in the center of Europe that Treasury Secretary Morgenthau had envisioned.

West German per capita income in 1990 stood at $20,775.00.[2] What is remarkable about this per capita income is not simply its level, or even its rapid rise over the past several decades; it is that it has occurred without a massive investment in hours worked by West Germans. Despite the much-vaunted discipline and hard work of Germans, the fact is that West Germans work fewer hours per year than do workers in any other major industrialized nation. In 1988, the average West German worked 215 hours a year fewer than his American counterpart, and 452 hours fewer than his Japanese counterpart. This is a testimonial less to hard work and discipline than to efficiency and high productivity.

This economic record put the West German federal budget in solid shape. Net new West German government borrowing remained relatively low in the late 1980s, stabilizing at less than 1 percent of GNP. Between 1988 and 1989 tax revenues grew a full 12 percent. As reported in a State Department analysis, "From the standpoint of the West German federal budget, East Germany could not have picked a better time to open its borders."[3]

German economic growth has not been financed by foreign borrowing over the past several decades. To the contrary, with the exception of 1979–1981, the Federal Republic of Germany had a positive current account balance every single year since 1970. In

Hours of Negotiated Scheduled Work
Situation as of November 1, 1988

	AVERAGE WORK WEEK (HOURS)	ANNUAL VACATION PLUS ADDITIONAL FREE TIME (DAYS)	HOLIDAYS (DAYS)	AVERAGE WORK YEAR (YEARS)
F.R.G	38.4	30	10	1,697
Denmark	38	25	8	1,733
Belgium	38	20	11	1,748
Neth.	40	36.5	5	1,756
France	39	25.5	9	1,767
Italy	40	31	9	1,768
U.K.	39	25	8	1,778
Luxemb.	40	27	10	1,792
Spain	40	22	14	1,800
Greece	40	22	9	1,840
Ireland	40	20	8	1,864
Portugal	45	22	14	2,025
Austria	38.9	26.5	11.5	1,735
Norway	37.5	21	8	1,740
Switz.	41	22.5	8	1,890
Sweden	40	25	8	1,824
Finland	40	33	6	1,776
U.S.A.	40	12	10	1,912
Japan	NA	NA	NA	2,149

Source: Federation of German Employers Associations—Bundesvereinigung Deutscher Arbeitgeberverbaende (BDA)
(Drawn from the U.S. Department of Labor)

the late 1980s the West German current account balance surpassed Japan's, to place it squarely as the world's largest.

The greatest share of West German trade by far is with other European nations. In 1988, for example, the F.R.G. exported 54.3 percent of its exports to other European Community (EC) nations and 18.7 percent to non-EC European nations, for a total of 73 percent of its exports to Europe. In that same year, the F.R.G.

Current Account Balances in Billions of Dollars

	1987	1988	1989	1990
United States	− 143.7	− 126.6	− 122.0	− 118.0
Japan	87.0	79.6	61.0	61.0
Germany	45.2	48.5	61.0	71.0
France	− 4.4	− 3.6	− 4.0	− 4.0
Italy	− 1.5	− 5.6	− 12.0	− 13.0
United Kingdom	− 4.7	− 25.9	− 32.0	− 30.0
Canada	− 7.1	− 8.4	− 14.0	− 14.0

Source: Organization for Economic Cooperation and Development

imported 51.7 percent from other EC nations and 15.9 percent from non-EC European nations, for a total of 67.6 percent of its imports from Europe. In absolute terms, West Germany on the eve of unification was the largest exporting nation in the world; in the European context, it was totally dominant. Between 1985 and 1989, West Germany's trade surplus with other EC nations tripled, growing from DM32 billion to DM94 billion.[4] This accounted for more than two-thirds of Germany's worldwide trade surplus.

Despite some fluctuations, German exports to Europe are likely to remain fundamentally strong for several reasons. First, demand for German capital goods will remain high, as the economies of EC member nations are projected to continue generally healthy growth. Second, because of relatively high labor costs, Germany has automated its production to the fullest extent of any EC economy. Its capital products are likely to continue to set the standard for quality and to remain competitive even as the German mark grows stronger.

German success at home and abroad resulted in a cash surplus position. Many large German corporations retained large cash surpluses and were in a position to invest in expansion in the eastern part of Germany and abroad. Much of Germany's foreign direct investment, like its exports and imports, takes place in other EC countries. However, in the 1980s the United States proved an inviting field for selected acquisitions. At the end of 1988, German assets in the United States stood at $26.7 billion, $8.4 billion more than the $18.3 billion in U.S. assets in Germany.[5] At this time German acquisitions are turning increasingly toward Europe, and particularly toward expansion into the former G.D.R. In 1989 the number of German acquisitions in the United States fell to fourteen, from twenty-five in 1988 and twenty-one in 1987.[6]

Germany in turn has been of interest to foreign investors both in Europe and in America and Japan. The number of foreign acquisitions of German firms in the first half of 1989 was more than double the number of German foreign acquisitions.[7] Of the former, Japan represented less than 10 percent.[8] To this point, German firms have obviously proceeded cautiously. But the surplus position of large German firms will guarantee that when they act, they will act decisively.[9]

West Germany established this enviable record of growth at a time when it was required by its laws and mores to absorb a huge influx of refugees. In 1988 West Germany assimilated 240,000 ethnic Germans from East Europe and East Germany. In 1989, that number swelled to 720,000, or more than 1 percent of the entire West German population. Figures for 1990 prior to reunification far exceeded these rates. There were sizable fiscal and social costs of this influx. But one cannot reasonably conclude that the costs outweighed the benefits. As many as two-thirds of all East German resettlers found employment in West Germany in 1989. Perhaps as many as one-half of all East European ethnic Germans did so. These people provided much-needed skilled and semiskilled labor. In addition, they raised demand for consumer goods, automobiles, and housing. It is reasonable to conclude that the West German economy grew in part *because* of the influx of refugees, not despite it.

Even without reunification, West Germany would have been poised to grow rapidly in the 1990s. A cash rich, export-oriented, high value producing nation, West Germany was well positioned to reap the fullest benefits from EC 1992. As the most open European nation, West Germany had the least to lose and the most to gain from further West European economic integration. Very little economic restructuring was required. Finally, West Germany, like Japan, had developed only a limited arms manufacturing industry. Up to the present, it has ceded the rights to compete in this sphere of its natural competitive advantage to other nations, principally the United States, France, Britain, and Italy. Should Germany have taken a different course in terms of arms production, this could only have been a benefit to its economy. With the supplement of additional refugees to offset its very low birthrate, there was virtually no cloud on the horizon to affect West Germany's prospects for continued strong growth in the 1990s.

The Economy of the German Democratic Republic

What did East Germany bring to the table? How will the inclusion of this land into a unified Germany alter the prospects for continued German growth? Historically, it was very difficult to gauge the economic performance of the East German economy. Until November 1989, even such elementary information as net debt and exchange valuations were regarded as state secrets of the G.D.R. Given that many aspects of East German economic activity were (not surprisingly) overstated, it is not difficult to understand why this information remained classified.

In the past year, however, it has been possible for the first time to begin to develop an accurate account for the East German economy on the eve of reunification. This is a welcome relief from the admittedly clever, but still guesswork, approaches that had characterized economic analysis of the G.D.R. between 1950 and 1989.

The picture that emerges is of an economy that had very significant structural problems and limitations, and was able to survive only by destroying its capital base and its environment to cover its inefficiencies. To begin, the region of the G.D.R. is not especially rich in natural resources, the principal ones being coal, potash, and uranium. Historically, the region was predominantly an agricultural area including both small and middle-size farms and large estates. Beyond this, as has already been mentioned, what industrial capabilities had survived the war were largely removed by the Soviet Union between 1945 and 1955 as war reparations. Thus, the G.D.R. began its existence without any advantages at all, relatively devoid of natural resources, its historical trading patterns interrupted, and its national stock of capital forcibly removed by its so-called ally and protector.

Although the G.D.R. was a densely populated country by world standards, its population declined throughout its forty-year existence. This was not entirely, or even principally, due to its relatively low fertility rate, which was slightly higher than that of West Germany. It was rather a result of out-migration to the West—in large numbers from 1951 through 1961, and then again beginning in 1989. In the four decades of the G.D.R's existence, its population declined almost 2 million people, half of that loss occurring between 1951 and the closure of the border between the two Germanies in 1961. Throughout its forty years, the ratio of men to women returned to a more normal level from the disproportionately high percentage of women in the immediate postwar years.

The decline in population created problems for the G.D.R.'s labor force. This was particularly true because the people who fled the G.D.R. tended to be younger than the general population. Older East Germans were more likely to remain, either because of life-long attachments or because of relatively generous retirement programs. In order to meet labor shortages—and because of the ideological viewpoint regarding work and family—women made up a greater share of the work force than in Western countries, reaching 49 percent of the work force at the end of the 1980s.

The G.D.R. collectivized nearly 95 percent of its agricultural production. It appears, almost in defiance of logic and history, that these collectives were able to feed the East German population and actually increase yields over time. Nevertheless, yields per acre in the G.D.R. were only about three-fourths those of West Germany. To secure these yields, the G.D.R. employed far too many people in agriculture, resulting in per person yields less than one-half those in the West. Prior to reunification, about 10 percent of the East German work force was employed in agriculture. This was about twice the 5.1 percent share employed in agriculture in West Germany, where there also remains room to reduce subsidies and diminish the farm population to bring about maximum efficiency. Had the G.D.R. been able to achieve the productivity of the West in agriculture, it could have reduced the number of people employed in agriculture from 900,000 to 450,000. This would have freed up 450,000 people for industrial production, which experienced chronic labor shortages throughout the duration of the G.D.R. This 5 percent differential was the price of the inefficiency of the structure of collectivized agriculture in a centrally planned economy.

The key to the G.D.R.'s economic survival and to its relative success in the East bloc (it produced the highest per capita income of the centrally planned East European economies) lay in its industrial capability. Over time the G.D.R. centralized its heavy industrial production into 126 large-scale enterprises called *Kombinate*. These entities arose out of no particular economic necessities and had no particular economic rationale. They were the result of a politically driven organization of East German industry. Within the East bloc, these enterprises produced among the best industrial products. Over time, however, the inefficiencies of the *Kombinate* were felt increasingly in the areas of financial management and the rational allocation of materials. East Germany's growth rate slowed along with those of all the other centrally planned East European economies, coming to nearly a complete stall in the late 1980s. In the wake of reunification, the *Kombinate* have been broken up into nearly 8,000 more manageable economic units by the board empowered to privatize the East German economy. As in every sector of the East German economy, a far too high number of people were employed in these enterprises. Indeed, in the first month after monetary union in July 1990, unemployment in East Germany grew 60 percent, to 223,000 people.

Prior to the opening of the Berlin Wall, the G.D.R. maintained a military force of about 173,000 men. Official data presented the defense share of the East German economy at 5.5 percent in the mid-1980s.[10] As further evidence of defense spending patterns in each of the East bloc nations comes to light, it is likely to become clear that such costs took a significantly larger share than official data suggested. Indeed, an article from the Socialist Unity Party newspaper *Neues Deutschland* suggested that defense spending took an ever greater share of the East German economy in the 1980s, growing twice as fast as the economy.[11] At the same time, there is evidence that investment held a decreasing share of the East German economy between 1975 and 1985, shrinking from 23 to 17 percent.[12] Without ascribing too much accuracy to these specific figures, the general picture is one of an economy in deep and growing difficulty in the 1980s.

If there was any sector in which the G.D.R. did invest more productively, it was in human capital. To be sure, this did not include job training and skills to compete successfully in a world economy. But the people of the G.D.R. possessed near-universal literacy equivalent to that in West Germany. The basic educational building blocks are thus in place in eastern Germany, and there is every reason to expect that Germans from the former G.D.R. will rapidly become competitive with their counterparts in the West. After a transition period of no more than four or five years, differentials in worker quality between eastern and western Germany should be reduced to no more than standard regional differences.

In sum, the G.D.R. produced a highly literate, highly trainable, but poorly motivated, labor force which probably took the East German economy to the most efficiency possible within its flawed structure. It is of course difficult to assign a specific number to East Germany's GNP on the eve of reunification. Estimates in the late 1980s ranged from $66 billion to the one-time CIA assessment that the East German economy was as productive as the West's. Nevertheless, based upon various estimates and a common sense judgment vis-a-vis other economies, it is not unreasonable to place the East German GNP in the range of about $200 billion on the eve of unification.

The Unified German Economy: A Second *Wirtschaftswunder*

The simple addition of the two German economies late in 1990 produced a total gross national product in excess of $1.4 trillion. This was not only the largest GNP of any West European country (a designation the West German economy held in its own right), it was almost the size of the next two West European economies *combined*. We will explore these relationships in the next section of this chapter. Here we consider the great synergistic impact of unification on the economies of both former parts of Germany. If the currency reform of 1948 produced an "economic miracle" in the western portion of Germany, the integration of the two parts of Germany will almost certainly produce a second.

This is not to say that the process of economic integration will be easy or without cost. Clearly, initial estimates of how much West

German tax revenue will be required to cover the transitional losses were low. These were amended upward twice in 1990 alone, and Chancellor Kohl has had to backtrack on his "no new taxes" pledge and propose a $31 billion tax increase. Also, it is fair to say that the magnitude of the task of modernizing the former East German economy was also underestimated. Lacking firsthand experience of the actual condition of the East German infrastructure and the East German industrial base, West Germans could not have guessed the full extent of the problem.

It is also not to say that reunification will proceed without other economic and social difficulties. There remains always a possibility of inflation, although the addition of so many unemployed workers to the economy will likely restrain inflationary pressures. Massive —though temporary—unemployment will itself constitute a wrenching political problem. Estimates are that 3.7 million old jobs in the former G.D.R. will disappear (nearly 40 percent of the former employment base). At the beginning of 1991, 600,000 former G.D.R. workers were unemployed, and nearly three times that number were working reduced hours. A difficult transition is clearly underway.

But it is critical to distinguish between transitory problems and fundamental structural problems. It is all the more important to do so because not every political party in Germany and not every journalist has an incentive to do this. In this regard, it is well to recall some of the realities of the rosy days of the first economic miracle. As Ludwig Erhard, Adenauer's economics minister, learned from personal experience, the German boom of the late 1940s and early 1950s did not occur without serious birth pains. Inflation began nearly as soon as currency reform was put into place. Unemployment rose rapidly. The opposition Social Democratic Party called for the reintroduction of rationing and for an across-the-board freeze on prices. A general strike was called in November of 1948. Erhard tried to explain again and again—not always to receptive ears—the difference between short-term and long-term problems. He argued that patience was required and that temporarily high prices would bring forth a profusion of new goods that in turn would moderate price levels. To secure his policies he agreed to additional governmental regulations, thus creating the social market economy.

Such an outcome is not at all difficult to envision at the current time. Faced with substantial unemployment, the German government has found that it must adopt certain special policies for eastern Germany in order to weather the transition to a market economy in that part of the country. But for purposes of understanding the deeper possibilities for the German economy, we must focus not on temporary difficulties and expedients, but upon structural realities. And in this regard, one must simply say that East and West Germany could not possibly have been more suitable partners for marriage.

West Germany required a solid location for investing its cash surplus. This investment could have occurred to some extent in the western German economy itself, and indeed it will do so. But the massive surplus could not have been productively invested in this economy by itself. The East provides a ready-made location for this investment. It has a base of educated workers and consumers who speak German. It offers a reservoir for potential investment in which the West Germans have a natural competitive advantage over their industrialized competitors. And finally, just about the only difficulty that any observer could identify for West Germany in the years before reunification was the internal decline of the ethnic German population. This problem is resolved, at least for the time being, by the addition of 25 percent more ethnic Germans to its population.

From the standpoint of the East, reunification works equally well. It is clear from the long-term decline in growth rates that the East Germans had taken their economy as far as it could go without structural reorganization. The East German economy was simply not replenishing itself with adequate investment. Neither was it replenishing itself with productive workers, and of the available work force, many were underutilized and undermotivated. The East German economy needed a major infusion of new capital, of incentives, and of productive labor. All of this will be achieved by reunification.

Estimates for growth in the eastern portion of Germany vary, but are uniformly optimistic. Some former West German officials speculate that yearly growth could be about 10 percent a year.[13] This estimate is seconded by Axel Siedenberg of Deutsche Bank, who

sees growth in the 8 to 10 percent yearly range.[14] The Industrial
Bank of Japan suggests a growth rate of nearly 10 percent per year.
One thoughtful observer expects a growth of productivity in the
eastern portion of Germany in the range of 20 percent per year for
the next several years.[15] In short, prospects for rapid growth should
be very good over a multiyear period until eastern Germany reaches
the level of the western portion of the country.

Can the western portion provide help for the East without damage
to its own economic standing? Some critics have said that a unified
Germany will be economically weaker than West Germany alone.
But the experience of recent years, in which the West German
economy grew rapidly even as it assimilated many new refugees,
suggests that the former West Germany will strongly benefit from
unification. Indeed, economic results to date suggest that unification
has been a powerful economic stimulus for growth in the former
West Germany. In the third quarter of 1990 economic growth raced
along at 8 percent, helping to put overall real growth for 1990 at
4.6 percent. Employment in the western part of Germany rose
775,000, the largest increase in more than thirty years.

But who will pay the costs of modernizing the East? First, many
of the costs of modernizing the East's industry will be borne by
private firms in the West. These are the very firms that are flush
with financial reserves. To the extent that additional borrowing is
required, in many cases it will be backed by new assets of land (or,
less likely, useful industrial plants) in the East. It seems well within
the capacity of West German industry to provide the necessary
capital for modernization over a period of five to ten years. To the
extent that foreign investors participate, this process will be
speeded up.

Funds for the modernization of infrastructure may be somewhat
more difficult to attain in sufficient quantities to make the kind of
progress that Germans in both the East and West desire. One source
of funding will be the sale of former G.D.R-owned enterprises.
How much money this will raise is uncertain at this time. More
likely will be direct German federal funding for the cost of envi-
ronmental and other infrastructure problems, supplemented in turn
by growing revenues from the five federal states in the East. But
infrastructure modernization is by its very nature a time-consuming

process that cannot be completed all at once. It requires substantial planning to make major changes in local transportation systems, utilities, sewer systems, and communications systems. These are long-term projects that do not always require substantial funds up front. Often, these monies are expended more slowly than either planned or hoped, and it is likely that the German government will find that these funds will spend out more slowly than anticipated.

The German government will be required to assume the direct costs of reunification. These will not be insignificant; health insurance and unemployment compensation for formerly employed workers in the East will be costly. But there are several reasons for optimism. First, the former West German government all along allocated funds within its budget that were associated directly or indirectly with the existence of two German states. In 1989, for example, direct subsidies from West to East Germany totaled about DM2.5 billion. Of these funds, nearly DM1.4 billion was paid directly to the G.D.R. for postal and communications facilities, for transit fees, and for the release of political prisoners. Additional funds were expended on resettlers and immigrants from the East, as well as for "welcome money." The former West German government offered subsidies for home loans and furnishing to resettlers, as well as unemployment compensation for those unable to find work. In addition to these payments, the West German government forgave duties and value-added taxes on intra-German trade. In all, these costs ran to perhaps DM5 billion. The German Unity Fund of DM115 billion will be funded by DM20 billion from government revenues and DM95 billion borrowing. The DM20 billion will be composed of the above-mentioned funds the former West German government would have spent between 1991 and 1994 on subsidies that are no longer needed.

More significant, however, is the projected growth of German tax revenues from reunification. For 1990, the increase of one percentage point of economic growth in West Germany (from three to four percent) resulted in increased tax revenues of DM12 billion over initial projections. Over the next four years, increased tax revenues are now estimated at DM115 billion more than initially forecast.[16]

These numbers should not be surprising. What they reflect is that the entire German budget will be far larger in coming years, both on the expenditure side and on the revenue side. Those analysts who focus exclusively on the costs of reunification (which have been estimated to be variously between DM500 billion and DM1.1 trillion) are bound to produce a pessimistic picture. The fact is, however, that although German government borrowing will rise, the growth of revenues in both the western and eastern portions of Germany will over time offset a great share of the federal costs associated with reunification. One should note that in addition to the large West German firms going into the East, many small new businesses are springing up there. In the first half of 1990 alone, 100,482 applications to begin new businesses were registered in the East.[17] Some of these businesses will not succeed, but many others will, providing both additional employment and state and federal tax revenues in the eastern portion of Germany.

None of this is intended to minimize the pain of transition which will be experienced by many Germans who are unemployed or working reduced hours. Clearly, the hope that reunification could be financed without a tax increase has disappeared: new taxes on income, gasoline, cigarettes, and consumption will be in effect over the next several years.

But when looked at in the large, the outcome will inevitably be highly positive. Reunification puts an end to a great many structural inefficiencies and irrationalities that limited the economies of both former Germanies. A skilled, labor-short West has joined a capital-short, structurally deficient East. The result has provided a new internal market 25 percent larger than the previous F.R.G. market. It has almost overnight reduced the structural inefficiencies of combined German agriculture by half. It has matched pent-up consumer demand with high-quality products. And it will allow a nearly 50 percent reduction in German armed forces from a combined East and West total of 670,000 to 370,000, at the same time resulting in greater security.

Let us consider a combined German economy in which the eastern portion grows rapidly, say at 10 percent annually, and the western portion grows at 4 percent. After five years the eastern and western portions of Germany grow at an average combined overall rate of 4 percent. The following chart reflects these assumptions:

German GNP (in billions of dollars)

	WEST	EAST	TOTAL
1990	1,290	216	1,506
1991	1,341	237	1,578
1992	1,395	260	1,655
1993	1,451	286	1,737
1994	1,509	315	1,824
1995	1,569	346	1,915
1996			1,992
1997			2,071
1998			2,154
1999			2,240
2000			2,330

As this chart shows, the German economy would reach nearly $2.5 trillion by the turn of the century. If, in response to strong growth the value of the mark should increase against the dollar by even 1 or 2 percent a year, the relative value of the German economy could approach $3 trillion by the year 2000. It is perhaps worth noting that these assumed overall German growth rates are *less* than those actually registered in the West German economy in the years 1948–1953.

The German Economy in Europe

As the European Community has moved toward elimination of trade and investment barriers, the economies of these nations have prospered. From the beginning of the 1980s, when American economic growth and job creation far outpaced West Europe's, the tables have turned; Europe looks toward a decade of solid growth and is frequently mentioned as a "locomotive" of the western economy. As the largest trading nation within the EC, Germany is positioned to benefit most from this growth. Indeed, Germany's success over the past two years traces in part to its extraordinary record of export sales. In the first three months of 1990, West German exports were up 18 percent over the previous year, to $99.8 billion, and surpassed total United States exports. What benefits each EC nation will benefit them all, but no nation stands to gain more than Germany. One system for rating who will gain most and who least from EC 1992 has been developed by the *Economist*, and appears on the following page. The relative preponderance of Germany in the EC will grow throughout the 1990s. This is so not only because of the addition of East Germany, but because of trade and investment capabilities already in place in the Federal Republic prior to reunification. Although all EC nations will become richer, the richest will become even richer, faster.

Beyond this, no region stands to gain more economically from the liberalization of Eastern Europe than does the EC, and no nation within the EC should gain more than Germany. In 1989, EC nations exported roughly three times as much to East European nations as did the United States and Japan combined. The ratio of imports from Eastern Europe into the EC was even higher, as the chart entitled "Eastern Europe's Trade Partners" illustrates. The Federal Republic of Germany was the largest single trading nation in the EC with Eastern Europe. Even without reunification with East Germany, West Germany was poised to make the most gains in Eastern Europe. A reunified Germany will reinforce and magnify this position. The G.D.R. conducted fully 40 percent of its trade with the Soviet Union, and another 25 percent with other East European countries. These patterns will be intensified for a reunified Germany which is able to provide credits for the purchase of German exports. The chart entitled "West German Lending" outlines the growth of West German commercial credits to East European nations in the 1980s. German commercial lending activities in Eastern Europe are in stark contrast to the lending activities of U.S. commercial banks in the 1980s, as is reflected in the chart comparing U.S., U.K., West German, and Japanese lending in 1981 and 1988. These charts display a "sharp divergence in lending strategies among German and Japanese banks on the one hand and U.S. and (to a lesser extent) U.K. banks on the other," suggesting that at least in part this divergence can be accounted for in terms of trade flows.[20] Whatever else one makes of this, it is clear that West Germany saw a degree of security and/or necessity in lending to Eastern Europe that was missing in American assessments.

Who Will Gain Most from Europe's Boom?

| RANKING | AS % OF TOTAL EXPORTS | | AS % OF GDP | | | INFLATION % | HOURLY LABOR COSTS W. GERMANY = 100 |
	EXPORTS TO W. GERMANY	EXPORTS TO EASTERN BLOCK	TOTAL EXPORTS	NET CAPITAL EXPORTS OF GOODS	CURRENT ACCOUNT		
1 W. Germany	n/a	5.0	32.6	3.9	5.4	2.3	100
2 Austria	31	11.9	35.7	−0.4	0.0	3.1	73.7
3 Switzerland	21	4.1	36.3	4.1	3.5	4.6	124.0
4 Holland	27	1.8	54.8	−1.6	1.9	2.1	81.4
5 Ireland	11	1.3	72.0	6.3	1.4	4.2	55.7
6 Denmark	18	2.0	34.1	0.0	−1.1	3.0	81.7
7 Belgium	18	1.2	69.0	−2.2	2.2	3.2	79.3
8 France	17	2.0	21.5	−0.3	−0.4	3.2	68.1
9 Italy	16	7.1	18.1	1.0	−1.4	5.8	74.6
10 Portugal	17	3.3	33.0	•	−3.1	12.8	18.1
11 Sweden	12	3.5	33.1	0.8	−2.3	10.1	95.1
12 Greece	17	6.5	24.4	•	−4.7	17.8	29.1
13 Britain	12	1.8	23.3	0.2	−3.4	9.4	59.5
14 Spain	12	2.8	19.5	•	−3.8	7.0	43.0

Latest available figures except current account, 1990 forecast; • net importers

Sources: OECD; IMF; Swedish Employers' Confederation

Eastern Europe's Trade Partners*

US$ MILLION	US		JAPAN		EC	
	EXPORT TO	IMPORT FROM	EXPORT TO	IMPORT FROM	EXPORT TO	IMPORT FROM
Soviet Union	4,201	802	3,053	2,525	12,425	15,303
Romania	86	463	40	166	624	2,565
Bulgaria	160	117	114	46	1,476	561
Czechoslovakia	46	102	63	120	2,533	2,557
East Germany	457	151	97	63	6,473	5,252
Hungary	116	360	92	142	3,192	2,779
Poland	183	495	148	94	4,166	4,224

*Annualized 1989 totals

Source: Economic Commission of Europe (Drawn from *Far Eastern Economic Review*)

West German Lending[18]

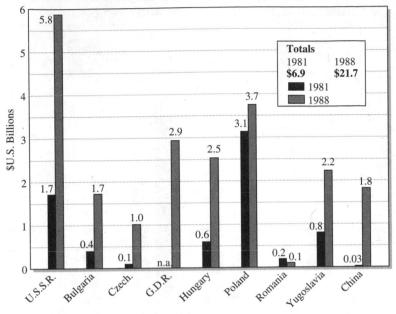

Source: Lawrence S. Brainard, Bankers Trust Company

Having experienced difficulties with risky foreign debt in the early 1980s, U.S. lending institutions have been shy about increasing their exposure in Eastern Europe. Germany is therefore well positioned from the standpoint of both financial ability and practical experience to expand its relationships in Eastern Europe. Economist Norbert Walter of Deutsche Bank has predicted that the 5 percent share of West German exports going to Eastern Europe could triple to 15 percent in the next decade.[21]

German government-guaranteed credit will also deepen German commercial activities in Eastern Europe. Germany has offered guaranteed credits to the Soviet Union, to Hungary, and to Poland. In some of these cases, geopolitical factors play a role, and hence it is difficult to predict how economically significant the results will be. But the German interest in Poland, Hungary, Czechoslovakia, and the Soviet Union is unmistakable. So, too, is the growing German economic influence in each of these nations.

Commercial Lending by Four Major Western Nations to the Soviet Union, Eastern Europe, and China[19]

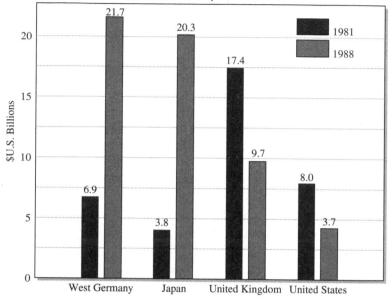

Source: Lawrence S. Brainard, Bankers Trust Company

If we draw together these elements—German reunification, West German integration, and the liberalization of Eastern Europe—we find a vivid picture of German dynamism. Each of these factors by itself would benefit Germany more than any other single nation; together their impact on German economic strength is bound to be reinforcing, sustained, and powerful.

If we compare this German economy to that of the Soviet Union, the results are unambiguous and striking. Even assuming a Soviet economic growth rate of 2 percent a year, the German economy will surpass the Soviet Union's by 1993. Assuming a more realistic no-growth or negative growth scenario for the Soviet Union, this will occur in 1992. *By the end of the decade the German economy will be 20 percent larger than the Soviet economy*—assuming, of course, that the Soviet Union remains intact as an entity for that long.

This result is both the stimulus for and, ironically, the inevitable result of Gorbachev's reforms. But it is a result that is surprising only when considered in light of the postwar period. For it represents a fundamental return to the Europe of a century ago. John Maynard Keynes wrote of this Europe in his 1920 classic, *The Economic Consequences of the Peace*: "The whole of Europe east of the Rhine thus fell into the German industrial orbit, and its economic life was adjusted accordingly." Today's Europe has not only its geographical center but also its economic center in Germany. Europe as a whole will became stronger and richer vis-a-vis other regions, particularly the already poor ones; but Germany will become stronger and richer than the rest of Europe. Whether, how, and in what degree Germany can exercise this strength depends upon how much independence of action it retains as a nation within Europe.

CHAPTER THREE

The Politics of Germany: Brussels vs. Berlin

The Politics of Postwar Germany

THAT THE POLITICAL LIFE of postwar Germany could not be predicted in 1945 goes without saying. As the allies laid plans for the postwar democratization of a defeated Germany, they must have known that there did not yet exist a successful model of a nation compelled by outside powers to become a democracy. Experience with the post-World War I creation of the Weimar Republic did not offer strong grounds for optimism. The Weimar experience may have provided some guideposts as to what to avoid in constructing a viable democracy, but it certainly did not prove that constructing a viable democracy was possible.

Indeed, looking back at the postwar democratization of both West Germany and Japan, one cannot help but be struck by the confidence of the American conquerors that democratization could and would succeed. Even now, as we survey the landscape of American democracy-building projects over the past forty-five years, it is not clear that the United States possesses a good recipe for creating democracies. In 1945, there was no track record of success at all. But in Germany and Japan, the U.S. did have a free hand in remaking political institutions from the ground up, and a military government to enforce the new conventions until they took root. This was no small advantage.

In Germany the picture was clouded by the Soviet Union. As American plans were drawn and redrawn for occupied Germany, the Kremlin was also busy in 1944 and 1945 developing plans of its own. Along with the Soviet troops who captured Berlin came Soviet operatives and, in turn, anti-Nazi German Communists who had resided in the Soviet Union during the war. The Soviet Union set about promptly in the summer of 1945 to establish political groupings dominated by their own people. The core of their activities centered around Berlin, for it was still the working assumption of each of the allied powers that Berlin was and would remain the key to all of Germany. The Soviet Union hoped to blur public distinctions between their own militant communist organizers and the social democrats, and hence to secure pliable regimes. They failed to achieve this even in their own zone of occupation, much less in the allied zones.

For the Americans, creating a theoretical political structure for Western Germany was the easier part; it was more difficult to determine how to put it into practice. Americans held their usual doubts about whether democratic ends could or should be achieved by nondemocratic means. It was clear enough that all vestiges of Nazism should be banned; there was no sentiment anywhere for tolerating this form of politics. But should the United States ban other political parties? Should it ban the Communist party? Should it give public and private encouragement to the political parties and candidates it favored? These were issues of considerable debate in the immediate postwar years, just as they have remained for American democracy builders ever since.

The politics of democratization in Western Germany were favored by two positive factors. As political parties were allowed to reorganize, Western Germans resumed the traditions that had existed before 1933. They began to group themselves around the Christian Democratic Party (CDU) and the Social Democratic Party (SPD).

In addition, other smaller parties including the Communist party—which the Americans decided to permit—came into existence. The first positive factor for West German democratization was the caliber of leadership offered by the Christian Democratic Party. Konrad Adenauer aligned his party, and the emerging nation, on a course fully committed to the democratic ideals of pluralism, tolerance, and individual liberty. He also set both his party and his new government on a course that could only be described as unabashedly pro-American. In these ways, Adenauer provided reassurance to the American occupiers that West Germany was on the road to becoming a reliable democratic ally.

But no less significant was the leadership of the SPD in the early postwar years, and particularly that of Kurt Schumacher. A man of impeccable anti-Nazi credentials, Schumacher accomplished an absolutely critical task for the new West German democracy: he insulated the main left-leaning political party from the blandishments of the antidemocratic Communist party. In the Soviet sector of Berlin, the less popular Communist party forced a merger upon the more popular SPD to create a new "unity" party (the Socialist Unity Party, or SED). This merger was intended to create the appearance of democracy and the reality of communism. In the western sectors of Berlin, however, the SPD voted freely *not* to merge with the small Communist party. By a plurality of 82 percent, the SPD voted to retain its independence. This was an extraordinary service to the emerging West German state, for it guaranteed that the essential core of both major political parties would be democratic. This is indispensable for a viable democratic government.

But if the SPD settled firmly in the camp of democracy, it nevertheless diverged strongly from American views on many issues. The SPD was at that time a socialist party, historically oriented toward labor. It was not until the adoption of the Bad Godesberg Program in 1959 that the SPD abandoned its orientation as a working man's party and became a broad-gauged "people's party." This step, taken after a decade of federal electoral defeats, further clarified the distinction between democratic socialism and communism.

But the SPD differed with Adenauer and with the Americans on other fundamental issues as well. The SPD believed that Adenauer's firm alignment of West Germany with the West jeopardized the prospects for German reunification. They attacked Adenauer for his allegedly slavish devotion to America and presented themselves as the political party of reunification. This view extended to Adenauer's decision to rearm and to join NATO, a move that the SPD attacked as another step away from the reunification of Germany.

In short, although the SPD shared with Americans the root value of democracy, it also possessed from the beginning a certain independence and a certain critical distance from the United States that has not characterized the CDU. This was observable during the period of SPD dominance between 1969 and 1982. During these years, the relationship between the Federal Republic and the United States remained very solid at its core. But relations were at their most formal in the postwar period. Perhaps this was a result of the unpopular American war in Vietnam. Yet there remains an inescapable sense that the SPD—as indeed, the Left in Germany generally—harbors serious reservations about the United States and prefers, where possible, to follow a more independent course.

Indeed, it was during the years of SPD dominance that the policy of *Ostpolitik* was developed. To say the least, this was not an American creation. It should be said directly that *Ostpolitik* operated well within the conceptual framework of Western values and the Western alliance. In fairness, it should also be noted that the fruits of this policy, which was subsequently also adopted by the CDU, were many. But there is no doubt that *Ostpolitik* reflected a substantial German independence of tactics, if nothing more. From time to time it also betrayed a certain moral relativism on the German Left that saw few, if any, significant differences between the United States and the Soviet Union.[1] The less pleasant side of this tendency included a latter-day enthusiasm for Erich Honecker that is difficult to imagine today.

These tendencies found their fullest expression in the left party of the Greens. The Greens expressed in words what lay in the hearts of many on the German Left: that West Germany would be better off pursuing its own course than aligning itself with either the United States or the Soviet Union. As there was no prospect of alignment with the Soviet Union, this meant in practice that West Germany should distance itself from the United States.

Americans have up until now tended to interpret the independence of the German Left through their own political vocabulary; that is, they have seen it as an *ideological* matter. They have interpreted —perhaps correctly to an extent—independence as ideological neutrality between the values of the West and the values of the East. But this is no longer relevant. At a time when the former ideals of the East have collapsed, the ideological question is no longer significant. It matters not at all that the German Left should be in any way sympathetic to the ideals of the former East Germany, for eastern Germany now holds the ideals of the West. So, too, with regard to the Soviet Union. Is it meaningful, for example, whether the German Left holds any particular view of perestroika? *Ideology no longer matters*. There is no longer any meaning to the question of whether Germany will become ideologically "neutral."

But what does remain, and what does matter, is that the German Left retains its tradition of independence even while the ideology on which that independence was fixed has disappeared.

The question arises now as to what that spirit of independence will attach itself. Germany *will* become more independent in the next decade. It is uncertain how that independence will express itself, but it is not uncertain how that independence will first assert itself: it will arise from the place it has been nurtured for forty-five years—on the German Left. The Left in postwar Germany was invariably the party that fostered go-it-alone, split-the-difference tendencies in the politics of the Federal Republic. This will be fateful now precisely *not* because of a connection to Marxism, but because of the effect it will have on the way in which a unified Germany will be integrated into Europe in the West and in the East.

This characteristic left-leaning independence will have its effect on domestic German politics. As Soviet and American military forces recede in central Europe, and as the Soviet gift of reunification and the American gift of protection are given and gone, there will be domestic political pressures for the CDU to display a new degree of independence from American views. The fundamentally new political-military situation, fueled by pressure from the German Left, will bring an end to the "American party" as we have known it.

It was predictable sooner, but obvious as early as November/ December 1989, with Chancellor Kohl's ten-point plan for reunification, that the politics of Germany had assumed new and broader parameters. Had it been possible for Chancellor Kohl to speak at that time about reunification for German ears alone, one supposes this would have been the first choice. Having to choose between a speech on reunification heard by Germans and by all the world, or no speech at all, the demands of internal politics prevailed. This new independence was again expressed in Chancellor Kohl's announcement in the Soviet Union that he had agreed with General Secretary Gorbachev on new limitations on German armed forces in exchange for Soviet acquiescence in continued German membership in NATO. Likewise, the simple announcement that American troops would depart from Berlin when Soviet troops left eastern Germany reflected a unilateral self-certainty not evident in German politics up to that time.

The Force of the East

These tendencies toward new independence from America are likely to be subtly reinforced by the integration of East Germany into the unified German political system. In light of the many fatuous predictions about the impact of the East, one must state this as carefully as possible.

To begin, the impact of the East on German politics does not mean reversion to the failed ideology of communism. Who knows better than the former East Germans the futility of this? Nor does it imply any significant support for a "third way" between capitalism and communism, as was so widely predicted prior to the East German elections in the spring of 1990. The so-called third way has never been anything more than a way for certain intellectuals to stand aloof from the realities of politics and look down on all genuinely practical systems. There will be no third way that emanates from the eastern portion of Germany.

What *is* likely to occur, however, is a pronounced reinforcement of German independence. Citizens of East Germany never developed a pattern of looking to reconcile their views with Western nations, and particularly with the United States. They will be integrated into the tradition of West German politics. But they will also have an impact upon those traditions. This will not occur all at once, and its effects are likely to be subtle. But there will come a time within several years in which politicians of the eastern portion of Germany will assume leadership roles in Germany, and they will tend to shift the balance of domestic German politics eastward. What occurs in Poland will be equally or more significant to the federal state of Brandenburg as what occurs in Holland or Belgium or France.

This tendency was obscured by the March 1990 elections in the G.D.R. West German social democrats had hoped to capitalize on traditions of East German socialism to attract a sizable vote to the SPD in the March 1990 elections. This did not occur, because the March 1990 vote was above all a vote on speedy reunification with West Germany. The SPD had raised concerns and issues about reunification on every occasion, suggesting it would be too expensive and that it should take place in a gradual, measured way. Helmut Kohl, on the other hand, left no doubt as to the importance he attached to speedy reunification. Having waited patiently for forty-five years for an opportunity to escape the Soviet-supported failure of communism, the voters of the G.D.R. were not about to miss a chance that might come only once. As a result, the alliance of parties including the CDU did very well.

It is unlikely, however, that the CDU will retain the kind of dominance in the east it enjoyed in the March 1990 elections. Indeed, although the SPD campaigned in 1990 on the worst imaginable platform—resentment, second-guessing, and an inability to grasp the true interests of the people of the GDR—its fortunes are likely to rise in a unified Germany. Indeed, it is interesting to note that had the December 1990 German election been restricted to voters under the age of forty-five years, the SPD/Green coalition would have won. Ironically, the SPD's fortunes will improve for reasons related to its current misfortunes. For once the country is firmly reunified and Soviet troops have departed in large numbers, the international situation that has favored the CDU will begin to disappear. Politicians of both parties will be freer to stake out essentially German positions that will be justified in terms of their adequacy for German voters in all the federal states stretching from the Rhine to the Oder-Neisse.

In the East one will still find a reservoir of support for more state-

Performance of G.D.R. Parties in the Regions (Länder) and East Berlin
(percentage of valid votes)

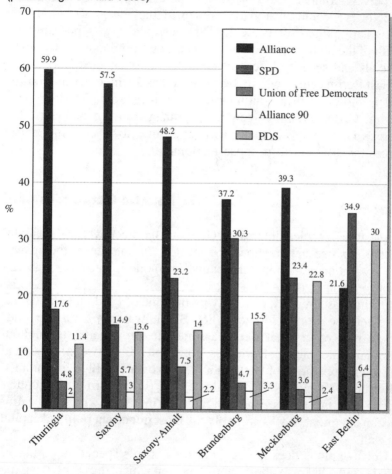

Source: *German Comments*

oriented social ideals. The tradition of liberal individualism has always been stronger in western Germany than in eastern Germany. A poll taken in early 1990, at about the same time as the CDU victory in the East, offers much to think about. Two-thirds of all East Germans thought that the collapse of East Germany was caused by ''incompetent politicians'' rather than the failure of socialism.[2]

Of further interest is the voting pattern in East Berlin. There the SPD performed at its very best in the March 1990 elections, gaining 35 percent compared to less than 22 percent for the CDU alliance. The former communist party, renamed the Party of Democratic Socialism, polled 30 percent. This percentage was probably the result of the high proportion of votes cast by Communist government officials and security forces in East Berlin. But the SPD's success in East Berlin cannot wholly be explained as a temporary aberration, and is more likely a continuation of historic socialist strength in Berlin. Given the left-of-center's dominance in West Berlin, Germany's new capital is likely to operate in a local environment of forces far different from those in Bonn.

Berlin: The German Capital

A question of topical interest in Germany has been where the capital of the reunified nation should be located. In one sense, the answer has always been obvious: the capital of modern Germany was and is once again Berlin.

Berlin was already a large city by the time of Frederick the Great, who reigned from 1740 to 1786. But it was not until the mid-nineteenth century that Berlin assumed its prominence throughout Germany and much of what is now Poland. Between 1860 and 1880, the population of Berlin doubled, to over 1 million inhabitants; between 1880 and 1900 it doubled again. By the turn of the century Berlin was the largest, most significant industrial city on the European continent. It was arguably the most important political capital as well.

But size alone does not account for Berlin's special importance. As the city that was the locus of power which drew together the German nation, Berlin assumed for Germans a different status from other capitals in the modern period. Cities such as London or Paris had played a similar role centuries earlier, at a time when the essential national borders of England and France were defined.

That Berlin would remain the capital of the newly organized, postwar Germany was not doubted by the allied nations in their postwar planning. Although German political life was to be decentralized as well as demilitarized, the allies regarded Berlin as a singular place that would have a different status than the remainder of occupied Germany. The special arrangement for Berlin spelled out in the London Protocol of September 1944 served two purposes. First, it was designed to prevent "for the time being" the emergence of a central German government while principles of local self-government were restored and progress toward demilitarization was achieved. This was thought to be especially important because of the association of Berlin/Prussia with militarism and Nazism in the view of the allied powers. Second, the special status of Berlin guaranteed that no single allied power could use its occupation of Berlin to wield undue influence over the whole of Germany.

The allies established both a Control Council for the governance of Germany and a Kommandatura for the governance of Berlin in the capital of the former Reich. Had it been possible to work successfully with the Soviet Union on the future of Germany, Berlin would gradually have reemerged as the capital of the German nation. This of course did not occur. As the gulf between Western and Soviet objectives widened, Berlin became an unintentional but nevertheless highly critical problem. As the two parts of Germany each consolidated into a separately governed state, Berlin remained a unique enclave for the continuation of four-power administration. In practice, however, Berlin too began to parcel itself into two sectors under the respective dominance of the Western powers and the Soviet Union. When the Communist party's attempt to merge with (and then control) the more popular Social Democratic Party failed in 1946, the Communist hope to secure power in Berlin through the appearance of democratic means was doomed to failure. From that time, Soviet-backed members of the new German Socialist Unity Party (SED) resorted to violence and irregular means to try to control Berlin's politics. After the city's municipal council was moved to the British sector because it had been unable to function in the context of demonstrations and the absence of police protection in the Soviet sector, the SED members of the council declared themselves to be the true municipal council. Thus, there came to exist by 1948 two separate municipal councils, each under the protection of its respective occupation power.

Realizing that its attempts to gain control of Berlin by parliamentary chicanery, veto power, violence, and blockade had all failed, the Soviet Union began in 1949 to integrate East Berlin into the German Democratic Republic. Although some legal conditions continued to differentiate East Berlin from the other fourteen political districts of the G.D.R. right up until the state's dissolution, East Berlin was more or less fully integrated into the G.D.R. East Berlin became the official capital of the G.D.R. in 1968.[3] The Western position that Berlin was legally under four-power control did not change until the fall of 1990.

Had the United States retreated from Berlin in 1948, the question of the German capital might have remained in doubt. By remaining in Berlin, the United States preserved the condition in which Berlin could retain a vibrancy that makes it the preeminent German city. Consider what Berlin would be today had the Soviet blockade succeeded and the entire city had fallen under Soviet domination. Even if the West had maintained the line at the inner-German border after 1948–1949, Berlin would stand today as the capital of two back-to-back tyrannies. Such discredit—not to mention the physical condition of both the eastern and western sectors of Berlin—would have made it symbolically more difficult for the Federal Republic to consider locating any national governmental functions in Berlin.

As it stands now, however, Berlin has been at the fulcrum of Europe for the past four and a half decades. Its recent history has made it a greater, not lesser, candidate to serve as the capital of Germany. Beyond this, moving the German capital to Berlin offers to the people of East Germany about the only consolation possible for their failed experiment of forty-five years' duration. Opinion polls taken in 1990 revealed that 72 percent of all Germans favored Berlin as the German capital. In East Germany, however, fully 91 percent chose Berlin.[4] These figures guaranteed that however much speculation to the contrary occurred in journals and press articles, Bonn would not remain the seat of all government functions in a unified Germany. Berlin's symbolism is too rich to permit this.[5]

Transition of some government functions to Berlin will occur gradually. The allied powers have now ceded to Germany formal rights over the city. The continuation of those rights beyond the time required for legitimate security purposes would have exacerbated the feeling that resides within many Germans that they have paid an adequate bill for their mistakes in World War II, especially when so few Germans are alive who actively participated in that war. Certainly Germany will not move its essential legislative, security, and foreign policy functions permanently to Berlin as long as substantial numbers of Soviet troops remain in the eastern part of Germany. Also, considerations of cost, location, and timing will enter into the transition of various governmental functions to Berlin.

It might also be said that haste to move the German capital to Berlin would be disconcerting to Germany's allies and neighbors —both those away from whom it is moving and those toward whom it is moving. To be sure, a nation's choice of its capital city is rightly its own internal affair. But the event itself—even if it is argued that it is a restoration or a continuation—is not a meaningless occurrence. What if the United States should decide to locate its capital in California? Would Germans assume this step to be wholly without meaning?

As Germany seeks to assure the West of its implicit commitment, many of its governmental functions will be moving east. They will be moving east by nearly 200 miles, to the eastern border of its territory, as far east as Prague, and in the very center of a broader territory that Germany once controlled. What does this mean? Germany will not move away from Western liberal democracy because its capital moves to the east. But does such a step mean nothing at all? To think so would be an almost equally serious misunderstanding. To assume it means nothing is to assume that the now vanishing ideological rivalries between East and West are the only rivalries possible.

There is an old saying that where one sits determines where one stands. Even though Germany is not a large country, one can feel tangibly in Berlin that the perspective is not that of Bonn. The Polish border is one hour away by automobile. One senses the presence of Russia lying behind that experiment in revolutionary capitalism that is now Poland. The center of gravity in Germany is bound to move eastward—again, not in an ideological sense, but in a geographical and political sense. One can predict different tendencies between Germany and America in how to deal with a U.S.S.R. that is not a strong union of militant communism, but a weaker, inward-looking nation. One can predict differences in how to deal with

Poland if its economy does not revive. These are honest differences, better understood and accommodated than ignored or, worse yet, assumed not to exist at all. The city of Berlin symbolizes these issues.

The Question of German National Identity

It is widely acknowledged, most frequently by Germans themselves, that Germans have had difficulty in being unself-consciously patriotic. It has never been as easy for a German as, say, an Englishman or a Frenchman or an American, to adopt a measured, nonreflective attitude of pride in his country. Either patriotism is forced down and denied, or it becomes a fundamental organizing point for the interpretation of life. There seems to be no middle course.

Why should this be so? Perhaps it is a result of the fact that Germany did not develop a set of unifying political institutions until relatively late in the modern period. Not having the benefit of a settled tradition of governmental authority (as, say, France or England), Germans sought the identification of national character with factors outside the sphere of everyday political institutions. Germanness thus resided in a common language, or in common traditions of thought or emotional response. Often, these were idealizations rather than reflections of actual conditions. At times, Germans have seemed to define Germanness by what it was not, rather than by what it was, thereby distinguishing themselves from other nationalities or from foreigners generally. To some extent, this situation persists to this day. Virtually no German regards a Turk residing in Germany as German, regardless of how long he has lived there.

It is fair to say that the shifting politics and geography of central Europe have made it very difficult for Germans to fix their national identity upon a stable locus of political authority. One has only to look at the map of central Europe over time to see the changing shape of the country.

This difficulty was in no way mitigated by the post-World War II division of the country. To the contrary, the dilemmas caused for a sense of national identity by the division of Germany represent *continuity* in this aspect of German political history. It was often said that East Germany was an ideology in search of a nation. Despite the propaganda efforts of the East to discover a unique East German identity, such a thing never came to exist at all. Having spent nearly two decades fostering an East German identity, the government—and the state—of East Germany were swept away at the first possible moment.

The situation was hardly more normal in the Federal Republic. While the East was doing its best to promote a sense of national identity, the West was working no less diligently to deny that it had one. There was in West Germany for four decades a desire to remain inconspicuous from a national point of view. Cosmopolitan German youth, thinking that they were rejecting their legacy and striking out anew, were in fact confirming the orientation of their elders. Across all generations in West Germany, there was a decidedly unnatural embarrassment at discussions of national identity. Frequently this was misconstrued by professional conference participants from other countries, who mistook this surface appearance for the fact that Germans had actually renounced or overcome their Germanness.

If there was any doubt, however, that a quest for German national identity still beat strongly beneath the surface of cosmopolitanism, that doubt surely must have been dispelled by the extraordinary reaction to the opening of the Berlin Wall in November 1989. A feeling of national identity is still very much present in Germany. The question is, to what will that feeling of national identity attach itself?

The incredible economic success of the Federal Republic has not fulfilled the German need for identity.[6] Having dug out of the rubble of near-total destruction, the West Germans could say to themselves, "Wir sind wieder wer" (We are somebody again). But who? That question has not yet been answered. Professor Werner Weidenfeld, the German government's coordinator for German-American cultural relations, wrote in 1986:

> The German need for collective identity obviously has not been adequately satisfied as of today. . . . There is a "roving identity need" of which one does not know yet what it will attach itself to.[7]

Although Weidenfeld's words were spoken of West Germany, they are all the more relevant today. What was true of West Germany is all the more true of a unified Germany, a nation whose modern history constitutes the history of a "roving identity need." Today the search for German identity will occur in the whole of the German nation.

Material achievements will be no more sufficient today to answer the question of national identity than they have ever been. Americans are rightly proud of their material accomplishments, but one could neither produce nor deduce American patriotism from those accomplishments. This is no less true of Germany. To what, then, shall Germans attach their sense of identity? Weidenfeld writes of two available options:

> From the sociopsychological point of view, European unity and the German nation offer central solutions to this need. . . . The political pragmatism of the European Community's severely restricted room for maneuver can hardly exert an emotional appeal. Against that background, the community component of the "German nation" is likely to grow in importance for people in the Federal Republic in the 1980s, not least because this community component can be given a broader cultural interpretation.[8]

As Germany has just now come together and is experiencing its new identity, it would be surprising if its first conclusion were to absorb itself and disappear into a larger entity. This is not to say that it could not happen. But despite repeated assertions to the contrary, the relationship between full political integration in the EC and German reunification has always been problematical. West Germany did not need to become neutral in order to become whole; it did not need to leave NATO; and it did not need to slow down EC integration. But these formulas put the cart before the horse. A certain degree of independence; a diminution in NATO's meaning; and a limit to the value of full integration into the EC are the *results*, not the preconditions, of German reunification.

Almost no one expected reunification would be so rapid or so easy. In 1988, one German commentator could say:

As a united Germany would be overwhelming in its economic power, neighboring countries are bound to do all they can to prevent reunification in any form and to maintain the status quo.[9]

This was not an isolated view. As recently as January 1990, 46 percent of all West Germans thought that the victorious powers of World War II would try to prevent German reunification, as opposed to 27 percent who thought they would agree to it.[10] This was two months after the opening of the Berlin Wall, and at roughly the same time that an American poll found that 67 percent of all Americans, 74 percent of all French, and 61 percent of all British supported reunification of Germany.[11] Clearly there was a mismatch between what Germans thought their neighbors and allies would tolerate and what in fact happened. Germans could hardly have asked for more accommodations than General Secretary Gorbachev agreed to; nor could they have found a more supportive government than they did in America. If Germans come to harbor any resentments over the manner in which reunification occurred, it will not be fair to lay them at the doorstep of their neighbors and allies.

There has been underway for several years a race for Germany's soul. The nations of Western Europe, including the Federal Republic, have moved step by step toward economic integration. Had the EC moved faster, or had the Soviet empire not disintegrated so rapidly, perhaps a unified Germany would have had fewer choices. Perhaps West Germany would have ceded in advance essential elements of its sovereignty to Brussels. But as matters stand now, Germany possesses a full panoply of choices, and those choices will set the terms and conditions for all of Europe. This is surely the sign of a great power.

CHAPTER FOUR

A United Germany in the "Common European House"

EC 1992 and Beyond—The Race for Germany's Soul

THE FEARS THAT UNITY would be purchased at the expense of German neutrality were not well-founded. The government of West Germany was good to its repeated commitments to remain an integral partner in the Western alliance. What was surprising was not what occurred in West Germany, but the speed at which the Soviet Union's East European empire crumbled.

Now that Germany is reunified, what does this mean for European integration? European Commission President Jacques Delors has said that since history has speeded up, so must West European integration. By this he meant, of course, that no one had anticipated how quickly Germany would become unified. Most participants in the process of European integration thought they would have far more time within which to draw Western Europe together in a web of common institutions and policies. Most participants believed that West Germany would be more fully entwined in these institutions before reunification became a serious prospect. Under this assumption, West Germany would have had far fewer options when reunification came, its latitude to choose as an independent actor being greatly constrained.

The rapid reunification of Germany has thus added a new urgency to West European integration for those who seek this goal. Perhaps these individuals recall the utterances of Adenauer in the 1950s when European integration first emerged as a serious goal. In explaining to his countrymen why West Germany should favor integration—when it appeared this would cement the division of East and West Europe, and therefore of East and West Germany—Adenauer explained that West European integration was a means to German unification. This was consistent with his overall philosophy of building firm relations with the West. Advocates of European integration must wonder whether after several decades of European integration, the means have at last become the end.

Whether that is the case or not, supporters of European integration are not prepared to risk a period of lengthy deliberation over the answer. These supporters—including many Germans—believe that it is now more important than ever to press forward. Indeed, some German advocates have made the argument that "the achievement of German unity will accelerate rather than delay the course to closer European unity."[1] No longer must West Germany concern itself with how each new step of West European integration will affect fellow Germans in the East.

The agreement to form a single West European market by 1992 is being implemented smoothly. A majority of the 279 measures to harmonize the economies of the twelve European Community nations have already been put in place. This is an important and complex undertaking, and one that merits praise. Yet it is important to understand the limits of the EC 1992 agreement. For the most part, the provisions address matters such as harmonizing product standards, streamlining professional qualifications and requirements to do business, and standardizing customs documents. Although EC 1992 creates movement toward commonality in Europe, it by no means implies the creation of a meaningful transnational European authority to address fundamental matters of state. Indeed, it is clear to all participants that if EC 1992 is put in place, *and nothing further*

occurs, there is a strong chance that European integration will end
as little more than a glorified customs union. It is for that very
reason that supporters of further European integration have concluded that they must not wait to press beyond the agreements of
EC 1992.

This process is well underway. It consists of two additional steps
to deepen EC integration. In April 1990, the members of the EC
agreed in Dublin to meet at the end of the year to discuss the
development of a common monetary system referred to as Economic
Monetary Union (EMU) and further steps toward centralizing foreign affairs and defense policies. The December meeting produced
agreement to create two intergovernmental conferences to suggest
amendments to the EC's organizing Treaty of Rome in these two
areas.

On the monetary side, the goal of the intergovernmental conference is to amend the Treaty of Rome to create a European central
bank and a common European currency. Such steps would compel
a common economic, as well as fiscal, policy among the member
states. Though Britain has dragged its feet on these proposals, it is
also clear that Germany will not agree to any centralized financial
structure which would permit the possibility of an inflation rate
higher than German authorities find acceptable. The outcome of this
conference is therefore not yet clear.

The second aspect is political unification. This will be the most
difficult step for the member nations of the EC. In 1970, the EC
members set up a process of European Political Cooperation (EPC).
This was essentially a consultative process, and its record of success
has been modest. In the Single-Europe Act, however, EC members
committed themselves to find ways to implement "a European foreign policy." In the late 1980s, EPC coordination become more
regularized and its role in European dealings with the third world
grew. However, it is fair to say that to date the EPC has not
tackled—nor has it been required to tackle—issues of potential
divisiveness either among its own members or with the United
States.

Steps toward harmonizing the foreign policies of EC nations are
likely to occur. But it is less clear that power to handle these issues
directly will be ceded to the EC in Brussels by member governments.

This is so for several reasons. First, Britain has been a reluctant partner in progress toward both monetary and political integration. In part, this was caused by deep personal suspicions that Margaret Thatcher harbored about European integration. But it was not simply the personal taste of Prime Minister Thatcher that accounted for British policy. With regard to the more conciliatory approach of Prime Minister John Major, French President Mitterrand has said, "There has been a change of personalities but not of policies." We will see how far Britain's change of leadership changes Britain's attitude. Britain's entire modern history displays a desire to maintain some distance from the continent. Britain has invariably sought a degree of independence from the continent, even while expressing deep and abiding interest in it.

So long as the United States exists outside the framework of the EC, Britain is likely to try to have its cake and to eat it, too. It is

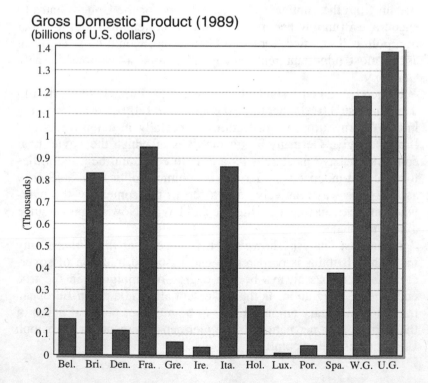

Gross Domestic Product (1989)
(billions of U.S. dollars)

likely to seek to be part of the continent when it wishes, and to fall back upon its "special relationship" with the United States when it does not. Skepticism about merging the U.K. into a political unit dominated by the continent runs high across the spectrum of British politics, and it is no certainty that a different British government would make the process of integration any easier from the British standpoint.

Britain is certainly concerned about ceding powers to an entity dominated by the German economy. Germany already possesses a far larger economy than any other EC partner. Given reasonable expectations of growth in the coming years, the German economy will likely become double the size of its nearest competitor, and more than equal to the next two leading economies together. But British concerns are not a matter of numerical calculations alone. They derive from centuries of habit and a continuing overestimation of the importance of the narrow channel of water that separates Britain from the continent. The surest way for the United States to encourage Britain to become a willing, if not enthusiastic, member of a politically unified European Community would be to cultivate as its most important relationship in Europe a relationship with Germany.

France has taken a somewhat different position. It seems to understand instinctively that its best course is to fully enmesh Germany into Western European institutions, especially in defense matters. It aims to give Germany a hug the likes of which the Soviet bear could never have mustered. Its aim is to constrain the possibilities for free and independent German economic, political, and security action. This was relatively easy to do in the context of the overwhelming Soviet threat during the Cold War. Now it must assume a new rationale.

In the last analysis, however, it is no clearer that France, any more than Britain, is prepared to end its proud tradition of sovereignty. There has always been a degree of ambiguity in the true ends of EC integration. Is the EC essentially to be a pan-European trade and monetary union, or is it to be a deeper political union of the current member nations? The German commentator Christoph Bertram raises this point:

In the past, the EC has reconciled these objectives by refusing to accept the contradictions between them. The difference between members unwilling to support political unification and those actively seeking it was bridged by the argument that integration was required for economic reasons, and that more economic integration would somehow demand, and thus lead to, more political integration as well.[2]

This question has not yet been answered, rather, it has been cleverly finessed. The answer will in large measure turn on what Germany decides. At this time, Germany is moving toward additional European integration with a commitment and energy no one could reasonably fault. But the EC will soon confront a fundamental question, the question of width versus depth. Many of the new governments of Eastern Europe have expressed interest in joining the EC. They do not wish to be excluded from the economic benefits of EC integration. In this they have added their voices to other nations including Austria, the Nordic countries, and smaller countries like Cyprus and Malta.

Can the EC absorb these new nations? If the point of EC integration is a broad single economic market, they could be integrated without conceptual or practical difficulty. But if the goal is monetary and political union, it is difficult to see how it will be possible to take these nations into the new union. Many of these countries have only recently made the transition away from command economies; they have had no track record of experience with markets or the political conditions necessary to preserve them. The Eastern Europeans have had no substantial economic interchange with the EC. Their industrial products and processes are based on different standards altogether. Moreover, their governments have had little of the kind of experience in foreign policy, monetary policy, or economic policy that would make them attractive candidates to be digested in a deeper union. For all these reasons, the leadership of the EC is reluctant to admit new members in the near future, having concluded that widening the EC will jeopardize the goal of deepening it to include economic and political union.

Germany will remain committed to the EC; of that there can be no doubt. Yet Germany will also inevitably be an advocate for widening the EC. If Austria, Czechoslovakia, Hungary, and Poland have democratic governments that do not threaten the West, and if they are prepared to accept the conditions of EC membership, why should they be excluded from the broad single market of the EC? It is Germany above all which has a tradition of trade and interchange with the nations of Eastern Europe. It is Germany above all which is creating new ties of trade and investment in these nations. It is Germany above all which would benefit from inclusion of Eastern Europe into the single market. The issue is summarized succinctly by Bertram:

> What Germany's West European partners may be worried about (and what should concern the Germans themselves) is not a united Germany's continued formal adherence to the rules and regulations of the EC, but its continued political and emotional commitment to the political union of Western Europe.[3]

Germany sits astride East and West in Europe. Its interest must inevitably be to incorporate the East into arrangements of which it is a part. Perhaps the issue of a wider EC versus a deeper EC can be accommodated by clever statesmanship. Perhaps all parties can be brought to see the wisdom of two concentric rings of members, one of which has developed deeper monetary and political ties among its members. But it is well to remember that while constituent governments can find institutional advantages in broader economic intercourse, they will *not* find similar advantages in putting their sovereignty aside. Perhaps the American experience is instructive. It required a secret extrapolitical gathering in Philadelphia in 1787 to create a United States of America. The governments of the colonies were not eager to cede their authority to a new central government, even after having created a more or less national army during the War of Revolution.

One thing is certain. The impetus for both wider and deeper integration must come above all from Germany. West Germany lay at the core of the Western alliance; East Germany lay at the core of the Warsaw Pact. Each was a necessary condition for its respective alliance to succeed. A united Germany, however, will not merely be a large player whose cooperation must be secured in any European project. It will, through its actions or inactions, decisively shape whether, and to what degree, European integration occurs.

Military Power in the Common European House

In no sphere are the consequences of Germany's decisions more critical than in the military sphere. Even the hint of an independent German military course will be sufficient to set capitals from London to Moscow off in search of new alliances in the old game of national power politics. And in no place has the full impact of the end of the Cold War been less easy to discern than in the military sphere. For in this area above all it was assumed that change would come most slowly. It was assumed that even if the nations of Eastern Europe and the Soviet Union itself experimented with market economies, the Soviets would insist to the bitter end on their postwar security prerogatives stretching as far West as the inner-German border.

This of course did not happen. General Secretary Gorbachev's decision to move Soviet forces out of central Europe came upon everyone, including the Soviet Union, extremely rapidly. Gorbachev's agreement with Chancellor Kohl in July 1990 to take this step and to allow Germany full latitude to choose any military relationship it wished has transformed the military picture in Europe entirely. On its face, it appears to be a complete and total abdication of Soviet influence in Europe. And indeed, to an extent that is the case. It is an abdication, however, of what could no longer be sustained in any event: Soviet domination of all aspects of East European life.

In the longer run, though, the Soviet Union's political and military influence in Europe will not disappear. The U.S.S.R. is far too large a nation—in whatever shape it assumes—for its influence to descend to nil. Its power will doubtless be expressed in more subtle, less domineering, and more seductive ways. Since the Soviet Union has turned away from efforts to dictate to Germany, it is difficult to envision how Germany can remain permanently a part of an alliance dedicated to opposing the Soviet Union. Indeed, it is difficult to envision how that alliance can permanently sustain and refresh itself in the absence of any organizing threat.

By mid-1991 Soviet forces will be gone from Hungary and Czechoslovakia; by the end of 1991 Soviet forces in Poland will be cut in half; by 1994 all Soviet troops are to have departed from Germany. Let us consider the consequences of these steps for various parties. First, it is already clear that Soviet reductions are causing reciprocal reductions in West European forces. Belgium has announced that it will remove its 37,000-member NATO contingent from Germany. Undoubtedly many of these troops will be decommissioned altogether and Belgium's total military force will be smaller. Britain has announced that it will cut its NATO contingent in Germany in half. Further, it has said that it will cut its total armed forces from 320,000 to 267,000, an 18 percent reduction. The fact is that virtually every West European member of NATO will reduce its armed forces in the coming years.

The same is true of the United States. Washington has announced plans for an initial reduction of 50,000 U.S. troops in Europe, but it is clear that this is simply the first installment of what will be several rounds of additional cuts. It is conventional wisdom in Washington that the United States is likely to reduce its ground forces in Europe by anywhere from two-thirds to three-fourths during the 1990s. Reductions have not and will not result from the usual Cold War arms limitation negotiations. Indeed, it had never been possible during the Cold War to achieve any conventional force reduction agreements at all. In the post-Cold War period, the pent-up desire for reductions has raced far beyond the slow and tedious pattern of previous arms control negotiations. Announced reductions will be more or less ratified in successive rounds of conventional force negotiations. Political pressures have pushed beyond the usual pace of diplomacy.

It is of course in Germany that the military consequences of Soviet withdrawal have been most pronounced. In an effort to encourage General Secretary Gorbachev to continue his liberalization and withdrawals, the West German government announced in 1989 that it would cut the federal defense force, the Bundeswehr, from 495,000 to 400,000 men, a 20 percent shrinkage and the largest reconfiguration of the force in its thirty-five-year history. This announced reduction was barely in place six months when it was superseded by Chancellor Kohl's agreement with General Secretary Gorbachev to limit combined German forces to 370,000 troops.

However, since the mid-1980s West German forces have confronted an ever less favorable demographic picture. As the following chart suggests, the pool of available young men in West Germany would not have been sufficient to maintain the Bundeswehr at 495,000 men much beyond 1990 in any event. The West German government had already announced its intention in 1989 to extend conscription from fifteen to eighteen months to offset a portion of the demographic pressure. The reunification of Germany has totally reversed the picture for the Bundeswehr. Now it must achieve an end strength of only 370,000 and it can draw from a population 25 percent larger. Indeed, the combined end strength of the West and East German armies in 1989 was approximately 670,000 men,

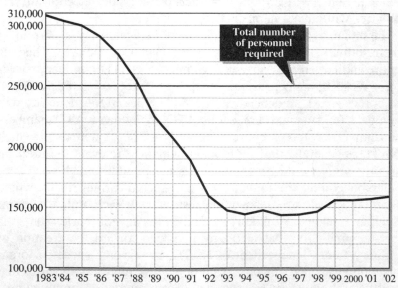

Annual Availability of Young Men
(armed forces, police, federal border patrol, disaster relief, development service)

Total number of personnel required

Source: German Press and Information Office

nearly twice the size of the forces now needed. Overall wartime strength is also slated to decline from West German forces of 1.34 million men to unified German forces of 950,000. This unified force will include about 580,000 reserves and 370,000 active forces.

Given their training and equipment, the German military will be the most capable conventional forces on the continent. At 370,000 men (and with the capacity to mobilize its 580,000 reserves rapidly) they will clearly be the strongest conventional force outside the Soviet Union. The German government calculates that with Soviet force reductions, with the lengthened warning time of a Soviet attack, and with generally less hostile Soviet intentions, forces of this magnitude will offer sufficient insurance against Soviet conventional force aggression against Germany.

How will Germany decide to orient itself in the new Europe? No answer can be given with assurance. What can be said, however, is that Germany will clearly no longer tolerate different treatment than is received by other European countries. The Germans have made clear that a policy of ''singularity'' according to which Germany is expected to operate under special conditions not shared by other nations, will no longer be acceptable. The rejection of singularity will have a number of consequences.

First, other NATO nations currently dedicate only a portion of their military forces to NATO; West Germany alone has had its entire military force subsumed within the NATO command structure. West Germany possessed no military forces (with the exception of border guards) independent of NATO. An end to singularity will compel a fundamental choice for NATO. Will other NATO members subsume their forces entirely under NATO? At a time in which NATO is generally thought to be growing less relevant to European security, this would be an unusual step. In addition, there is considerable complexity in the creation of such an arrangement, which for all practical purposes would constitute a de facto military union. Such an outcome is unlikely in the near term. For that reason, it is a safer prediction that Germany will tend toward the creation of military forces independent of NATO, or of some successor organization, with perhaps only a portion of its forces assigned to that multilateral body. Such a step would be regarded as highly significant in European capitals.

Second, Germany will not agree to outside limits on its forces or on its policies that are not also binding on other nations. She will therefore not agree to binding troop ceilings unless these are part of a broader negotiated set of limits that are placed on all nations. Limitations on German armed forces to a level of 370,000 men—or any other level—will be understood as a self-imposed German decision. Such a limitation can change as circumstances may require in the eyes of the German government.

Third, Germany will not agree to foreign forces on its soil if such forces are not stationed elsewhere as well. It is distinctly possible that the time will come when Germany will oppose foreign forces within its borders under any conditions; but it is certain to do so if it is singled out as the locus for foreign troops. Although German forces have been subsumed under the NATO command, foreign troops have always served in the Federal Republic at its invitation. If that invitation were to be withdrawn, foreign forces would have no choice but to depart.

Finally, Germany will also regard all commitments regarding levels and types of armaments as self-imposed commitments unless they are agreed to in a general formula limiting all parties. This is true of conventional armaments as well as of chemical, biological, and nuclear armaments whose production and possession Germany has to date forsworn. It is also true of conditions or understandings relating to the deployment of Bundeswehr forces along Germany's eastern border or anywhere else within German territory.

What difference does an end to singularity make to anyone outside Germany? Are not the abovementioned consequences an exercise in hair splitting with no practical meaning? After all, Germany has agreed to impose on itself all of the conditions that any other nation reasonably seeks. Further, the German populace is in a thoroughly antimilitary frame of mind. Isn't a force level of 370,000 troops the maximum level that German domestic politics would permit? Has not the SPD called for a reduction of the Bundeswehr to 240,000 men?

There is no doubt that current German sentiments toward the military are not favorable. But this should not really be difficult to understand. Germany has been more or less occupied by foreign forces since its defeat in 1945. It has not possessed the strength to end that state of affairs on its own. The western portion of Germany was pressed into an alliance to contain the force of one of its conquerors in World War II; the eastern portion of Germany was pressed into an alliance directed against the other conquering nations. That there should be no special fondness for military matters is hardly surprising. Indeed, it is predictable that for a brief time longer, the German people will become even less positively inclined toward military spending than they now are.

German leaders may offer all manner of security commitments. But it will take at least several years before it is certain what the German people will decide about Germany's security relationships. If the United States withdraws its forces too quickly, or if Germany seeks their withdrawal too quickly, a downward spiral will result that will ultimately loosen Germany's military ties with the West. It seems evident that this would be in no one's interest—not America's, not Europe's, not the Soviet Union's, and not that of Germany itself. As former U.S. Army General William Odom has written, an American military role in Europe seems nearly indispensable to the credibility of American engagement there. And American engagement in Europe, in turn, is the key to peace and stability:

> When Germany and the United States have had strong ties, Europe remained stable. When they have not had such ties, there has been war. In the context of current slogans, the record of peace in the "European House" has been poor. The record of peace in the "Atlantic House" has been perfect.[4]

This is not to say that a loosening of these ties cannot or will not occur. It is an unfair use of historical example to hold up earlier aggressive German regimes and to argue that Germany will necessarily revert to them. But it is equally unfair to make selective use of historical example and to assert that because West Germany has had forty years of postwar military ties to the West, that it will therefore necessarily maintain these ties in the future. The fact is that German options have expanded widely and rapidly, and it cannot yet be said how Germany will decide to proceed in this new environment.

Nuclear Weapons in the Common European House

Conventional forces alone did not protect the Federal Republic of Germany for forty-five years. NATO conventional forces were part of an overall defense posture that was firmly anchored in a nuclear deterrent, principally that of the United States. NATO doctrine always retained a degree of public ambiguity about when nuclear weapons would be used in the event of a conventional attack from the East; sometimes it served NATO's interest to be more public about the urgency to "go nuclear," and other times not. But there have never been sufficient reasons to doubt the intention or the willingness of NATO to utilize nuclear weapons in the defense of Europe. The structure and number of American forces in Europe— not enough to stop a Soviet drive by themselves, but not an insignificant number either—made the necessity of using nuclear weapons plain.

During the period of reunification negotiations in 1989 and 1990, Western observers initially feared that the Soviet Union might make the removal of Western nuclear forces from Germany a precondition of reunification and the removal of Soviet forces from eastern Germany. It was supposed that without nuclear weapons in Europe, America would withdraw its ground troops. This condition was not raised for two very good reasons. First, as 1990 unfolded it became clear that the Soviet Union's ability to place any conditions on German unification was severely limited. Second, the fact is that the Soviet Union did not need to concern itself excessively with demanding the withdrawal of weapons that the Germans themselves would soon enough insist be removed from their soil. With the removal of intermediate-range missiles from Europe under the Intermediate-Range Nuclear Forces (INF) agreement, the only remaining nuclear weapons stationed in Germany had too short a range to strike the Soviet Union itself. They would be useful only against targets on German soil or, potentially, on Polish soil.

The Soviet Union will secure the withdrawal of non-German nuclear weapons from Germany not by its demands, but by its own actions. The Soviet withdrawal behind its own boundaries clearly rendered short-range nuclear weapons far less useful in any purely defensive NATO strategy. Whether short-range nuclear weapons are now thoroughly useless, as some have asserted, or are a hedge against a Soviet return, as others have argued, will turn out to be irrelevant. Whatever one believes, the utility of these weapons is so diminished that there will be no *political* possibility to retain them in Germany for anything beyond a brief transitional period.

With or without short-range nuclear weapons, the presence of 300,000 U.S. troops in Europe carried the implication of an American nuclear umbrella over those forces. But if U.S. ground forces were to leave Europe, or to be so reduced as to be militarily insignificant, where would the nuclear umbrella that protects Germany be? The answer is unavoidable: it would no longer exist. It would then be every bit as clear that the U.S. would not—just as it seems clear that the U.S. would now—launch nuclear weapons from outside European territory to respond to a Soviet invasion of Europe. In other words, deterrence would have failed—and deterrence is, as it has always been, the critical goal.

In the absence of a sizable U.S. force in Germany, there will be no nuclear umbrella over a unified Germany. Where, then, does that leave Germany? It could be argued that Germany does not require nuclear protection. After all, against what is protection required if the Soviet Union has reduced its conventional threat to the point that there is no current reason to expect attack? This is a fair point. But it is no less fair to ask why, then, does the Soviet Union require nuclear weapons? Against an attack from the United States? From Britain or France? From Germany? Although there is no fully satisfying answer to that question, it is certain that the Soviet Union will not eliminate its own nuclear weapons. This is so not only because these weapons are the chief thing that distinguishes it from less-developed nations; it is so because *every advanced, powerful nation in the world is somehow protected by a nuclear umbrella.* It would be doubly foolish to suppose that the Soviet Union would forgo its possession of nuclear weapons if all other nations did not do so as well.

And this is precisely the point: As one of the three most productive and powerful nations on earth, Germany, too, will expect and require nuclear protection so long as other nations possess nuclear weapons and enjoy that protection. Who will offer this protection? One possibility is that Britain and France will provide a nuclear umbrella for Germany. Under this scenario, a division of labor will emerge between Germany, with its conventional force superiority, and Britain and France, with their nuclear arsenals. This of course supposes that the current political/military alignment of Europe, which is firmly rooted in the Soviet threat, will persist after that threat has diminished. It also supposes that Germany, a larger and more powerful nation than Britain or France, will choose to rest its ultimate security in the hands of its smaller neighbors over an extended period of time. These are not farfetched suppositions; they are suppositions without any foundation at all.

Alternatively, would it not be possible for the United States to provide a nuclear umbrella over Germany even if substantial numbers of U.S. ground forces do not remain in Europe? Technologically, there is no reason this could not be done. Nuclear weapons on ships or on aircraft based in Europe could provide a powerful nuclear force. U.S. strategic forces based in the United States could respond to a nuclear or conventional force challenge to Germany. But a realistic political assessment suggests otherwise. No rhetorical assurance is likely to give sufficient credibility to a U.S. nuclear umbrella over a Europe where U.S. conventional forces are no longer deployed. From time to time Europeans have doubted whether the United States would suffer its own destruction to defend Europe. Without U.S. forces in Europe, these doubts would achieve a far greater validity, thus jeopardizing the goal of deterrence.

Perhaps it could be argued that a nuclear umbrella is not required at all. Given the diminution of the Soviet threat and the unlikely event of conflict with Britain or France, why does Germany need it at all? This is not a question without merit. Asking why *any* nation requires nuclear weapons given the small likelihood of their use is to pose a difficult question. But to ask why Germany alone does not require nuclear protection is a different question altogether. It asks again that Germany be treated in a singular way, and as we have already discussed, this will not be acceptable to Germany. In this sense, it appears that General Secretary Gorbachev knew precisely what he was doing when he sought a *German* reaffirmation that Germany would not develop nuclear weapons rather than seeking that Germany require all NATO short-range nuclear weapons to leave German territory. The long-term interests of the Soviet Union have more to do with German nuclear intentions than they do with the disposition of more or less outmoded NATO short-range nuclear weapons.

Unless Germany accepts "singularity," there appear to be only two possible outcomes: either all nations' nuclear weapons will decline toward zero or Germany will have nuclear weapons as well. Could movement toward the elimination of nuclear weapons occur? The Soviet Union will not permit this so long as the Americans and the Chinese possess them. The British and the French will come to see their nuclear capabilities as the unique advantage that they possess over a far stronger Germany. And these five nations whose nuclear rights are recognized in the Nuclear Nonproliferation Treaty are only the tip of the iceberg. For one must think as well of eliminating the nuclear capabilities of India, Pakistan, Israel, South Africa, and perhaps four or five additional nations by 1995 before this becomes realistic. The existence of French, British, and Soviet nuclear weapons does not obviate the German need for nuclear protection; it guarantees it.

Is it reasonable to suppose that a nation like Germany will permit its security to be guaranteed by other nations when perhaps as many as ten or twelve nations have both nuclear weapons and the ballistic missile capability to deliver them on German soil? Would we expect this of ourselves? Of the Soviet Union? Of France? Why, then, would anyone expect it of a unified Germany whose economy is the motor of Europe, and who arguably has the most to lose from war? Deterrence is deterrence, and it is a most peculiar argument that what works everywhere else does not or need not work in Germany.

But what of German views regarding nuclear deterrence? Is Germany somehow special? The first argument for the special character of Germany is the constitutional argument. The nation is restricted in its Basic Law from the use of force to resolve international problems. But how significant a stricture is this? The Basic Law is not inconsistent with the maintenance of a large standing army. Nor is there a specific constitutional bar to German possession of nuclear weapons, except insofar as the 1954 agreement not to maintain nuclear weapons is "consistent" with the Basic Law. Let us recall, too, that the constitution of East Germany established a special governing role for the Communist party. In the face of rapid changes, this provision—which was integral to the structure of governance in the G.D.R.—was cast aside within a period not of months, but of weeks.

Constitutional strictures can be very effective in shaping attitudes and outcomes. But constitutions cannot survive if they are too far divorced from the realities of national life. At this time, German attitudes toward nuclear weapons are decidedly negative.[5] The promise of no German nuclear weapons, which Chancellor Kohl reaffirmed to General Secretary Gorbachev in 1990, was not a difficult political pledge—it was wholly within the mainstream of current German sentiments about nuclear weapons. But inasmuch as up until now the nuclear weapons deployed on German soil have been those of other nations, to be used essentially against *German* forces and *German* cities, this view may not be too difficult to understand. There are undoubtedly many Germans who despise all things nuclear, including nuclear power plants, just as there are in every industrialized nation. But there has not yet been a fair referendum on the Germans' view of *Germany* possessing nuclear weapons. Nor is such a referendum likely until the consequences of reunification and changing European security relationships have been absorbed.

Let us imagine a United States divided into two separate states at the Mississippi River. In the east, German forces possess a nuclear arsenal pointed at the western United States. In the west, Japanese forces possess an equivalent arsenal pointed at the eastern half of the U.S. It is not difficult to predict American attitudes toward nuclear weapons under these circumstances. This is more or less the situation confronting Germany for the past four decades. The German view on nuclear weapons has not yet emerged; simply put, it has been Soviet nuclear weapons and American nuclear weapons on which Germans have rendered judgment to date. In the one area in which the West German government has dealt with German nuclear capabilities—the export of nuclear technology to third world nations—it has not displayed an especially obvious "allergy" to nuclear weapons.

In assessing Germany's future view of nuclear weapons, one must think of weapons that are not pointed at Germans. In a world in which small, backward nations as well as three of Germany's neighbors possess nuclear weapons, could a responsible German chancellor simply turn his back on nuclear weapons? Germany is presumably already the target of Soviet nuclear weapons. Will not the same realities that have led other governments to conclude that nuclear weapons enhance deterrence also operate on Germany?

It is not realistic to expect that Germany alone of all leading nations in Europe will cavalierly dismiss the issue of nuclear weapons. Free of outside constraints on its sovereignty, Germany will utilize its diplomatic abilities and its highly advanced technological skills to guarantee not only its survival, but a serious role in the world. There *will* be some credible nuclear umbrella over Germany; the only question is whose? The question of how Germany defends itself as large numbers of American troops and nuclear weapons leave Germany is critical for the future of European security arrangements. The current defense structure should not be dismantled until and unless a broadly acceptable alternative is in place. This is an issue for the near term.

Have the Germans Changed?

What is an acceptable defense alternative? The answer depends in large measure on the tendency and direction of the new Germany. This is itself a question that is as unfair to ask as it is difficult to answer. Is not an unbroken record of forty years of commitment to freedom, democracy, and Western values proof enough in itself to make the very asking of the question not only superfluous, but even insulting? What more proof could one ask? Four decades of representative government; a highly progressive role in world organizations; reparations to Holocaust victims; and, above all, a democratic temper and spirit—these cannot fail to impress anyone familiar with the Germans of the Federal Republic. Then, too, at the first possible moment, the East Germans acted upon on a long-held desire to renounce the totalitarian regime imposed upon them by the Soviet Union for all those years. In all, this is a record that is not only hard to fault, *it is impossible to fault.*

But for the sake of understanding, it is well to ask again about Germany. And the German people must also do so, in a deep and truthful way, if they are to know themselves better and to guide themselves well. For it cannot be ignored that the Germany of the past forty-five years has not been in the fullest sense of the word a German Germany; it has been an American Germany and a Russian Germany. While freely choosing within the political environments they inhabited, the two Germanies acted within very narrow parameters. Neither the Germans nor the world have yet seen what kind of nation they will choose to become when the political environment is no longer so closely constrained. Committed German democrats may be frustrated by this assessment. But let us once again be aware of the uses of historical argument. One cannot argue that the last century of German history is irrelevant to today's Germany, and then turn around and prove this proposition by referring to the last forty years of German history.

But is there reason to wonder about German intentions? Is it not peculiarly unfair to question them just because Germany has again grown large and powerful through benign economic activities? The fate of any powerful country is to have its intentions questioned. In the postwar world, the United States has had its policies attacked and its motives questioned at every turn. It will require a high degree of political maturity for the German people to submit to the scrutiny that attaches to any great nation. To ask about Germany today is not necessarily to hold that nation to a higher standard than the rest of the world. Let us leave moralism aside and say only this: When a new and great power emerges in the world, one has every reason to ask about its tendencies.

There is no doubt in this author's mind that the current generation of German leaders are infused with democratic principles. Indeed, in emulating Americans there is scarcely another people who could have done it so well. This has been variously noted with positive and negative connotations by Germans of high culture. But the Germany of the next decade will not find its hopes and ideals so fully reposed in America. There are already signs enough of this. It is unlikely that either all things American or the persona of General Secretary Gorbachev will ever stand so high in the German consciousness as they do at this time.

The next Germany is just now being born, and we do not yet know what its features will be. How will this nation orient itself in regard to its newfound independence? Will Germany choose to renounce its independence and sign it away in a deep grant of sovereignty to the European Community? This would be an extraordinary step for a country that has just achieved the object of forty-five years' longing. Will Germany choose to set itself on a course of European integration that will inevitably diminish its latitude for action? Will it opt for an arrangement that would in effect give it the same status as an American state within the United States? Will Germany choose to become the California of the United States of Europe?

As the most populous, most economically powerful American state, California has an important role in America. But it exercises no independent point of view within the United States national government. Perhaps with the exception of issues relating to wine, there is no "California point of view" when it comes to federal or international issues. California retains a certain cultural image in America, as does each state; but federal legislators from California are little different from any others—they are liberal or conservative, for or against national health care, defense cuts, agricultural price supports, and so forth, in the same ways as are other federal legislators. There is a necessary and inevitable homogenization in a federal political entity like the United States. Will Germany agree to become the California of Europe, the largest, most productive unit of a broader federal system? Had European Community integration continued for an additional five to ten years before Germany was reunified, the answer would have doubtless been affirmative. Now it is by no means certain.

In estimating the prospect for a United States of Europe, it is well to consider the American experience. The states of the new republic in 1789 had far more than a common currency. They shared a language and inherited traditions that far surpassed even the multilingual and cosmopolitan tendencies of modern West Europeans. And although they shared a single national government for the next seventy years, they fought a civil war over secession. On the positive side, perhaps there is no issue on the European horizon to equal the explosive, unresolved issue of slavery in the new American republic.

But the reconciliation of national traditions and attitudes in a United States of Europe would not be easy.

The process of German unification occurred very rapidly. Changes in both constituent parts of the new country took place virtually overnight. Such rapid changes have frequently characterized German politics. The goals of these politics have shifted markedly over time, and it is facile to assume that they cannot and will not do so again. Why has German political life undergone so many changes in the past century? Each transformation must be considered in its own specific terms. But throughout their modern history, Germans have always had very lofty expectations of politics. The Western tradition of limited government promises at best an outcome of security and physical comfort. That is both a great deal and also not very much. The politics of liberal democracy pursues essentially material goals. By not aiming too high, it seeks to achieve decent and modest goals. But it does not speak to the interior life of human beings; it does not ipso facto promote a *community* within which members can realize their social, moral, intellectual, and spiritual strivings. These it leaves to individual men and women to secure or not as they please.

German politics often has been imbued with higher ideals. It has not infrequently sought to find in the political realm the answer to what is missing in modern life. Whether from the right or the left, it has been Germans who have offered the most incisive criticisms of modern liberal democracy and its limitations. Modern liberal democracy has definite limitations, and is therefore always susceptible to criticism. It does not enjoy any mythic defense or support against such criticism. It is not difficult to see that the ideal of "a chicken in every pot" is hardly uplifting.

Today one senses among some German democrats a certain discomfort with the modest, essentially material goals that are now the end of German politics. On the left of the political spectrum one certainly finds a decided tendency toward a view of politics that transcends the goal of material prosperity. Americans on the left seek wider access to and sharing of these very material ends; they are essentially egalitarian liberal democrats. Germans on the left, particularly as embodied in the Green Party, want more thoroughgoing goals; they hope for a transformation of the limited politics of liberal democracy. They still seek some special, presumably higher, way.

Will the Germans decide once and for all to accept the limits of modern liberal democratic life and not to pursue higher aspirations through politics? There are many promising signs that they understand the grief to which these loftier notions have led. But there is no answer to this question yet. What we can learn from the past forty-five years is this: three-fourths of Germans became better democrats than the Americans, while the other one-fourth became better Communists than the Russians. This period is now over. German choices will now be based upon principles other than emulation of outside powers. Decisions previously made in the shadow of others will now be made as German decisions.

"Have the Germans changed?" is not really the appropriate question. Of course they have, many times. The "political culture theory" school of political science once spoke of a congruence between a people's values and the kind of political regime(s) it would have. But consider the German experience. In the relatively brief historical time of 150 years—less than the entire existence of that parvenu, the United States—the Germans have lived under: a collection of petty principalities of regions and towns; the Reich of Bismarck; the Weimar Republic; Nazi totalitarianism; liberal democracy; and a rigid one-party Marxist state. What is the "political culture" that could permit or explain such a bewildering array of virtually every form of political life in the modern world? This history has led that most urbane and thoughtful of modern commentators, Luigi Barzini, to conclude that this very mutability is the essential characteristic of the Germans. The question then becomes: Will the Germans change again, and if so, how?

That these choices will matter so much to people outside of Germany's borders signifies the breadth of initiative that Germany will possess. Having such initiatives and options in world affairs is the very meaning of a great power, or as we now say, a superpower.

PART TWO
Japan – The Sun Rises Again

Japan, an ancient state, with the highest sense of national honor and patriotism and with a teeming population and a remarkable energy.

—*Winston Churchill*
[Hansard, Record of Parliamentary Debates, *February 12, 1933]*

CHAPTER FIVE

Economic Dominance: Financing the Next Generation of Technology

The Initiative Passes to Japan

THE SOVIET UNION ALONE was able to prevent post-World War II Germany from assuming the initiative in Europe. This capacity came to a practical end when the two portions of Germany agreed on a single economy; its end was officially recognized when Gorbachev agreed in July 1990 to allow a unified Germany to retain its membership in NATO.

The United States alone has the capacity to forestall the initiative in the Pacific from passing to Japan. As with the Soviet Union and Germany, the time within which to exercise this capacity is rapidly drawing to a close. To a certain extent, Japan has already been freer to act than Germany for some time, because it did not have to receive from the United States what the Soviet Union finally gave Germany in 1989–1990: the gift of unity.

Japan escaped being a divided nation in a far more painful way at the close of World War II. On August 6, 1945, the city of

Hiroshima was destroyed by an atomic bomb. Three days later, a second bomb destroyed Nagasaki, and the following day—August 10—Japan offered its first surrender message. But one other event occurred within that same four-day period. On August 9, the day of the Nagasaki bomb, the Soviet Union declared war against Japan. Coming as it did, when the war with Japan was all but over, Soviet entry into the conflict was transparent in its motivation. Stalin hoped to gain a share in the disposition of a defeated Japan. Unfortunately for him, but fortunately for the Japanese, the war ended too soon for the Soviet Union to lay plausible claim to a role in the settlement of Japan. Thus was averted what would have been an all but certain Soviet invasion of the northern island of Hokkaido.

As it was, the Soviet Union took control of the Kurile Islands in September 1945. Though the Kuriles are not an insignificant set of territories, whose reversion to Japan could simplify Japanese naval planning, Japan did not lose its major northern island, Hokkaido. Thus, Japan was spared the fate of Germany, which was to have major portions of its territory fall under the control of divergent occupying powers.[1] Had the division of Japan occurred, a Soviet-controlled sector of Japan, with predictable attempts to undermine the American sector, would have made U.S. efforts to protect the Western Pacific during the Korean War and afterward far more parlous.

But that did not occur. All of Japan fell under the sway of American rule, and the nation remained united as it sought to work its way back from the destruction of the war. In this, it possessed a major advantage that Germany did not enjoy. The United States had learned, at Germany's expense, about Soviet intentions between June and August of 1945. Japan was the principal beneficiary of this learning.

Although it did not face a deep internal political division and the need to spend huge sums of money to deploy armies of Japanese facing one another across an internal border, in other respects Japan underwent the same difficult problems as did Germany in rebuilding its economy, its political structure, and its self-image in the years after World War II. It did so with such vigor and with such success that it now stands on the verge of entering into its own leadership role, not only in the Pacific but in the world.

While the United States cannot now offer the reconciliation of the Japanese nation, as the U.S.S.R. did Germany, it still has several tools with which to affect Japan's fundamental decisions about its role in the world. The first of these is the huge U.S. market for Japanese goods. The United States is by far the largest consumer of Japan's products. Fully one-third of all Japanese exports go to America, more than one and one-half times Japan's exports to all West European nations combined. The U.S. market is essential for Japan's continued economic success. To be sure, the United States also finds a large market in Japan. In 1988 and 1989, 22.4 percent and 22.8 percent, respectively, of all Japan's imports came from the United States. But the relationship has been an unequal one, and each year since 1965 the balance of trade has favored Japan.

This is not to suggest, of course, that the United States has anything to gain by closing off or even threatening to close off Japan's markets in the U.S. But it does imply that Japan is far more dependent upon the American market than vice versa. Ironically, this inequality remains a factor that can and will help to affect Japan's decision making. The Japanese trade ministry, MITI, has estimated that a total halt in U.S.–Japan trade would result in a short-term reduction of the Japanese economy of 5 percent, compared to only 0.6 percent for the United States.[2] Substantial U.S. federal borrowing has been taken up by Japanese investors, and this is frequently mentioned as a form of potential Japanese leverage over the United States. Short-term financial stability and the orderly sale of U.S. notes depend upon Japanese purchases. But the long-term leverage inherent in these purchases has never been proven. To the contrary, historical examples suggest that freezing or blocking assets is perhaps a more powerful tool.

Secondly, the United States faces a fundamental set of decisions about its military role in the Western Pacific in the 1990s. The United States can give Japan more, or less, pretext to fill a power vacuum in that region. If the U.S. withdraws from the Western Pacific, the resulting instability will inevitably draw other nations to attempt to fill this vacuum. Efforts by China, the Soviet Union, Japan, and the smaller nations of the region to project power and to form new alliances will occur. Of these nations, Japan is best

U.S. Merchandise Trade, 1950–1986
(Billions of Dollars)

	WITH REST OF THE WORLD			WITH JAPAN		
	EXPORT	IMPORT	BALANCE	EXPORT	IMPORT	BALANCE
1950	10.23	9.10	1.13	0.418	0.179	0.239
1951	14.25	11.18	3.08	0.695	0.185	0.510
1952	13.43	10.85	2.58	0.768	0.229	0.539
1953	12.40	10.98	1.42	0.758	0.227	0.531
1954	12.93	10.35	2.58	0.847	0.277	0.570
1955	14.43	11.52	2.90	0.772	0.449	0.323
1956	17.58	12.80	4.78	1.065	0.543	0.522
1957	19.55	13.30	6.25	1.618	0.597	1.021
1958	16.40	12.98	3.42	1.054	0.680	0.374
1959	16.48	15.30	1.17	1.113	1.031	0.082
1960	20.45	15.23	5.22	1.545	1.083	0.462
1961	20.95	15.07	5.88	1.767	1.054	0.713
1962	21.73	16.85	4.88	1.540	1.358	0.182
1963	23.35	17.73	5.63	1.820	1.497	0.323
1964	26.70	19.38	7.33	1.974	1.769	0.205
1965	27.80	22.25	5.55	2.051	2.427	−0.376
1966	30.75	26.35	4.40	2.341	2.966	−0.625
1967	32.17	27.75	4.42	2.674	3.017	−0.343
1968	35.25	33.95	1.30	2.959	4.069	−1.110
1969	38.25	36.80	1.45	3.503	4.893	−1.390
1970	44.55	40.85	3.70	4.648	5.894	−1.246
1971	45.55	46.53	−0.98	4.069	7.280	−3.211
1972	51.72	56.85	−5.13	4.978	9.079	−4.101
1973	73.93	71.85	2.08	8.357	9.665	−1.308
1974	100.95	104.53	−3.58	10.723	12.414	−1.691
1975	109.60	99.00	10.60	9.567	11.257	−1.690
1976	117.47	124.30	−6.83	10.196	15.531	−5.335
1977	123.05	151.85	−28.80	10.566	18.565	−7.999
1978	144.68	176.48	−31.80	12.960	24.540	−11.580
1979	183.30	211.95	−28.65	17.629	26.260	−8.631
1980	225.05	247.45	−22.40	20.806	31.216	−10.410
1981	238.30	266.45	−28.15	21.796	37.597	−15.801
1982	213.98	249.48	−35.50	20.694	37.683	−16.989
1983	206.07	271.33	−65.25	21,789	42.844	−21.055
1984	224.07	334.25	−110.18	23.241	60.210	−36.969
1985	220.80	341.02	−120.22	22.145	65.653	−43.508
1986	224.88	367.52	−142.65	26.361	80.764	−54.403
Growth (%)[a]	8.96	10.82		12.20	18.50	

[a]**Compound annual growth rate.**

Source: U.S. Department of Commerce, *Survey of Current Business,* various issues/Drawn from Kar-Yiu-Wong, Makin, and Wong, *Sharing World Leadership.*

positioned to rapidly expand its power into the region. Even if the United States does not withdraw as a matter of policy, its own budgetary constraints and Japan's budgetary capabilities will lead inevitably to a far larger Japanese military role in the region. The farther this process advances, the less will be America's ability to influence it. For this reason, America's capacity to initiate and shape the outcome of events in the Western Pacific is temporary, and will soon pass to Tokyo. What occurs in that capital will be decisive for the entire region.

Economic Dominance

At the current time, Japan's capacity to affect the region rests entirely upon its economic power. The growth of this power has been nothing short of staggering. Like Germany, Japan's principal cities were virtually destroyed in World War II. It has been estimated that Japanese real national income in 1946 was 57 percent of that of the mid-1930s. In the early postwar years foreign trade was only 10 to 20 percent of its prewar levels. Japan's industrial production was decimated, its coal output was cut in half, and its shipping was totally destroyed.[3] Despite the loss of more than 3 million lives and the destruction of much of its infrastructure, by 1954 Japan had already exceeded its highest prewar level of production. From that time forward, Japan's economy made rapid strides that began to yield tangible results by the 1960s.

This process was all the more remarkable because it occurred without the infusion of large amounts of outside capital. Japan can truly be said to have pulled itself up by its own bootstraps in the 1950s. The capital that Japan invested in its economy in the first twenty years after the war was capital it accumulated from suppressing consumption in favor of saving. Compared with the United States, the current Japanese savings rate is still substantial. But at a time when most Japanese citizens owned little or nothing, this self-generated capital was a strong testament to the discipline and sacrifice of an entire generation of Japanese.

By the late 1960s, it was already clear to farsighted thinkers that Japan was on its way to becoming a major economic power.[4] This

Exchange Rates in Twelve Countries, 1950–1988
(Value of Foreign Currency Relative to the U.S. Dollar)
(Indexes: 1977=100)

YEAR	UNITED STATES	CANADA	JAPAN	BELGIUM	DENMARK	FRANCE	GERMANY	ITALY	NETHERLANDS	NORWAY	SWEDEN	UNITED KINGDOM
1950	100.0	97.2	74.4	—	87.0	140.5	55.3	141.3	64.4	74.6	86.4	160.5
1955	100.0	107.7	74.4	—	86.9	140.4	55.2	141.2	64.4	74.6	86.4	160.0
1960	100.0	109.6	74.4	71.8	87.1	100.2	55.7	142.2	65.1	74.6	86.4	160.9
1961	100.0	104.9	74.2	71.8	86.9	100.2	57.8	142.1	67.6	74.5	86.5	160.6
1962	100.0	99.4	74.2	72.0	87.0	100.3	58.1	142.2	68.1	74.6	86.7	160.9
1963	100.0	98.5	74.1	71.8	86.9	100.3	58.2	142.0	68.1	74.4	86.1	160.5
1964	100.0	98.5	74.0	72.0	86.8	100.3	58.4	141.4	68.0	74.4	86.7	160.0
1965	100.0	98.5	74.1	72.2	86.8	100.3	58.1	141.3	68.2	74.4	86.6	160.2
1966	100.0	98.6	73.9	71.9	86.9	100.0	58.0	141.4	67.8	74.4	86.5	160.1
1967	100.0	98.5	73.9	72.1	86.0	99.9	58.2	141.4	68.1	74.4	86.6	157.6
1968	100.0	98.6	74.3	71.7	80.2	99.2	58.1	141.6	67.8	74.5	86.4	137.2
1969	100.0	98.7	74.7	71.4	79.8	94.9	59.2	140.7	67.7	74.5	86.4	137.0

Year												
1970	100.0	101.8	74.8	72.2	80.0	88.9	63.7	140.8	67.9	74.5	86.1	137.3
1971	100.0	105.2	77.1	73.8	81.1	89.2	66.8	142.8	70.3	75.6	87.5	140.1
1972	100.0	107.3	88.4	81.4	86.3	97.4	72.8	151.2	76.4	80.8	93.9	143.3
1973	100.0	106.2	98.9	92.3	99.7	110.8	87.6	151.8	88.3	92.6	102.6	140.5
1974	100.0	108.7	91.9	92.1	98.7	102.3	89.9	135.7	91.4	96.4	100.8	134.1
1975	100.0	104.4	90.3	97.6	104.7	114.8	94.5	135.3	97.3	102.1	107.9	127.3
1976	100.0	107.8	90.4	92.9	99.3	102.9	92.2	106.3	92.9	97.5	102.6	103.4
1977	100.0	100.0	100.0	100.0	100.0	100.0	100.0	100.0	100.0	100.0	100.0	100.0
1978	100.0	93.2	128.5	114.0	109.0	109.2	115.8	104.0	113.6	101.5	98.9	109.9
1979	100.0	90.7	122.7	122.2	114.1	115.5	126.7	106.2	122.3	105.1	104.2	121.6
1980	100.0	90.9	118.7	122.7	106.7	116.5	127.9	103.2	123.6	107.8	105.6	133.3
1981	100.0	88.6	121.4	96.8	84.1	90.4	103.0	77.5	98.6	92.7	88.2	116.0
1982	100.0	86.1	107.5	78.3	71.9	74.7	95.6	65.2	91.8	82.4	71.1	100.2
1983	100.0	86.2	112.7	70.1	65.6	64.5	90.9	58.1	86.0	72.9	58.2	86.9
1984	100.0	82.0	112.8	62.0	58.0	56.3	81.6	50.3	76.5	65.2	54.0	76.6
1985	100.0	77.8	112.3	60.4	56.6	54.7	78.9	46.2	73.9	61.9	51.9	74.4
1986	100.0	76.5	159.1	80.2	74.2	71.0	107.0	59.2	100.2	70.0	62.7	84.1
1987	100.0	80.1	185.2	95.9	87.7	81.8	129.1	68.1	121.1	79.0	70.4	94.0
1988	100.0	86.3	208.9	97.4	89.1	82.5	132.1	67.8	124.1	81.6	72.8	102.1

Source: U.S. Department of Labor, Bureau of Labor Statistics, June 1989.

was also clear to the financial markets, which reflected the judgment that Japan's economy was rapidly growing stronger and stronger. One measure of this was the continued appreciation of the yen once the decision was made to allow international currencies to float. From 1971 on, the yen appreciated against the dollar each and every year to 1989.

Many factors can influence the value of a currency in the short term. But the long term clearly bears witness to considerable confidence in the vigor of Japan's economy.

That strength is impressive by virtually any standard. Japan's economy, now the second largest in the world, is 60 percent of the size of the American economy. With a population of 123 million,

The World's Largest Financial Firms
Ranked by Market Capitalization

FIRM	COUNTRY	MARKET CAPITALIZATION ($ BILLIONS)
1. Industrial Bank of Japan	Japan	$86.2
2. Sumitomo Bank	Japan	67.9
3. Dai-Ichi Kangyo Bank	Japan	66.9
4. Fuji Bank	Japan	61.5
5. Mitsubishi Bank	Japan	60.7
6. Sanwa Bank	Japan	50.6
7. Nomura Securities	Japan	45.6
8. Long Term Credit Bank	Japan	34.1
9. Tokal Bank	Japan	33.2
10. Mitsui Bank	Japan	32.6
11. Mitsubishi Trust	Japan	25.2
12. Taiyo Kobe Bank	Japan	24.6
13. Bank of Tokyo	Japan	24.1
14. Sumitomo Trust	Japan	23.2
15. Daiwa Securities	Japan	21.7
16. Nippon Credit Bank	Japan	19.7
17. Nikko Securities	Japan	18.8
18. Daiwa Bank	Japan	16.9
19. Mitsui Trust	Japan	16.1
20. Yamaichi Securities	Japan	15.5

Source: Morgan-Stanley, *Capital International Perpective*.

just half that of the United States, it produces a gross national product three-fifths the size of that of the U.S. Japanese corporations now dominate the list of the world's largest business enterprises.[5] Japanese firms account for all twenty of the world's largest financial firms.

Japanese stock markets currently represent 46 percent of the value of the world's stock markets, compared to 27 percent for U.S. stock markets.[6]

Real economic growth in Japan was 4.5 percent in 1987, 5.3 percent in 1988, and 4.9 percent in 1989. Real growth, which for 1990 was estimated to be about the same as it was in 1989, actually came in above 5 percent.[7] Observers are once again suggesting a slow down for 1991, but to this point growth has continued in the 4–5 percent range for 1991. A Japanese government budget increase of 9.7 percent from 1989 to 1990 was easily digested, because tax revenues were up more than 13 percent. This allowed an increase in government spending of nearly 10 percent at the same time the deficit was cut by more than 20 percent from its 1989 level of ¥7.1 trillion.

However impressive statistics like these may be, they do not tell the whole story. Like all snapshots, they do not reveal underlying trends. No matter how large Japan's economy may be at any given time, one would draw different conclusions if that economy were rapidly shrinking rather than rapidly expanding. But as we shall see, the economic trends for Japan are everywhere positive.

Japan's So-called Limits to Growth

Much has been written and said in recent years about the problems that confront the Japanese economy. Many of these commentaries come from Japanese government officials, who naturally feel the weight of real problems and policy choices at first hand. Others emanate from officials who believe that Japan's best interests are served by minimizing the appearance of Japanese power. Still others come from scholars whose attraction to novelty is sometimes more than a match for reasoned judgment. Barely a week goes by without another newspaper article which suggests that Japan is now at the acme of its power and faces inevitable decline.

The arguments about limits to Japanese growth are in different forms, and each deserves to be considered briefly. The first of these theories rests on the premise that Japan's population growth has slowed to almost zero, and that as the population ages, its requirements must be met by an ever smaller share of youthful workers. This view seems to rest upon the premise that populations must be large and growing to insure economic, political, or military success. Yet the implicit egalitarianism of this view just does not hold up. Sheer size of a populace seems to guarantee little in the way of success if one considers many examples from past and present life. History is replete with examples of small nations that were able to dominate—often for long historical periods—by virtue of their advantages, natural and accidental. In any event, Japan's population places it squarely as the seventh most populous nation of the world. Beyond this, the size of one's populace is arguably less important now than at any time in history. Technology extends and multiplies the force of individual differences, and more than offsets sheer size. Finally, it should be considered that Japan has achieved its current success while laboring under obvious structural inefficiencies. Agriculture is a good example. As the following table indicates, Japan maintains a far higher proportion—nearly three times—of its populace in agriculture than does the United States:

Labor Force Distribution

	AGRICULTURE	INDUSTRY	SERVICES
Japan (1988)	7.9	33.6	58.0
United States (1987)	2.8	25.4	65.5

Source: U.S. Department of Labor

Approximately 4.75 million Japanese were employed in agriculture in 1988. If Japanese agricultural employment fell to only twice the percentage of U.S. agricultural employment over the next decade, this would free up approximately 1.25 million additional workers for its industrial and service sector, and result in a more efficient structural basis for its economy. A similar case could be made with regard to Japan's labor-intensive distribution system. These inefficiencies will be reduced over time, resulting in far more effective employment of several million people in the Japanese work force.

A second argument holds that Japan's economic success will itself be the cause of its undoing. It is said that the Japanese will succumb to the desire to work less and to enjoy the fruits of prosperity. The average Japanese factory worker labors 43.7 hours each week compared with the average American worker's 38.4 hours. Much anecdotal evidence has been produced to suggest that individual Japanese are fed up with long hours, long commutes to work, and cramped living quarters.[8] There is every reason to suppose that Japanese workers will choose to consume a somewhat greater share of their income than in the past. But the Japanese are not Americans, and it would be far wide of the mark to suppose that rampant individualism was about to break out in Japan. Traditions of discipline and sacrifice remain strong and they will change only very slowly. But even more significant, it should be noted that West Germans work an average week of only 35.6 hours, nearly three hours a week less than Americans, and this has in no way harmed the performance of the German economy or diminished its prospects for further growth.

A third argument suggests that Japan will be hampered by its homogeneity and lack of diversity. It is difficult to know what to make of this argument. Perhaps Japanese homogeneity does contribute to distrust of Japan among its neighbors, and perhaps this will offer some bounds to Japanese dominance in East Asia. To date, however, such limits have not been obvious. But it is unclear why domestic productivity and capability should founder as a result of Japan's racial and cultural homogeneity. America possesses, because of its diversity, a certain cultural richness and a tolerance that Japan lacks. But there is no known account of any positive correlation between social diversity and productivity.

Finally, it has been argued that Japan's lack of natural resources will jeopardize the country's success. So long as the international trading system remains at least as free and open as it is now, there is no reason why lack of natural resources should be more a problem for Japan in the future than it has been over the past forty years. Yet there is substance to this argument under a different set of circumstances. If Japan's access to natural resources is reduced, say, by an oil embargo, then its economy will suffer. In this regard, Japan faces the same problem it did between World Wars I and II.

When the Soviet Union temporarily cut off natural gas to Lithuania; when the United States suspended economic relations with China after Tiananmen Square; or whenever moral arguments shape economic decisions, as they have in the Middle East or South Africa—these were and are occasions on which the Japanese almost instinctively fear the precedents that are being established. Japan's lack of natural resources requires it to find a means of access to critical materials. The postwar trading system has proven to be a very successful means of doing so.

Under current and foreseeable circumstances, none of the above theories presents evidence of a significant barrier to Japan's continued economic growth, for none of them touches the essential core of what it will take to be successful in the 1990s: high investment in research and development; easy formation of huge amounts of capital to commercialize new products; and a commitment to excel in world markets. These are precisely the characteristics of contemporary Japan.[9]

Consider research and development. The old canard that the Japanese can copy and market but cannot create, is (if it was ever true) now wildly off the mark. A few statistics may be helpful here. First, more than half of all patents now granted in the world go to Japanese inventors. Fully 47 percent of all U.S. patents are granted to non-Americans, the largest share of whom are Japanese. Increasingly, these patents are granted not only for minor improvements in existing products, but also for essentially new products and commercial processes. Through domestic development and through licensing agreements for the purchase of foreign technology (principally, American technology), the technological base on which Japan builds is solid.

Japan now spends as much of its GNP as does the United States on research and development.[10] This is largely an expenditure of

the private sector, for Japan's government supports research and
development at only a fraction of the American expenditure. Where
the Japanese government *has* played a role has been in fostering a
broad-base educational system. This system now produces 5,000
technical workers per 1 million population, versus 3,500 in
America.[11]

Beyond this, Japanese companies are quickly stepping up the
pace of their investment in research and development. Between 1985
and 1988, research and development surpassed capital expenditures
for sixty-eight leading industrial companies.[12] The following table
shows the share devoted to research and development vis-a-vis capital expenditures for some of Japan's leading firms. By 1985 Japan
had become a net exporter of technology.

All of this fits very well with the Japanese desire to become world
leaders at the high end of high-technology products. Such products
have two advantages. First, they require the greatest added value
of any industrial products. Second, they are most immune to the
dangers of foreign competition from lower wage/cost producers in
Asia.

Japan's top ten in R&D, 1988

	R&D	CAPITAL EXPENDITURE	R&D AS % OF
	(BILLIONS OF YEN)		CAPITAL EXPENDITURE
Toyota	275	225	120
Matsushita Electrical Ind.	271	66	410
Hitachi	262	103	255
NEC	250	172	150
Toshiba	190	109	175
Fujitsu	184	119	155
Nissan	155	74	210
Sony	128	134	95
Mitsubishi Electric	122	59	205
Canon	75	45	165

Source: Japan Company Handbook

Japan's wealth permits it undisputed world leadership in capital formation. High domestic savings, large financial surpluses, and relatively low interest rates all combine to produce a virtual capital formation machine.[13] New Japanese capital investment in 1989 was, for the first time ever, larger *in absolute terms* than U.S. capital investment.[14] This cannot fail to have a pronounced effect in the coming years when the fruits of this capital spending are realized. The fact that Japanese capital expenditures will exceed U.S. capital expenditures in each of the next years for the foreseeable future— which is a certitude—will magnify this advantage.[15] The accumulation of huge surpluses makes it possible to dominate entire product lines from their infancy through maturity. In the words of one author, this has created a situation in which "Japanese industries [have] become 'supercompetitive,' " meaning that they are "so strong that they threaten not just to outsell the competition or gain percentage points of market share, but threaten to wipe out the competition completely."[16]

It is this very wealth that will permit Japan to take a world leadership role in the 1990s, not just in international markets, but in international market making. Japan has depended on world markets, and principally the U.S. market, to achieve its current success. But in the 1990s, no large firm can be a world leader if it does not sell to the world market. And the costs of doing so are substantial. In economist and management expert Peter Drucker's words, "Only a very big and cash-rich company can really afford today to go the multinational route."[17] He goes on to say, "Financially, only the Japanese can still afford to go multinational."[18] For other nations to play a role in world markets will require their firms to adopt different strategies, including joint ventures, partnerships, and other yet to be created hybrids of economic organization.

Given Japan's yearly surpluses, the cumulative transfer of wealth to Japanese ownership by the end of the 1990s will be enormous. It has been estimated—largely by extrapolating recent yearly surpluses—that Japan's cumulative surplus will grow from about $350 billion in 1989 to more than $800 billion in the 1990s.[19]

Among leading American economists, politicians, and academics, almost no one believes that Japan's surpluses will disappear; that its spending on research and development will be less; that its dominance in leading industries will be shakier; that its entry into new high-tech industries will be barred; or that its share of world production will be less in the next decade than now. Best estimates point to an economy that will continue to grow at or near current rates throughout the first half of the 1990s. Much of this growth will be fueled by increases in domestic demand. Demands for greater social welfare spending and for reduced working hours can be accommodated easily without substantial effect on Japan's world leadership in financial matters. Indeed, if Japan should undertake some of the steps desired by its trading partners, these steps are likely to strengthen its economy.

Let us suppose that the Japanese economy continues to grow at an average rate of approximately 4.9 percent a year over the next decade. Let us also suppose that under these circumstances of growth, the yen appreciates against the dollar an average of 1 percent in each of those same years.[20] Let us further suppose annual U.S. economic growth of 3 percent. Given Japan's economy currently at 60 percent the size of the U.S. economy, we find results as follows:

	JAPAN @ 4.9%	U.S. @ 3.0%	JAPAN @ 4.9% + 1% = 5.9%
1990	60	100	60
1991	62.94	103	63.54
1992	66.02	106.09	67.28
1993	69.25	109.27	71.25
1994	72.65	112.55	75.46
1995	76.2	115.92	79.91
1996	79.94	119.40	84.63
1997	83.86	122.98	89.62
1998	87.97	126.67	94.91
1999	92.28	130.47	100.51
2000	96.80	134.39	106.44

Under this scenario, by the close of the 1990s Japan's economy will grow from being 60 percent of the U.S. economy to 77 percent without yen appreciation, or to 79 percent with yen appreciation— and this with a population less than one-half that of the United States.

In short, whatever problems may lie on the surface for Japan, its economy is poised to be far more competitive in the 1990s than it was in the 1980s. The economic strength of Japan will grow vis-a-vis that of the United States and virtually all other industrial nations except a united Germany, whose own growth will maintain its relative size vis-a-vis Japan. Japan's economic strength will grow even faster than almost all of the less developed world.

The Goals of Japanese Economic Policy

If we were to speak of the "goal" of American economic policy, we would perhaps not know what to say. For in fact there really is no goal at all. There is instead a faith that allowing individuals and firms to be relatively free to compete will result in the best possible outcome; indeed, since choice is valued above all, this is by definition the best possible outcome. In cases where this system produces results that are manifestly at odds with good outcomes—results such as unemployment, homelessness, unsecured retirement, and so forth—tax dollars are directed to these problems. But the idea that there should be national economic priorities in any but a rhetorical sense is very foreign to the United States.

Only in times of grave crisis (as in World War II) or perceived grave crisis (as with the Sputnik threat) has the United States government genuinely directed resources so as to affect the domestic economy and the incentives for production according to a vision of the national interest. It is an open joke in Washington that legislation whose real motive is to reallocate domestic political priorities is most often called the "National Security Act of . . .". Domestic spending legislation masquerading as national security legislation results not only from appeals to patriotism, but from the fact that there existed throughout the 1980s a political consensus to increase spending on national security. But few Americans argue seriously that there is anything but the most remote and generalized connection between domestic funding priorities and the national security of the United States.

This is to say that the United States does not have an industrial policy that equates the success of industries with the success of the nation. There is simply no American consensus about what is national success, unless it is that as many people as possible have the fullest possible freedom of choice—regardless of what they might choose.

It is much different in Japan. One can point to certain Japanese assumptions about future economic necessities that are shared by Japanese politicians, officials, and businessmen—in fact, by most all Japanese who form opinions on these sorts of things. The core view is that Japan needs to dominate world markets in high-tech products. The goal is not merely to succeed, but to dominate. To do so, Japan must have a highly competitive industrial system with access to raw materials and to markets. In the words of Dutch journalist and author Karel van Wolferen, "Economic control, rather than profit-maximizing, is the main driving force."[21]

In Japan there is no radical disjunction between economics and politics, as there is in America. For that matter, there is a unity of view in Japan that extends beyond economics and politics to social and spiritual life as well. This unity informs the views of decision makers in the government, in industry, and in the financial sector. Mere choice for its own sake is not a sufficiently integrating principle in Japan. Rather, views are integrated as to the *kind* of choices that are made.

In recent years there has come to be a theory, subscribed to by some in the U.S. government, that there are two opposing forces in Japan, the internationalists and the traditionalists. The internationalists are said to believe that Japan must open its economy and its market to the world in order to play its proper role. The traditionalists are described as believing that there is no pressing need to reform the economy. The internationalists are said also to be in league with Japanese consumers, who seek access to the cheaper food and consumer goods that would come from a fuller opening of Japan's economy.

Without denying that there are individuals in Japan who hold views that are internationalist in the above sense, there is no such division in Japan as has been described. So-called internationalists in Japanese government and industry may believe that it is unavoidable that Japan will have to open itself more fully to world competition. But they do not see this as a virtue in the fashion of an ideological American free trader; they believe it to be a tactical necessity that must be managed so as to allow Japan time to position itself to accommodate this intrusion. Nowhere is this better said than by van Wolferen:

> Industrial expansion in the Western democracies aims to make life more livable and to expand choices for consumers. Japanese aims are much more political: Administrators in industry and government take it for granted that Japan should become ever more invincible in the face of a potentially hostile world. They strive for domination in as many industrial sectors as possible and believe it to be only natural to do this at the cost of other desirables in life.[22]

CHAPTER SIX

Japan's So-called Asian Competitors: The New Greater Asia Coprosperity Sphere

Japan's "Competitors"

ECONOMIC GROWTH IN EAST ASIA has been strong throughout the 1980s. On average, the rate has been between 6 and 7 percent each year for the region as a whole, with growth reaching as high as 8.6 percent in 1988. This has led to the impression that while Japan is growing stronger, so too are its neighbors, and that Japan is actually threatened by competition at the lower end of the scale of value-added products.

It is indeed true, as we shall discuss later in this chapter, that Japan has experienced strong competition in lower-end products. But Japan does not even contest these market sectors any longer, and is quite content to help create offshore production facilities for such products. What is important to note here, however, are the true dimensions of Japanese economic dominance in Asia. Asia is not a region of more or less equal nations, all of which are growing rapidly. To the contrary, there is no other nation, or even any combination of nations, in the region that is in the same league as Japan.

Let us try to put Japan's economic strength into perspective. The table on the following page makes the point as clearly as anything can. From these figures one can see that in 1989 the gross domestic product (GDP) of Japan was 1.7 times greater than that of all twelve other leading East Asian nations put together. Those twelve nations include both China and India. In short, the 123 million people of Japan produce more than the 3 billion people of the most populous region in the world.

Some of the magnitude of Japan's dominance reflects the strength of the yen in the late 1980s. But it is instructive to look at the beginning of the 1980s. In 1982, Japan's GDP was already larger than that of all twelve other nations combined. If the yen continues to strengthen against other Asian currencies, the disparities will grow even larger. Based on the DRI/McGraw-Hill estimates on which the above table was prepared, at an exchange rate of 105 yen per dollar in 1993, the Japanese economy would stand at $4.795 trillion, or almost exactly twice the value of all twelve other Asian nations combined.

To put these numbers into sharper relief, let us consider several specific comparisons. Taiwan is frequently mentioned as a nation that offers strong economic competition for Japan. Taiwan's total GDP is about 4 percent of Japan's. Put differently, the growth of Japan's GDP year by year in the 1980s has been greater than the entire size of Taiwan's economy.

Korea is another nation that is often mentioned as an up-and-coming competitor of Japan. Indeed, Korea has been widely touted as the "next Japan." Yet Korea's economy is only about 6 percent of the size of Japan's economy. And, as in the case of Taiwan, the dollar value of Japan's economy grew more in each year between 1985 and 1988 than Korea's entire GDP.

For comparison, the combined Korean and Taiwan economies together are about the same percentage of Japan's economy as Canada's is of the American economy. This was true at the beginning of the 1980s. Both Korea's and Taiwan's currencies appreciated against the dollar in the second half of the 1980s, just as did Japan's. After this appreciation, this comparison remains precisely the same.

Gross Domestic Product*

	1982	1983	1984	1985	1986	1987	1988	1989	1990	1991	1992	1993
Australia	165.6	160.0	177.4	158.2	165.6	195.0	247.5	275.1	271.3	287.9	309.9	334.1
China	259.2	276.4	280.2	282.8	271.7	293.6	370.6	425.3	455.7	480.3	513.6	554.9
Hong Kong	30.7	28.6	31.8	33.5	38.6	47.2	54.5	60.8	72.0	81.9	92.7	105.2
India	187.8	205.2	202.0	211.6	232.2	254.1	283.8	282.0	299.0	323.8	351.4	380.8
Indonesia	94.7	81.1	84.9	85.1	75.2	67.1	74.1	79.5	86.3	94.7	104.0	114.0
Korea	75.7	82.3	90.1	92.9	105.9	131.3	171.3	205.4	226.8	258.5	302.2	348.5
Malaysia	26.8	30.0	33.9	31.2	27.6	32.0	34.6	38.0	42.0	46.7	51.8	57.8
New Zealand	23.4	22.9	21.9	22.2	27.6	35.1	41.8	40.4	42.7	45.2	48.2	51.3
Philippines	39.9	34.6	32.4	32.9	30.6	34.3	39.0	43.4	48.2	54.4	61.1	68.0
Singapore	15.3	17.4	18.8	17.7	17.6	20.0	23.9	27.6	31.5	34.7	38.5	42.3
Taiwan	48.1	51.6	57.7	59.9	72.9	98.5	116.2	143.6	170.6	196.0	221.9	250.6
Thailand	35.7	39.6	41.2	37.4	41.6	48.0	57.9	66.0	73.4	82.3	92.1	102.0
12-nation total	1,003	1,030	1,072	1,065	1,107	1,256	1,515	1,687	1,820	1,986	2,188	2,410
Japan	1,084	1,181	1,256	1,341	1,977	2,392	2,861	2,894	3,221	3,731	4,351	4,795

*Billions of current U.S. dollars
1982–1988 actual; 1989–1993 projections
Totals may vary due to rounding

Source: DRI/McGraw-Hill *Asian Review* and DRI/McGraw-Hill *Japanese Review*

Exports of Goods and Services*

	1982	1983	1984	1985	1986	1987	1988	1989	1990	1991	1992	1993
Australia	24.68	23.21	26.79	26.07	26.30	31.46	39.69	42.97	43.82	48.72	54.95	60.36
China	21.87	22.18	24.83	27.54	31.34	39.92	47.64	49.78	57.63	66.61	76.32	87.31
Hong Kong	26.03	27.20	33.93	36.07	42.39	57.48	74.17	82.73	99.48	117.20	135.09	154.54
India	12.34	13.11	14.04	12.18	13.48	15.44	17.47	19.42	22.00	24.36	26.70	28.88
Indonesia	23.17	22.49	22.40	19.51	15.63	18.68	21.06	24.27	27.08	30.95	35.44	40.01
Korea	26.30	29.37	32.41	32.11	40.88	54.77	69.85	74.29	80.35	92.31	106.12	120.06
Malaysia	13.64	15.64	18.42	17.13	15.77	20.13	23.48	25.97	29.30	33.37	37.93	42.83
New Zealand	6.84	7.15	7.55	6.94	7.86	9.60	11.08	11.23	12.20	13.26	14.49	15.57
Philippines	6.57	6.77	7.05	6.80	7.61	7.95	9.05	10.24	11.47	12.95	14.60	16.23
Singapore	30.49	31.14	31.65	29.19	27.61	34.72	47.30	53.83	60.07	66.96	76.48	85.16
Taiwan	24.26	27.82	33.18	33.59	43.92	58.85	66.40	81.72	99.57	114.92	131.69	149.90
Thailand	8.39	8.05	9.15	9.03	11.03	14.44	19.98	24.42	27.03	31.13	35.73	40.24
12-nation total	224.6	234.1	261.4	256.2	283.8	363.5	447.2	500.9	570.0	652.7	745.6	841.1
Japan	180.0	183.0	211.0	218.0	257.0	301.0	372.0	421.0	459.0	523.0	591.0	644.0

*Billions of current U.S. dollars
1982–1988 actual; 1989–1993 projections
Totals may vary due to rounding

Source: DRI/McGraw-Hill *Asian Review* and DRI/McGraw-Hill *Japanese Review*

Japan's dominance in the region is also revealed in other ways. As the table opposite shows, Japan's exports in the 1980s constituted between 80 and 85 percent of the value of all other twelve Asian nations' exports combined. Furthermore, this percentage was just about the same at the end of the 1980s as it was at the beginning. This is hardly the picture of a nation losing ground to more competitive neighbors.

Imports into Japan grew throughout the 1980s, particularly in 1988 and 1989. Yet as the following table reveals, imports into Japan at the end of the 1980s were about the same share compared to the rest of the region—70 percent—as they were at the beginning of the decade. Japan imports more than four times as much as its leading competitor; it exports more than four and one-half times as much.

As a region, the Asian nations have enjoyed a current account surplus beginning in 1983. But if Japan is broken out from this group, the remainder of the region has actually run a current account deficit each year. Some nations like Taiwan, Korea, and Hong Kong have consistently run surpluses; others like Australia, China, and India have run deficits. In short, Japan alone accounts for the substantial surplus registered by the entire region.

Finally, five of the region's thirteen leading economies, including Japan's, have no net external debt. The remaining nations have a combined external debt nearing $300 billion. This debt is nearly twice the value of all 1989 exports of these eight nations, whose exports and imports were in rough balance that year. It is nearly 40 percent of the combined GDPs of these nations.

There are no serious competitors to Japan in the region. Its economic position is absolutely dominant, dwarfing any combination of other nations. The growth of other nations in the region will require Japan to adapt its policies to the realities of competition from low wage-rate competitors. Japan is already doing so, and has found that a strong yen will not jeopardize Japan's success, it will reinforce it.

Imports of Goods and Services*

	1982	1983	1984	1985	1986	1987	1988	1989	1990	1991	1992	1993
Australia	30.17	25.61	30.75	30.32	30.96	34.19	42.91	47.63	47.87	50.63	54.43	58.74
China	18.90	21.34	25.95	42.83	43.39	43.86	55.36	62.08	67.52	77.98	87.75	99.45
Hong Kong	27.14	27.78	32.60	34.16	40.59	54.71	71.33	81.27	96.73	114.59	132.24	151.08
India	16.72	17.44	17.19	17.68	18.20	18.76	21.63	22.58	25.46	28.06	30.60	33.12
Indonesia	22.79	23.35	18.16	17.86	17.04	17.54	19.29	22.57	25.16	28.86	32.47	36.35
Korea	27.59	29.71	32.31	30.94	34.45	44.20	55.25	67.21	73.37	83.59	97.65	112.63
Malaysia	15.97	17.23	17.77	15.53	14.04	15.75	19.81	23.17	17.45	31.70	36.20	40.57
New Zealand	7.74	7.41	8.42	7.46	7.81	9.21	10.50	10.60	11.38	12.40	13.55	14.66
Philippines	9.29	9.10	7.09	5.83	5.70	7.65	9.12	11.87	13.53	15.20	17.15	19.14
Singapore	31.16	31.46	32.17	29.62	27.52	34.76	46.31	52.67	59.20	66.06	75.46	84.19
Taiwan	21.77	23.25	26.61	25.04	29.00	41.04	53.99	70.78	91.77	108.35	126.16	145.85
Thailand	9.01	10.92	10.94	10.09	10.16	14.32	20.99	25.43	28.26	31.57	35.10	39.02
12-nation total	238.0	244.6	260.0	267.4	278.9	336.0	426.5	497.9	567.7	649.0	738.8	834.8
Japan	171.0	161.0	174.0	168.0	170.0	211.0	288.0	346.0	396.0	464.0	530.0	586.0

*Billions of current U.S. dollars

1982–1988 actual; 1989–1993 projections

Totals may vary due to rounding

Source: DRI/McGraw-Hill *Asian Review* and DRI/McGraw-Hill *Japanese Review*

Current Account Balances*

	1982	1983	1984	1985	1986	1987	1988	1989	1990	1991	1992	1993
Australia	−8.41	−5.88	−8.54	−8.83	−9.75	−8.73	−11.22	−14.50	−13.93	−12.02	−9.88	−8.61
China	5.95	4.63	2.71	11.28	−7.00	0.25	−3.99	−8.72	−6.51	−8.14	−8.31	−9.15
Hong Kong	−1.12	−0.58	1.34	1.90	1.80	2.78	2.84	1.46	2.75	2.60	2.85	3.47
India	−2.52	−1.93	−2.34	−4.21	−4.63	−4.40	−5.27	−4.61	−4.67	−4.39	−4.68	−5.20
Indonesia	−5.32	−6.34	−1.86	−1.92	−3.91	−2.15	−1.23	−1.60	−1.61	−1.82	−1.29	−1.00
Korea	−2.65	−1.61	−1.37	−0.89	4.62	9.85	14.16	6.44	5.00	6.45	6.33	5.60
Malaysia	−3.60	−3.50	−1.67	−0.61	0.05	2.57	1.88	0.83	−0.27	−0.64	−0.68	−0.60
New Zealand	−1.61	−0.97	−1.75	−1.41	−1.48	−1.76	−0.76	−0.71	−0.58	−0.47	−0.38	−0.36
Philippines	−3.21	−2.75	−1.27	−0.02	0.97	−0.50	−0.37	−1.11	−1.08	−1.22	−1.30	−1.23
Singapore	−1.21	−0.58	−0.38	0.00	0.54	0.55	1.66	0.46	−0.02	−0.23	−0.28	−0.28
Taiwan	2.25	4.41	6.98	9.19	16.22	17.61	11.23	11.14	11.00	10.03	9.90	9.80
Thailand	−1.00	−2.87	−2.11	−1.54	0.25	−0.37	−1.67	−1.90	−2.19	−1.89	−1.12	−0.65
12-nation total	−22.46	−17.96	−10.28	−19.62	−2.31	15.72	7.26	−12.82	−12.10	−11.74	−8.84	−8.21
Japan	6.85	20.80	35.00	49.17	85.85	87.02	79.63	68.51	57.22	53.32	53.89	50.51

*Billions of current U.S. dollars

1982–1988 actual; 1989–1993 projections

Totals may vary due to rounding

Source: DRI/McGraw-Hill *Asian Review* and DRI/McGraw-Hill *Japanese Review*

Japan and China

It is worth a brief excursus to discuss China specifically. With its large population, its large land mass, and its tradition of education and culture, China is frequently mentioned as a "great power" in the region. China holds one of the five permanent seats on the United Nations Security Council. It is one of the five nations in the official nuclear club. It has had a tradition of high culture dating back thousands of years, a culture from which Japan's originated. Upon these, and perhaps other even less justifiable grounds, a mythology has grown up around China that suggests it is—or soon will or could be—in a league with Japan.[1]

If a great power is measured by its capacity to affect people outside its own borders, then China is not now and will not in the foreseeable future be a great power. Faced in the north by overwhelmingly stronger Soviet armies; essentially defeated by Vietnam in a border skirmish in the south; a net importer and debtor; and unable to govern a nearby island territory it claims as its own—this is China, both before and after the crackdown in Tiananmen Square in June 1989.

Prior to the crackdown, some observers pointed to a growing tendency toward a so-called Greater China composed of the mainland, Hong Kong, and Taiwan. Typical rhetoric found China "threatening" Japan:

> Greater China threatens not just Indonesia and Thailand, but such advanced nations as Korea and even Japan.

And:

> Some advocates of a Greater China like to use the metaphor of a flock of geese. Japan leads the flock, followed by Taiwan, Korea, Singapore and Hong Kong, then other Asian exporters. All fly in formation toward modernization. But China, instead of flying in place behind the pack, threatens to dominate the laggards and is closing in on the leader.[2]

Events have changed this view of China somewhat since the summer of 1989, and the passage of time has permitted a more sober assessment of the actual situation. First, it has become apparent that Hong Kong will not slide easily into the People's Republic of China (P.R.C) without loss of both economic power and its class of most creative entrepreneurs. The mainland still retains some capacity to affect this outcome, but it is a much diminished capacity. Trust can be broken overnight, but takes many years to repair.

More importantly, the conditions for integration between the mainland and Taiwan are not present. In fact, the realities seem to be moving the opposite way. On Taiwan, it has been the ruling Kuomintang (KMT) party that has preserved the view of "one China." Both Taiwan and the P.R.C. support the contention that "there is but one China and Taiwan is part of China." But as the KMT has liberalized the political process on Taiwan, opposition groups—and younger citizens of Taiwan who have no personal connection with the mainland—have openly doubted the value of unification with the mainland. In the fall 1989 election, the KMT captured 59 percent of the electorate; on the issue of independence from the mainland—which it is still sedition to discuss—the KMT will have to walk delicately in the coming years if it is to stake out a politically popular position.

Other nations reflect this situation in their relations with the mainland and Taiwan. Taiwan's economy is now actually stronger compared with the P.R.C. economy than it was at the time of U.S. derecognition in 1979. Given that success, and given Taiwan's financial and foreign assistance resources, many nations are rethinking where their longer term interests genuinely lie. Relations with both countries would be the first choice; but if that is not possible, Taiwan's standing as the thirteenth largest trading nation in the world makes it an important country with which to maintain a positive relationship.[3]

As the postwar division of Germany disappears, some observers have asked whether the other Communist/noncommunist divisions, including that between the People's Republic and Taiwan, will also disappear. But there is an important difference between the German and Chinese situations. In Germany it was the noncommunist sector that was the larger, dominant partner; in China, it is not. To understand the significance of this, think for a moment about how difficult German reunification would have been if West Germany had been the size of the East and vice versa.

In recent years China has begun to reduce its expenditures on military modernization. Of funds expended, the navy has received an increasingly large share, a reflection of the fact that the Pacific is essentially a naval theater. But despite improvements in both the quantity and quality of the navy, China's naval capacities do not approximate those of Japan.[4] Fully three-fourths of China's fleet of 1,296 ships consists of coastal patrol boats. Its 149 major combat ships are not in the first rank of technological capability, and thus the numbers are misleading as to China's true strength. The fact is that, unlike Japan, China will remain fully technologically dependent upon Western nations for meaningful improvements in the quality of its air and naval forces for many years to come. And the repression of June 1989 has diminished the willingness of the United States to assist in China's military modernization. Beyond this, as the Soviet Union recedes as a threat in the world at large, American policymakers will and should have every reason to slow China's military modernization. The fact is that in the coming years China will have a far greater need of American goodwill than vice versa.

Japan currently feels no sense of threat from China. To the contrary, it looks to China much as it has throughout the last century, as a place to turn for resources, markets, and influence if other regions are cut off. The Japanese private sector has been active in China, having replaced American businesses since 1987 as the second leading source (behind Hong Kong and Macao) of foreign direct investment. Even so, Japanese businesses have been guarded in their enthusiasm by the realities of China's limited profitability for their investments.

It is the government of Japan that has been more enthusiastic about China all along. The government has from time to time urged business leaders to look at China as a place for investment. While Japan adopted sanctions against China, albeit limited ones, in the wake of Tiananmen Square, it was the first nation to remove them and to urge the restoration of normal relations. Japan has been the leading provider of foreign assistance to China, giving approxi-

Foreign Direct Investment, by Country/Region

COUNTRY/REGION	1986		1987		1988	
	VALUE ($1,000)	COMPOSITION (%)	VALUE ($1,000)	COMPOSITION (%)	VALUE ($1,000)	COMPOSITION (%)
Hong Kong, Macao	1,328,710	59.2	1,598,210	69.1	2,095,200	65.6
Japan	263,350	11.7	219,700	9.5	514,530	16.1
U.S.A.	326,170	14.5	262,800	11.4	235,960	7.4
U.K.	35,260	1.6	4,550	0.2	34,160	1.1
Norway	n.a.	n.a.	1,500	0.1	32,010	1.0
Italy	29,400	1.3	16,260	0.7	30,540	0.9
Singapore	13,620	0.6	21,630	0.9	27,820	0.9
France	43,630	1.9	15,550	0.7	22,670	0.7
Netherlands	2,490	0.1	210	0.0	20,620	0.6
Denmark	1,410	0.1	2,420	0.1	19,800	0.6
Total (including the others)	2,243,730	100.0	2,313,530	100.0	3,193,680	100.0

Source: *Zhongguo Tongji Nianjian, 1989 / China Newsletter No. 84/JETRO, p.21.*

mately ten times as much aid as the second leading nation, Italy. In 1987 Japan provided in excess of $550 million, more than the total for all other leading donors combined. In 1990 Japan announced the resumption of its planned six-year program worth $5.4 billion, an average of $900 million a year. The United States provides no direct foreign assistance to China.

Hopes for mainland China's imminent development have long been misplaced. As one shrewd observer says, China has been on the verge of great market potential ever since the time of Marco Polo. Indeed, in the past century China has been largely distinguished by its weakness rather than its strength. The Japanese war with China in 1894–1895 was largely a result of that weakness; the "open door" policy was an attempt to preserve China from its own weakness; the Russo-Japanese War was a struggle for hegemony in Chinese and Korean territory; and the Japanese aggression in the 1930s that helped to propel Japan into full-scale war in the Pacific can be traced to that weakness as well.

In this context, China's decision to crush the democracy demonstrations of 1989 does not appear as a unique, isolated event as much as another instance of self-imposed Chinese weakness. The best judgment about contemporary China is predictably not that of a "China hand," but of a farsighted thinker unburdened by professional associations or mythology. Peter Drucker rightly speaks of a China that "will feature in world affairs mainly because of its weakness and fragility."[5] If China is a sleeping giant, it is a sleeping giant under heavy sedation, and it is not likely to awaken soon.

Japan's Regional Economic Policies

The dynamic nations of East Asia do compete with Japan, but only at the lower end of technological sophistication. Japan's ministries and industrial leaders have adopted strategies to make the most of this competition. It has kept the economy at a fever pitch by continually pressing Japan forward into ever more advanced high-end technological and value-added products. Consider the following table of products and their per pound added values:

The Higher the Better

PRODUCT	ADDED VALUE ($/LB)
Satellite	20,000
Jet fighter	2,500
Supercomputer	1,700
Aero-engine	900
Jumbo jet	350
Video camera	280
Mainframe computer	160
Semiconductor	100
Submarine	45
Color television	16
NC machine tool	11
Luxury motor car	10
Standard motor car	5
Cargo ship	1

Source: *The Economist*

The *Economist* has written that "more and more of Japan's national wealth is coming from industries that add value to their materials at rates in excess of $100 a pound."[6]

All other things equal, Japan might wish that Taiwan, Korea, Hong Kong, and now increasingly Thailand, Malaysia, and other nations were not pressing on the lower end of the competitive scale. But Japan is not looking back or down; it is looking ahead and up. Japan has learned in twenty brief years that there is no way to win except to stay ahead and to be in the very first rank of nations on the cutting edge of technology.

Japan has adopted two principal responses in relation to its low-end competitors: direct foreign investment, and foreign assistance. The major response is foreign direct investment in the economies of its competitors. Japanese foreign direct investment has undergone several phases since World War II. Initially, Japan had no funds available for this purpose. When it began to invest abroad in the 1960s, its first efforts were limited mainly to basic production facilities in an attempt to gain access to needed raw materials.

As the Japanese began to succeed in manufacturing products for

the world market in the 1970s, their foreign direct investment began
to change. Faced with competition from lower wage-rate neighbors
like Korea, Taiwan, and Hong Kong, Japanese companies started
to invest directly in these economies. The creation of Japanese-
owned parts and assembly facilities served several purposes. First,
it brought down costs for Japanese firms. Second, it assured participation in the growing markets of the newly industrializing economies.

In the 1980s, two new trends emerged. Overall Japanese foreign
direct investment increased enormously. This was given a huge
impetus by the so-called Plaza Accord of 1985, which forced a rapid
rise in the value of the yen. As Japanese manufacturers tightened
their profit margins and slashed costs in order to remain competitive
with a higher yen, they simultaneously discovered that the purchase
or creation of foreign subsidiaries was both inexpensive and highly
advantageous. This was true not only in developing countries, but
also in regard to its most advanced competitors in the United States
and Europe, and the first consequence was a huge increase in Japanese direct investment in those markets. As the following table
shows, Japanese direct investment increased sevenfold in the U.S.
and more than twelvefold in the United Kingdom between 1984 and
1988. Investments in the United States had the additional advantage
of damping down, to some degree at least, concern over Japanese
competitiveness. In preserving old jobs and in creating new ones in
basic American industries like automobiles, steel, and electronics,

Japan's Foreign Direct Investment by Country, FY 1984–FY 1988 (in millions of dollars)

	FY 1984	FY 1985	FY 1986	FY 1987	FY 1988	CUMULATIVE MARCH 31, 1989
United States	$3,360	$5,395	$10,165	$14,704	$21,701	$71,860
Canada	184	100	276	653	626	3,231
North America	3,544	5,495	10,441	15,357	22,328	75,091

	FY 1984	FY 1985	FY 1986	FY 1987	FY 1988	CUMULATIVE MARCH 31, 1989
Indonesia	$374	$408	$250	$545	$586	$9,804
Hong Kong	412	131	502	1,072	1,662	6,167
Singapore	225	339	302	494	747	3,812
Korea	107	134	436	647	483	3,248
China	114	100	226	1,226	296	2,036
Thailand	119	48	124	250	359	1,992
Malaysia	142	79	158	163	387	1,834
Taiwan	65	114	291	367	372	1,791
Philippines	46	61	21	72	134	1,120
Asia	1,628	1,435	2,327	4,868	5,569	32,227
Panama	1,671	1,533	2,401	2,305	1,712	12,858
Brazil	318	314	270	229	510	5,596
Caymans	1	132	930	1,197	2,609	5,085
Bahama	97	298	792	734	737	2,718
Mexico	56	101	226	28	87	1,671
Bermuda	29	148	16	36	337	991
Netherlands Antilles	66	62	66	199	172	747
Peru	6	10	—	1	—	696
Latin America	2,290	2,616	4,737	4,816	6,428	31,617
United Kingdom	318	375	984	2,473	3,956	10,554
Netherlands	452	613	651	829	2,359	5,525
Luxembourg	315	300	1,092	1,764	657	4,729
West Germany	245	172	210	403	409	2,364
France	117	67	152	330	463	1,764
Switzerland	229	60	91	224	454	1,432
Spain	140	91	86	283	161	1,045
Belgium	71	84	50	70	164	1,027
Europe	1,937	1,930	3,469	6,576	9,116	30,164
Australia	105	468	881	1,222	2,413	8,137
Oceania	157	525	992	1,413	2,669	9,315
Liberia	281	159	289	267	648	3,658
Africa	326	172	309	272	653	4,604
Kuwait	55	34	41	54	20	1,383
Iran	0	0	—	—	1	1,005
Middle East	273	45	44	62	259	3,338
Total	10,155	12,217	22,320	33,364	47,022	186,356

Source: Ministry of Finance/JEI REPORT

Japanese firms created counterpressures against efforts to restrict their access to the American market.

Second, the need to remain competitive in the face of a more highly valued yen has caused Japanese firms to look further abroad for lower cost labor. At the same time the yen was forced upward against the dollar, so also were the currencies of Korea and Taiwan. Wage rates in these nations have become far less favorable for Japanese investors than those in Southeast Asia. As a result, the second trend of the 1980s has been rapid increases in Japanese foreign direct investment in the six countries of the Association of Southeast Asian Nations (ASEAN). In addition to providing high-quality, low-cost workers, the ASEAN nations offer one additional benefit: they export heavily into the United States. More than 30 percent of ASEAN exports go to the U.S., thus masking the fact that Japanese firms are profiting substantially on trade that does not show up in charts and tables as a specifically Japanese trade surplus.

Japanese foreign direct investment in nonindustrialized economies is by no means uniform throughout the lesser developed world. To the contrary, this effort is focused almost exclusively on East Asia.[7]

A similar picture emerges with respect to the other economic tool with which Japan is expanding its export markets and economic dominance: foreign assistance. Western nations, particularly the United States, have pressed Japan throughout the 1980s to use its financial surpluses to provide economic assistance to less developed countries. This, it has been argued, could be her unique contribution to international well-being, making up for the fact that Japan's defense spending has been a smaller portion of its GNP than is the case in other industrialized nations.

Japan began to respond to these entreaties in the mid-1980s. In 1987 it pledged to provide $50 billion in economic assistance over the five-year period from 1988 to 1992. Three-fourths of the way through this period, Japan is on course to achieve that goal. In 1989 it surpassed the United States as the largest provider of economic assistance in the world, with Official Development Assistance payments of $8.95 billion.

In part, Japan's title as top foreign aid donor has resulted from the decline of American aid as a proportion of the U.S. federal budget. As the following chart displays, U.S. aid as a share of GNP declined about 50 percent, from 0.027 to 0.015 percent of GNP. Japan's economic assistance has remained stable at about 0.32 percent of its GNP, with absolute increases in aid reflecting the strong growth of Japan's economy.

Japan has concentrated its foreign assistance on Asia, with nearly 70 percent of its Official Development Assistance flowing to Asia, the majority going to Southeast Asia. The following table breaks down Japan's 1988 ODA to Asia by region. This concentration in Asia gives Japan enormous influence there. Last year, 60 percent of all economic assistance received by Asian nations was provided by Japan—which is to say that Japan provided more aid to Asian nations than did all other nations of the world combined.

In individual instances, the contrast is even more striking. For example, Japan provides resource-rich Indonesia with more than ten times the amount of assistance that the United States provides. Even in the Philippines, an American-oriented nation for the whole of the twentieth century, and a nation brutally occupied by Japan during World War II, Japan now provides more assistance than does the United States. And this is to a Philippine government that was in part the creation of the United States. The following table, which compares U.S. and Japanese bilateral assistance to ASEAN members, reveals Japan's clear dominance.

Japan's Official Development Assistance (Asia) 1988 (in millions of dollars)

REGION	GRANTS		LOANS	TOTAL ODA
	GRANTS	TECHNICAL ASSISTANCE		
East Asia	$ 52.4	$182.7	$ 494.9	$ 729.9
Southeast Asia	260.7	342.6	1,593.0	2,196.6
South Asia	370.9	78.1	660.5	1,109.5
Other Asia	—	2.7	—	2.7

Source: Ministry of Foreign Affairs/JEI REPORT

Official Aid, by Donor
Net disbursements as % of GNP

■ 1980
▨ 1989
0.0 Total $ billion 1989

%

	0.9	Norway
	1.0	Denmark
	1.8	Sweden
	2.1	Holland
	7.5	France
	0.7	Finland
	0.7	Belgium
	2.3	Canada
	5.0	West Germany
	3.3	Italy
	1.0	Australia
	46.5	Total OECD
	9.0	Japan
	2.6	Britain
	0.6	Switzerland
	0.3	Austria
	0.1	New Zealand
	0.1	Ireland
	7.7	United States

Drawn from *The Economist*

Japanese and U.S. Assistance (including Economic & Security) to ASEAN Countries (Japanese Figures in million US $)

YEAR	INDONESIA	MALAYSIA	PHILIPPINES	SINGAPORE	THAILAND
1983	141 (235)	5 (92)	155 (147)	0.05 (4)	129 (248)
1984	167 (168)	11 (245)	158 (160)	0.06 (28)	139 (232)
1985	149 (161)	5 (125)	282 (240)	0.1 (8)	144 (264)
1986	119 (161)	2 (37)	177 (438)	0.05 (15)	99 (261)
1987	140 (707)	1 (276)	500 (379)	0.05 (11)	74 (302)
1988	71 (985)	0.92 (25)	417 (535)	0.05 (11)	66 (360)

Source: Hudson Insitute/Agency for International Development

This picture is likely to become even more pronounced in the coming years. U.S. budget pressures make increases in foreign assistance unlikely. In addition, new recipients in Eastern Europe will compete with traditional U.S. beneficiaries for scarce aid dollars.

But it is more than the amount of the aid Japan offers that makes it a useful tool of Japanese economic policy; it is also the *manner* in which that assistance is given. Japan offers most of its aid as loans. It ranks eighteenth—dead last—among aid donors in the percentage of its aid offered in the form of grants or technical assistance.[8]

In the past, Japan "tied" a large percentage of its economic assistance loans to the requirement that the money be used to purchase goods and services in Japan. Because the most efficient use of aid (in principle) would not be tied to any such requirement, the industrialized nations have adopted through the Organization for Economic Cooperation and Development (OECD) an export credit regime that requires donors to sharply limit tied aid. Japan now follows the letter of this agreement, and offers more than three-fourths of its aid under untied terms.

However, there are many ways to escape the spirit of OECD export credit arrangements even while following their letter. For instance, Japan regularly utilizes Less Developed Country (LDC) untied aid. This approach restricts bidding on projects funded by Japanese loans only to Japanese companies and to companies from LDCs, thus effectively excluding American firms and those of other industrialized nations from competition. In addition, Japan utilizes "tied feasibility studies." Under this procedure, Japan offers a less developed country a grant—permitted by OECD rules to be expended directly in the donor nation—to undertake a feasibility study on a large project. The large project is financed by a Japanese government loan, but the feasibility study has established project specifications that favor Japanese bidders.[9] This approach is more complex, but yields the same result: loans for programs whose work is effectively limited to firms from Japan.

Often, Japan will mix private investment with government development assistance. The 1990 announcement that Suzuki would build an automobile plant in Hungary that will produce 15,000 cars a year offers a good example. A $140 million plant will be constructed. Fifty million of these dollars will be provided by Japan's foreign assistance program. All of this was planned, decided, and announced while General Motors was still debating whether or not to move into Hungary.

It is difficult to fault such a strategy. What should be understood, however, is that Japan's foreign assistance program is devoted to wholly different ends than America's. American foreign aid is given for three reasons: to relieve pressing humanitarian needs, to provide security assistance to allies and friends, and to provide development assistance and economic support for selected nations.[10] The latter two forms of aid—security assistance and development assistance —are given to further American interests. This is not disinterested philanthropy, as successive administrations have argued each year in presenting the foreign assistance budget to the Congress. But the perceived interests of American assistance are not commercial at all. They are *not* designed to foster new markets for American exporters. They are designed first and foremost to defend friends and allies from instability or the threat of attack from the Soviet Union or its proxies.

U.S. economic assistance has been based on the argument that poverty breeds radicalism; that prosperity breeds democracy and stability; and that democracy and stability breed friends of the United States and of freedom. There is no such chain of logic behind Japanese assistance. Japanese aid goes hand in hand with Japanese export market development. Japan will soon be in a financial position to utilize foreign assistance as a tool in the creation of new competitive industries in Japan itself. One market to which it aspires is commercial aircraft.[11] This is a natural market for Japan, with very high value-added content. It is also one in which the two dominant American firms, Boeing and McDonnell Douglas, have years of backlog orders for the delivery of new planes. Japan has considered giving away, through the Japanese foreign assistance program, replacement aircraft to countries that would purchase Japanese planes. Further, parts fabrication factories could be located in customer nations, thus providing employment in these nations and assured markets for an emerging Japanese commercial aircraft industry. Foreign parts fabrication is used by both U.S. commercial aircraft leaders. However, Japan's interest in giving away aircraft and in providing government aid to locate facilities outside of Japan can be contrasted to frequent congressional objections to locating manufacturing plants for the U.S. aircraft industry offshore.

In short, both Japan's and America's foreign assistance programs pursue visions of self-interest. But the visions are different. With the exception of its small humanitarian aid component, Japan's aid program is thoroughly motivated by the desire to expand its export markets.[12] This may change over time as Japan accumulates its own assistance clients and as it ventures into more political uses of aid. Perhaps, too, the U.S. foreign aid program will change in the post-Cold War world. At the current time, though, Japan's foreign assistance program is uniquely oriented to serve its regional economic goals.

Japan's Prosperous Asian Sphere

Japanese economic leadership in the Pacific region is obvious. This leadership has been achieved in spite of strong distrust of Japan by its neighbors. Much of this mistrust derives from Japan's often brutal efforts to colonize the region in the first half of the century, a campaign that began on the Asian mainland in the days of great power rivalry in China, moved to the Korean peninsula in 1910, and ultimately extended as far south as Burma and the islands of the Pacific almost to Australia.

At least three nations—China, South Korea, and the Philippines—still observe Japanese defeats in World War II on their official calendars. Anti-Japanese sentiment has surfaced publicly in rioting in Indonesia, in Thailand, and in the Philippines. There is especially deep hostility toward Japan in Korea, a country whose heritage Japan attempted virtually to stamp out during its thirty-five years of colonial rule. Precise limits against Japanese culture remain in place, and polls reflect that only about 14 percent of South Koreans have positive feelings about Japan, with more than 50 percent harboring negative feelings. Interestingly, it is younger Koreans, not those who lived through the period of colonial rule, who are most negative about Japan. And it is certain to be the case if and when the nation of Korea is reunited, that there will be an upsurge of Korean national sentiment directed against China, the United States, and, above all, Japan.

Despite this context, Japan has by virtue of its sheer power and success succeeded in drawing nearly all of these nations into its orbit. Korea has emulated not only Japanese business practices and strategies, but also its ruling political party's way of assuring dominance in the parliamentary arena. Both Malaysia and Singapore have sponsored "Learning from Japan" campaigns in an effort to achieve the success that Japan's model provides. There is a sense that the region is fated to deal with Japan. This sentiment is expressed in the carefully chosen words of the head of Indonesia's Bank Perkembangan: "We are tied to Japan, but there is no alternative."[13]

Indeed, there is not. We have already noted the dominance of Japanese trade and foreign assistance in Asia. The situation is much the same with regard to direct investment. When the yen was re-valued upward beginning in 1985, Japan surpassed the United States as the leading foreign investor in Asia for the first time. Last year, Japanese investment in Asia was more than two and one-half times the U.S. level. In some nations, Japanese investment dwarfs that of the United States, its closet competitor.

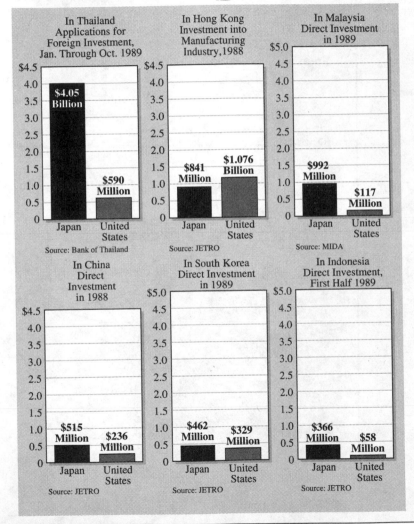

In Thailand
Applications for
Foreign Investment,
Jan. Through Oct. 1989

$4.05 Billion — Japan
$590 Million — United States

Source: Bank of Thailand

In Hong Kong
Investment into
Manufacturing
Industry, 1988

$841 Million — Japan
$1.076 Billion — United States

Source: JETRO

In Malaysia
Direct Investment
in 1989

$992 Million — Japan
$117 Million — United States

Source: MIDA

In China
Direct
Investment
in 1988

$515 Million — Japan
$236 Million — United States

Source: JETRO

In South Korea
Direct Investment
in 1989

$462 Million — Japan
$329 Million — United States

Source: JETRO

In Indonesia
Direct Investment,
First Half 1989

$366 Million — Japan
$58 Million — United States

Source: JETRO

Source: *The Washington Post*

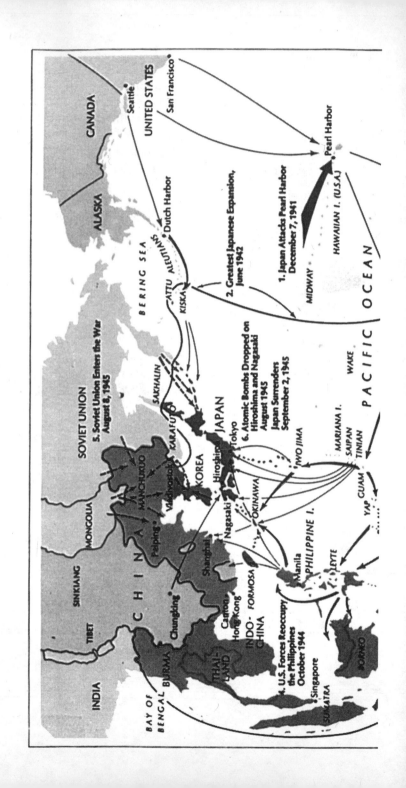

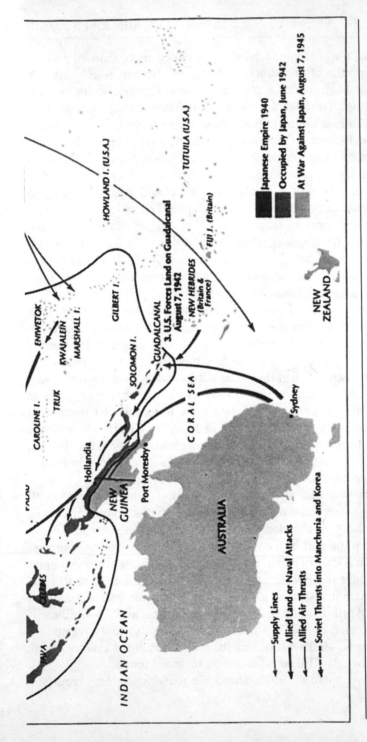

Source: *A History of the Modern World*/R.R. Palmer & Joel Colton

Japanese Empire 1940

Occupied by Japan, June 1942

At War Against Japan, August 7, 1945

Supply Lines

Allied Land or Naval Attacks

Allied Air Thrusts

Soviet Thrusts into Manchuria and Korea

HOWLAND I. (U.S.A.)

TUTUILA (U.S.A.)

Fiji I. (Britain)

NEW HEBRIDES
(Britain &
France)

3. U.S. Forces Land on Guadalcanal
August 7, 1942

GUADALCANAL

SOLOMON I.

GILBERT I.

MARSHALL I.

KWAJALEIN

ENIWETOK

CAROLINE I.

TRUK

PALAU

CELEBES

JAVA

INDIAN OCEAN

Hollandia

NEW GUINEA

Port Moresby

CORAL SEA

Sydney

AUSTRALIA

NEW
ZEALAND

In Thailand, for example, Japan has provided more than 70 percent of all foreign direct investment for each of the past four years.

Much has been made of the new "sense of community" in the Pacific region. To date, the evidence for this appears rather slim. Certainly there are no institutions comparable to those that are growing up in the European Community. Indeed, it is the residual concern about Japan by its neighbors that ironically has prevented integration from occurring. Japan would be the natural leader of a genuine Asian community, but it is unclear who would wish to belong to such an organization. It is not simply Japan's record in the first half of the twentieth century that concerns her neighbors. Germany and her neighbors have managed to develop common institutions to a far greater extent than is the case in East Asia. It is rather that Japanese practices and attitudes at the *current* time do not fully reassure Japan's neighbors.

It has been said that Japanese businessmen no longer differentiate between Japan and her Asian neighbors, and that they regard Asia as one undifferentiated region for investment and development.[14] Indeed, East Asia and Southeast Asia have been fertile grounds for Japanese investment. But this does not in and of itself testify to any emerging sense of community—only to the fact that wage rates in Singapore are 20 percent of Japan's; in Bangkok, 10 percent of Japan's; and in Jakarta, 4 percent of Japan's. Clearly, investment has flowed to politically stable nations with low wage rates. In this, Japanese investors do no more or less than American, European, or any other rational investors.

One rightly speaks of "community" only if there is some sympathetic self-identification of members within that community. And that is precisely what is lacking in Asia at this time. Japan has not undertaken to be part of a community in any way. To the contrary, it remains in a state of relative self-imposed isolation from its neighbors. Consider foreign direct investment flowing into Japan. Total foreign direct investment in Japan for the most recent full year available, April 1989–March 1990, amounted to $2.86 billion.[15] This represented only 4.3 percent of Japanese external investment. In other words, all the nations of the world combined invested there about one twenty-fifth of what Japan invested abroad.

To be sure, there are understandable reasons for this. Land and labor in Japan are expensive, and stock prices are very high. The highly valued yen makes prices relatively high. But it should be noted that foreign direct investment of $2.86 billion in 1989–1990 represented a *decline* of 11.8 percent from the previous year, and this at a time when the value of the yen actually declined vis-a-vis the dollar. The fact is that Japan does not want substantial direct foreign investment, and the higher yen has assisted in preventing what would have been unwelcome in any event.

What has emerged in Asia is not a community, but a yen-dominated trade zone.[16] This Japan-dominated zone has not emerged from the collective intention of the nations of the region; it has emerged from the commercial success and the policies of Tokyo. Japan has discovered that a highly valued currency is not an insuperable problem for an exporting nation. A successful exporting nation must adopt strategies including a focus on high-end technologies and superior products; a decision to invest in competent, stable low-wage countries; and a willingness to purchase outright that with which it cannot successfully compete.

Machiavelli said that it is best to be loved *and* feared, but that if one must choose, it is better to be feared. The Japanese are not loved. Indeed, for its Asian neighbors the development of deeper economic relations with Japan has been likened less to love than to a kind of sexual temptation. The benefits of succumbing to temptation are obvious.[17]

It is fair to conclude that a sense of community is precisely what is not emerging in the Pacific. The further evolution of the region will depend in large part on what happens in Tokyo. Whether Japan can and will attempt to foster institutions of community or whether its economic energy will spill inevitably and imperceptibly into political and military realms is the subject of the next two chapters.

CHAPTER SEVEN

The Demise of the "American Party"

The LDP and the Politics of Postwar Japan

AT THE CONCLUSION of World War II, it was not obvious what would be the evolution of Japan's political institutions. With the previous political structure—reaching all the way to the transpolitical standing of the emperor—thoroughly discredited, new arrangements had to be created from scratch. This was precisely what General Douglas MacArthur set about to do.

In his capacity as Supreme Commander of the Allied Powers (SCAP), MacArthur faced a daunting set of challenges, including the rebuilding of much of the political, economic, and physical infrastructure of Japan, and particularly of Tokyo. But he enjoyed one considerable advantage not possessed by his counterparts in Berlin: Japan was America's alone to shape without interference from militantly ideological Soviet opposition or aggravating injections from other allied powers.

MacArthur set about to construct a new political system for Japan.

He made an early decision to retain the institution of the emperor, a move that put him at odds with the State Department. The key to MacArthur's reforms was a new constitution, a document that established a parliamentary democracy based upon the sovereignty of the Japanese people and that renounced the use of force to resolve conflicts. The acceptance of this war-renouncing clause was, in effect, the price for maintenance of the emperor.[1] This was an arrangement that the new prime minister, Shigeru Yoshida, was prepared to accept. The new Japanese constitution became effective on May 3, 1947.

The capacity of Japan to absorb the many changes imposed upon it, including the new parliamentary democracy, was nothing short of astonishing. In developing a working relationship with not only parliamentary leaders, but also bureaucratic officials, American occupation rulers gained confidence in the capacity of the Japanese to govern themselves in a democratic way. Full sovereignty was restored to Japan on April 28, 1952, with the treaty of peace between the United States and Japan. Without the complexities of four-power rule, Japan achieved its new constitutional form a full two years earlier than the Federal Republic of Germany (and thirty-eight years before a comparable step occurred with regard to Berlin). Japan displayed every bit as much capacity to be efficiently democratic as it had been antidemocratic a decade before.

MacArthur offered every form of encouragement to the political forces of the Japanese Left, whom he regarded as less inclined to militarism than the Right. They held power briefly for a year in 1947, but soon lost again to Yoshida. It is difficult to predict how political factions in Japan would have developed had no further external factors intervened. But massive changes lay on the horizon. Just as the Soviet Union was affecting the development of the European peace, so also was the specter of communism in Asia forcing changes on America's hopes for Japan. Japan was to become another link in the new U.S. policy: the containment of communism.

The creation of a new ally was conceptually difficult to superimpose on a nation whose constitution obliged it never to create armed forces and to renounce war. The complexities of Japanese politics between 1949 and 1955 can be accounted for in part by the two contradictory ends of American policy: to pacify Japan and to encourage an ally against communist expansion. Japanese conservatives found a new lease on life in the American desire to create a new security treaty and a Japanese defense force. The socialists, with MacArthur's support, defended the no-war constitution. Ultimately, the key to the future lay in the clever Prime Minister Yoshida himself. He endorsed the no-war constitution and opposed for as long as he could the creation of the Japanese defense force. At the same time, he clearly aligned himself with the United States and against those who favored neutrality. Yoshida was criticized from every side, both for opposing the defense force and for his alleged subservience to the Americans.

But Yoshida was not Adenauer, and under his leadership Japan took a different course than West Germany in the 1950s. His attempt to have both the no-war constitution and the security treaty altered the political landscape of Japan. It enabled the party to the left, the Japan Socialist Party (JSP), to root itself outside the essential anticommunist alliance with the United States. At first, this appeared to be a winning hand: an increasingly radicalized JSP gained votes each year in the early 1950s.

But the growing strength of the JSP provoked countermeasures among the conservative parties. In 1955 they joined together to create an umbrella party known as the Liberal Democratic Party (LDP). The essential core relationship with the United States in a period of intense cold war was not in doubt, and the LDP has governed continually since 1955. Initially, the political situation was confused because the LDP prime minister in 1955, Ichiro Hatoyama, a long-standing adversary of Yoshida, moved to the left in foreign policy. He was supported in this by Japanese socialists. But there has not been an election since 1958 in which LDP control of the government was seriously in doubt.

Although the LDP was essentially assured of dominance after 1955, the complex requirements of the constitution and the security treaty continued to offer up new political combinations as those who favored one or the other, but not both, sought the upper hand. Finally, in 1960, Yoshida was able to resolve this issue in favor of both the constitution and the security treaty when he was able to install Hayato Ikeda as prime minister. This has formed the outline of Japanese policy ever since.

It has been a dominant theme in LDP circles that Japan would focus on economic growth and not on self-defense. Indeed, the rate of economic growth was very high throughout the late 1950s, even before Ikeda's so-called income doubling plan of the 1960s. The focus on economic growth was a long-held view of Yoshida's, who saw wisdom in making a virtue of necessity. Unable to move freely in the field of defense and foreign policy, he argued that Japan should concentrate on expanding its economy. When challenged about his country's subservience, Yoshida is reported to have said, "When it is objected that Japan will become a colony of the United States, I always reply that, just as the United States was once a colony of Great Britain but now is the stronger of the two, if Japan became a colony of the United States, it will also eventually become the stronger."[2] Under this banner, the LDP has presided over a period of extraordinary economic growth, close cooperation with the United States, and, as we shall see, a substantial military buildup as well.

In retrospect, there appears to have been a shrewd political judgment at work in Yoshida. The dominance of the American military presence in Japan, and Japan's dependence upon the United States for its security against the Soviet Union, simply did not permit a party like the JSP to achieve power. The thirty-five-year dominance of the LDP can be understood only in relation to the Cold War, which broke out in the late 1940s. Without that external reality, Japanese politics would certainly have taken a different course. The LDP never settled its center of gravity firmly where the United States might have wished in terms of its enthusiasm to arm Japan against the Soviet Union. It preferred often to appear as the reluctant partner. Yet there has been no doubt that the LDP has been the political party in Japan most sympathetic to the requests and demands of the United States.

Is Japan a Democracy?

One-party dominance in Japan for the past thirty-five years has caused some observers to ask whether Japan is really a democracy at all. Strictly speaking, this is not a serious question. In a purely formal sense, it must be said that of course Japan is a democracy. The Japanese political system provides for nearly universal adult suffrage to choose political leaders without restricting or foreclosing the ability of candidates to compete for their votes. Its constitutional procedures offer the full range of policy options that any liberal democracy would permit.

Nevertheless, it is possible to point to other nations whose constitutions outline democratic structures, but whose practices do not permit them to function. For many years the Soviet Union has operated under such a system. Is it a reproach to the democratic character of Japan's political system that Japanese voters have opted for one-party rule since 1955? Here, too, one must say that it is not. For unless it could be shown that somehow opposition parties and candidates were denied access to advantages of the LDP, or were forced to compete under unfair circumstances, then it would be incorrect to suggest that Japan is not a democracy.

In fact, the LDP's continuous dominance can be traced to two factors, neither of which reflect negatively on Japan's democratic character. The first is the LDP's capability to realign itself and its coalition membership to reflect the dominant sentiments in Japan. The LDP has displayed a talent for arranging itself in a loose federation of factions that political parties in other democracies could only dream about emulating. To a certain extent, it could be said that the LDP has been assisted in this process by the fact that there have been no major swings in Japanese political sentiments since World War II. In turn, it could be argued that this stability of purpose rested upon the absence of any necessity to make full-fledged security or geopolitical judgments during this period of American tutelage. However that may be, the LDP should be given its due as an effective political machine.

LDP dominance is also testimony to the fact that opposition parties in Japan to date have been unwilling or unable to prepare themselves to govern. The viewpoints of the principal opposition party, the Japan Socialist party, have been far too radical to appeal to the majority of voters. After the war, it seemed that the JSP had every possible advantage. It derived its core support—as it still does—from the General Federation of Trade Unions (Sohyo). At the same time, its pacifist tendencies fitted well with the desire of the American occupation, which was deeply opposed to any vestige of Japanese rearmament in the immediate postwar years.

Yet lacking the manifestly repressive regime across its border that, say, East Germany offered to West Germany, the JSP was unable to settle its internal center of gravity firmly in the non-Marxist camp. When Japan's American patrons became concerned about Communist expansion in Korea, and thus sought to alter gradually their policy against Japan's rearmament, the JSP was unwilling or unable to make this shift. And it has made scant progress over the past forty years by straddling the fence between pragmatic and orthodox Marxist versions of socialism. The JSP was in need of a Bad Godesberg Program of its own. The JSP has opposed Japan's security relationship with the United States and argued for smaller defense budgets, though—like the more extreme Japan Communist Party (JCP)—it does not have a highly favorable view of the Soviet Union either.

Although the JSP has been arguably further to the left than have the social democratic parties of Europe, the phenomenon of seeming unprepared to lead is not unique to it. This was also true of the social democratic parties in Britain and the Federal Republic of Germany over the decade of the 1980s. Both the Labor Party in Britain and the SPD in West Germany betrayed grave uncertainty in the 1980s about precisely where they stood on core issues relating to nuclear weapons and to NATO roles, and thus to the defense of Europe. Both parties found that their electorates sought clarity and continuity on these core issues and were not attracted to nuance and internal squabbling. When Labor and the Social Democrats stood foursquare on core security propositions, they were able to capitalize on their domestic appeal in Britain and in the Federal Republic. This has not been the case for forty years with the JSP, which has endorsed discontinuity in Japan's postwar security policies.

A more subtle and more convincing challenge to Japan's status as a democracy has been raised by those who argue that it does not possess a sovereign elected government in the modern sense. This idea has been raised at least as far back as the second decade of the twentieth century. In 1918 Yukio Ozaki, the noted liberal statesman, said that in Japan the seed of democracy "germinates and grows according to feudal notions."[3] The latest variation on this theme arises in Karel van Wolferen's thought-provoking work on Japan. Van Wolferen argues that it is a "fiction that Japan is a sovereign state like any other, a state with central organs of government which can both recognize what is good for the country and bear ultimate responsibility for national decision-making."[4] Van Wolferen calls Japan's political structure an "anachronism," a system differing from the modern sovereign nation state and instead partaking of a centuries-old balancing of semiautonomous groups with no central ruling body. As he says, it is "a complex of overlapping hierarchies . . . but it has no top"[5]—which is precisely the definition of a feudal system.

There is indeed in Japan a different structural relationship between the elected government, the career government, and the large business conglomerates than exists in the United States. There is not an adversary relationship between government and business that is founded on the philosophical theory of limited government and the rights of private individuals and entities. This is why Japan's government, which appears to be less centralized than those in other liberal democracies, actually does more to support the ends of business. And that is why in Japan the career bureaucracy assumes a power far beyond that exercised by the civil service in America, where the nonelected bureaucracy is also criticized from time to time.

Is a nation a democracy in which only a very few individuals at the top are elected and all the rest remain more or less permanetly in place? For example, would America be a democracy if only the president were chosen and he could not alter the permanent cabinet or any subcabinet employees if he wished to do so? One might say that this would be a somewhat imperfect democracy or, at the very least, a democracy heavily weighted toward continuity. Here we are confronting the question of whether only democracies that look precisely like the American model are "genuine." It seems prudent to say that many forms of democracy exist (including some arguably more purely democratic than the American), and that Japan's certainly counts among democratic governments.

A similar question arises when one considers the importance of ethnic homogeneity in Japan. In America, racial and other minorities are often not treated in the same way as other members of society.

Yet there is no doubt that this treatment is widely understood to be an imperfection in the practice of American democracy, and not within its core philosophy. It is, in short, a failure of American practice to achieve its ideals. This cannot be said of Japan. There is no abstract model of citizenry that all human beings within Japan's territory embody. To the contrary, there is a decided importance to being a Japanese national. When someone proposed voting rights for resident aliens in Japan, the home affairs minister summarized this view succinctly: "Voting rights are guaranteed only for Japanese people."[6] This set of issues has arisen most clearly in Japan's treatment of its 700,000-person Korean minority. Many of these people are third-generation residents in Japan. Korean resident aliens are not permitted to work as teachers or as government employees. First- and second-generation Koreans are routinely fingerprinted upon their sixteenth birthday,[7] implying the need for a special watchfulness over this group. A Korean residents' association leader says:

> There are three pillars in Japanese policy toward Koreans: assimilation, expulsion, and control. The root of this policy is the Japanese belief that foreigners are different and so can't be trusted. . . . They have no basic idea to live together with something different.[8]

The question of the relationship between democracy and nationality will be increasingly pronounced in Japan in the coming years. As a prosperous nation, Japan is a magnet to less skilled Asian workers who are prepared to do difficult and menial jobs. Japanese business groups—particularly in construction, food services, and small industrial production—are pressing for new workers. They will press even harder as the Japanese population ages and as the number of new workers entering the labor force each year declines. It seems highly unlikely that Japan will open its doors willingly to an influx of less skilled workers. At the same time, it is safe to predict that the share of non-Japanese residing in Japan will gradually creep upward. This will turn an interesting footnote about democratic theory into a practical question much like that which has arisen in other parts of the world: Is a nation a democracy if it excludes from universal adult suffrage a certain class of people who reside in that land?

The Future of Japanese Politics:
The Demise of the American Party

The era of automatic LDP domination in Japan is nearly over. Aside from the temporary ups and downs of the political parties due to topical issues such as corruption, there is a long-term, fundamental shift beginning to occur in Japanese politics. Already the opposition parties control the upper house of Japan's parliament, the Diet, giving them the power to block LDP initiatives. It is probable that the general election of 1986, in which the LDP won 49.4 percent of the popular vote, will be the high-water mark for the LDP for the remainder of the century.

The reasons for this relate less to the intrinsic popularity of the opposition's views than to fundamental changes in the external world. At a time when the Soviet Union was a manifest threat to Japanese security, an essentially pro-American party possessed an overwhelming built-in advantage. To challenge the pro-American party was to challenge the security of the nation. This connection, however, is now becoming less and less clear. As the Soviet Union becomes increasingly caught up in the web of its own internal problems, and as progress is predictably made in settling the Soviet occupation of the Kuriles, the Soviet Union will seem less and less menacing. To be sure, long-standing rivalries and recollections of war will never transform the Soviet–Japanese relationship into one of genuine warmth. But it is likely that outright hostility can and will give way to less concern about the Soviet Union's intentions, and even capabilities, in the Far East. The Soviet Union will come to be seen as one of a variety of security problems for Japan. Under these circumstances, it will be less and less obvious to Japanese voters why they need to hew so close a line to the United States.

This dynamic will have profound consequences for Japanese politics. These will be felt first—as they are already—in the opposition parties. To be sure, the JSP did reasonably well in the February 1990 election, capturing 136 seats, a 64 percent increase from the eighty-three seats it had held. But, as was widely noted in the aftermath of the election, the JSP's gains came only partially from the LDP.

Japan's February 18, 1990, Elections (turnout 73%)

PARTY	SEATS WON	SEATS AT DISSOLUTION
Liberal Democrats	275	295
Socialists	136	83
Komeito	45	54
Communists	16	26
Democratic Socialists	14	25
Others	5	5
Independents	21	7
Total	512	495*

*17 vacancies

Drawn from: *The Economist*

Much of the gain came at the expense of the smaller opposition parties. Part of its success can be traced to its opposition to the LDP-imposed consumption tax, an advantage it cannot count on again in the future.

The 1990 election produced no watershed, only a hint of change. As the Soviet threat declines, the JSP is well positioned to take advantage of sentiments questioning the need for a close tie with the United States. But it can do so only if it distances itself more substantially than it has yet done from the failed policies of socialism.

Until now, the platform of the JSP—urging a more independent security policy and a less internationalist economic policy—has found only limited sympathy from Japanese voters. But while the JSP will benefit from the fact that the costs of abandoning the tight security relationship with the U.S. will become harder to discern, there is almost no vestige of support for adopting social or political policies associated with the failed socialism of the Soviet Union or China. The views of the JSP will necessarily have to adapt themselves to this reality. To date, it has only begun to alter its position on a host of issues deriving from the security questions that differentiated it from the LDP. For example, the JSP's position on relations with South Korea will have to continue to change right along with the shifting political realities on the Korean peninsula. Likewise, the JSP must emphasize even more strongly than it has already done its adherence to social democracy rather than its adherence to democratic socialism.

Here, too, Japanese politics is not dissimilar to the politics of other advanced industrialized nations. In West Germany, Britain, and the United States, it is the major party to the left of center that is more protectionist, less internationalist, and generally less committed to active alliance-making than is the party to the right of center. To some extent, this may reflect parties out of power looking for a way to distinguish themselves from ruling parties—which happen to be right of center in each instance. But it should be noted that this is a reversal of earlier roles, in which the Left was everywhere wedded, at least rhetorically, to internationalist positions, and the Right was committed to positions ranging from inward-looking isolation to aggressive nationalism. In each of these instances, too, the social strata that are extensively oriented to an internationalist outlook include political sectors that were historically reservoirs of support for inward-looking isolationist points of view. Even the agricultural community, which is threatened by declining barriers to agricultural imports, remains largely within the ambit of the LDP.

Changing realities have hit Japan's small center parties hardest. Caught between a dominant ruling party and an opposition unable to find a coherent viewpoint, the small center parties—the Democratic Socialist Party (DSP) and Komeito—are searching for a meaningful way to differentiate themselves in the Japanese political spectrum. Buffeted by losses in the 1990 election, these groups will seek—largely in vain—for a defining purpose. Nobuaki Futami, policy director of Komeito, states this problem clearly:

> We have to look for specific policies which we can present as particular to Komeito. To tell the truth, however, we are devoid of original and innovative policies, other than those on the environment, arms reduction, and welfare issues.[9]

Both the DSP and Komeito face the standard difficulty of smaller parties in liberal democratic governments today. In Germany, the

Free Democrats are also searching for a mission and hang on to power more through the force of the personalities who lead the party than on intrinsic differences in its viewpoint from the CDU/CSU. In a world in which the political spectrum splayed itself out from free market individualism to statist collectivism, there was room for a nuanced party of the middle. With the statist pole gone, and with the entire political landscape in disarray, it is doubtful that there will be room for such subtle distinctions as would make these parties necessary or useful. They will have a difficult task to prevent themselves from being swallowed up into one of the two larger political parties, particularly in Japan where the LDP has shown such a strong historical tendency to absorb members into its loose association.

Although the impact of changes in the world will be felt first by the JSP and by the smaller opposition parties, it will soon enough be felt forcefully by the LDP. By the admission of some of its own members, the Liberal Democrat Party has clearly been the "American party" for the past thirty-five years. Its defense and foreign policies mark it clearly. But so, too, does its internationalist economic policy. For however unsatisfactory Japanese economic liberalization has seemed to Americans, the LDP is the most willing of the political parties to open Japan's markets, to liberalize its financial sector, and to expand foreign assistance. The JSP, Komeito, the DSP, and the Communist party are all more protectionist, and further from U.S. positions than is the LDP.

The LDP came out of the 1990 elections in reasonably good shape, winning 275 of 512 seats and gaining the cooperation of eleven independents. But it is clear that this election was less a mandate for LDP policies than a reflection of the inability of the opposition to craft a credible and coherent viewpoint in order to govern.[10] In short—similar to the cases of Britain, Germany, and the U.S.— the voters of Japan found the left opposition party unprepared to govern. The politics of continuity retained enough appeal in 1990 to carry the ruling party to yet another term of governance without rethinking essential questions.

This will not be possible much longer. For if the decline of the Soviet Union makes possible new developments in Japanese politics, Japan's economic success—ironically, the fruit of LDP rule— makes them inevitable. As the Soviet menace declines, and as the

United States gradually draws down its military forces in the region, Japanese voters will ask in earnest questions that until now have been only idle speculation. What is the compelling need for a security treaty with the United States? Why do U.S. forces, subsidized by Japan at that, need to remain in Japan? Why does Japan need to open its markets further in response to American desires? What is the reason to have to satisfy all of America's demands?

As these questions assume a new reasonableness, the JSP will find its voice. And when it does, it will be a more moderate voice, a voice that will compel the LDP to move to the center of the political spectrum. It is not beyond imagination that the JSP will assume power sometime in the 1990s. *But whether it does or whether the LDP retains power, Japan will move toward a more independent position vis-a-vis the United States in the 1990s.*

There are already harbingers of this. Japan has undertaken new initiatives in the region without their being developed first in Washington. It is fair to say that at this time, Japan still largely follows the American lead in world politics, even in East Asia. But the intuitive wisdom of all things American will be increasingly called into doubt, particularly if the United States further reduces its military presence in the region. At a minimum, the LDP will retain power in the 1990s only by accommodating some of the new assertiveness that the Left and Right in Japan will promote. This is the way of democracy.

In its effort to move toward independence from America, the Left in Japan will play an unwitting role in the rearmament of the country. By urging greater independence from the United States, it will undercut its other major security plank, namely, reductions in Japan's defense budgets. The Left undoubtedly thinks it can have it both ways—less dependence on the United States *and* smaller military expenditures. It also argues simultaneously against nuclear power and against the military means to protect supplies of imported oil. These are positions which, taken together, do not make sense. The Left will discover that the military expenditures it wishes to further reduce are already limited, and that reliance on the United States is the reason for this. This is well stated by Shintaro Ishihara in *The Japan that Can Say "No"*:

Both the right and left . . . tend to become fanatical on the security treaty debate. It is most regrettable that we do not have a cool and rational forum where the objective profit and loss aspects of the issue can be analyzed. But the time will come when we will have to face this issue and this time is in the near future.

The current state of the Liberal Democratic Party means that it cannot afford a serious deliberation on this issue. Once the opposition parties dissociate themselves from a one-sided pro-Russia and Chinese policy and demonstrate their capacity to be able to replace the LDP as alternative political parties fully recognized by the voters, we will be in the position to examine our options with greater flexibility.[11]

Changes that are now occurring in the world, however, will make the newly moderated positions of the JSP seem less out of touch to Japanese voters. Faced with the reality of a choice between giving up the close security relationship with the United States and the continuing armament of Japan, it is not difficult to predict what the JSP will choose. With the usual cynicism of left-leaning parties confronted by such a choice, it will turn away from the internationalism of the security treaty—a turn that would find deep support on the political right as well. This will be a game that the ruling party can also play quite well, and the danger of this game is that, once begun, almost no one understands how quickly it will move.

Some observers have suggested that the United States plays the role of the opposition to the LDP. This is surely too clever and altogether misleading. It is far truer to say that the LDP has essentially functioned as the American party, a reality that will be altogether clear only when it has been replaced by a new state of affairs in which fundamental disagreements between the LDP and the United States come to exist. Whichever political group dominates Japan in the 1990s, there will no longer be an "American party." If the Japanese Left and Right conspire with the American Left and Right to reduce the U.S. presence in the region, this will provide the strongest possible rationale for accelerating fundamental changes in the U.S.–Japan relationship and for rapid increases in Japan's defense capabilities.

Have the Japanese Changed?

Have the Japanese become good democrats? Just as in the case of Germany, is not an unblemished record of forty years sufficient proof of Japan's commitment to democracy and to the democratic value of tolerance? The answer to these questions is significant. For if one supposes that Japan is set irretrievably upon a democratic course, then it might matter far less whether Japan pursues a political direction either more or less independent of the United States.

The most honest answer is that it cannot yet be said what course Japan will pursue in the future. The past forty years have been a time in which Japan has essentially emulated America's values. In the words of the eminent observer of Japan, Robert Christopher:

> So instead of hating America, they set about imitating us. They took the fact that we had beaten them [in World War II] as a demonstration that our system was better than theirs, so they adopted our system to a very remarkable degree.[12]

The Japanese became better Americans in some ways than the Americans themselves. They put into practice industrial processes and quality controls that they borrowed from America and that were only haphazardly practiced by U.S. firms. Japan showed an extraordinary capacity to adapt to and implement the new democratic structure imposed upon it. To be sure, it did so in its own national way. But it undertook the creation of parliamentary democracy and new political parties with a thoroughness and an enthusiasm that have not been matched in most other postwar American development projects. Beyond this, the Japanese adopted many other cultural and social innovations from America. These have been developed in a uniquely Japanese way, but the borrowing has been substantial, particularly for a nation that has long struggled with its own insular tendencies.

Japan displayed a surprising capacity to absorb all things American. This should be fully reassuring only to someone who subscribes in advance to the innate superiority of all things American. For unless one believes that the Japanese have now reached the rational pinnacle of their social and political existence, one would have to suppose that they retain the capacity to surprise. As Robert Christopher says, "There is no nation whose social and political course over the long term is as chancy to predict as Japan's."[13]

Japan now stands at the edge of a path that is less well marked than that of the past forty-five years. The older, postwar generation of Japanese was acquainted at first hand with American magnanimity. Upcoming generations, lacking experience either of the war years or of postwar reconstruction, have grown into a world where Japan has been prosperous and successful. They see no need to emulate America at all. This has been noted again and again both in polls and in anecdotal ways.[14] There is a quiet resurgence of national pride in Japan and continuing reflection about the objects to which that pride should attach itself.

Some of these changes have been institutionalized in recent years in the Japanese school system. The Ministry of Education has restored several trappings of nationalism, including raising the flag and asserting a more "normal" or regular degree of national pride than has been thought permissible until recently. A more balanced form of national pride might be a positive development in Japan— up to the point where it confuses the assertion of pride in the nation with the specific racial traits of the Japanese people.

With the American model in decline as a source of inspiration, to what will Japan turn next? Will it remain on the path of openness and liberal democracy? There is no particular reason to assume that this must be the case. Japan is not a nation with long experience with democratic institutions. Japan never experienced a true democratic revolution arising out of the concept of individual choice and the consent of the governed.[15] Movement toward democratic institutions in the 1920s foundered in the wake of challenge, just as in the case of Germany, though for far less reason. Japan, after all, had been on the victorious side in World War I and had emerged from that war as a potent force in East Asia. Although manifestations of racial discrimination against Japanese occurred in America in the 1920s, on the whole the period was one in which Japan was accorded new international respect and in which it opened itself to arms control negotiations with the Western powers. It was not a time of desperate challenge either at home or abroad.

Nonetheless, democratic reform tendencies were overwhelmed

by the doctrine of the Japanese nation-state. This doctrine was espoused most pointedly by the military. The military was the forceful
expression of the drive for Japanese security, and as such it overwhelmed and subordinated domestic reforms to its vision of a secure
and prosperous Japanese nation.

The idea that the policies of Japan should reflect a composite of
many millions of individual choices does not hold sway in Japan
as it does, say, in the United States. Indeed, the entire concept of
individual choice, in which the freestanding individual serves as
guarantor of his own choices, is largely foreign to Japan. The manner
in which the Japanese individual finds his place is rather better
expressed by a Japanese proverb: The nail that sticks up will be
pounded down.

Democracy is now the norm in Japan. But democracy exists there
more as a fashion than as an organic product of Japanese life. As
Christopher says:

> Japan's current dedication to democracy, an open society and ma-
> terial influence is not something that grew inexorably from purely
> Japanese roots; it is the product of a particular set of international
> circumstances and under other circumstances might well be
> superseded by other imperatives.[16]

Democracy is a highly abstract idea. Karel van Wolferen argues
effectively that *no* abstract political or philosophical idea has ever
held sway in Japan. This same conclusion has been reached by a
variety of observers of differing sectors of Japanese life.[17]

This point has been raised again and again by Japan's neighbors,
many of whom doubt that Japan has looked into itself and its own
actions prior to and during World War II with much genuine and
searching depth. Asian observers frequently contrast Japan's attitude
with the degree of self-examination undertaken by West Germany.
Perhaps on the surface this has changed somewhat since the emperor's 1990 expression of "deepest regret" for Japan's actions
against Korea. But beneath the surface there remains deep mistrust
of Japan by its Asian neighbors. An assistant of South Korean
President Roh Tae Woo summarized this mistrust: "Some Koreans
feel that what the Japanese regret is that they lost the war."[18]

What, then, will Japan stand for? The question betrays the difficulty, and the simplicity, of an answer. Japan stands for whatever the Japanese consensus supports.[19] This is surely not a product that can easily be exported, for the world cannot all become Japanese.[20] For this reason, although Japan's structures and procedures may to some extent be emulated by its aspiring neighbors, it is unlikely to become a source of new ideological inspiration around the world.

But this also suggests the difficulty of assuming with confidence that the essentially Western concept of democracy has taken permanent root in Japan. Twice since 1868 the Japanese have completely remade their society. There is nothing to indicate they could not do so again.[21]

The question with regard to Japan is not whether democracy there can survive failure. It is whether democracy can survive its own success and manuever through a world in which other regions challenged by this very success take actions that Japan finds difficult to accept.

How will Japanese energy express itself in a time in which it no longer emulates American ideals? What will it choose when it makes its own choices? Those who find comfort in the rapidity and thoroughness with which Japan embraced democracy could just as easily draw the opposite conclusion. The question is not whether the Japanese have changed in the past forty years; it is how they will choose to express their inherent changeableness in the future. This thought ought to guide American policy. There is no sector in which this is of more importance than defense policy. This will be the subject of the next chapter.

CHAPTER EIGHT

Surge Capacity: The Japanese Military Machine

Japan's Peace Constitution

VIRTUALLY EVERY DISCUSSION of Japanese military policies traces back to one article of the Japanese Constitution. Written, as was the rest of the constitution by the victorious Americans, article 9 states:

> The Japanese people forever renounce war as a sovereign right of the nation and the threat or use of force as a means of settling international disputes. . . . Land, sea and air forces, as well as other war potential, will never be maintained.

At this time, Japan's Self-Defense Force numbers nearly 246,000 men. Major ground equipment includes new battle tanks; artillery pieces; armored personnel carriers; antitank and transport helicopters; and both surface-to-ship and surface-to-air missiles. The Japanese Navy now possesses sixty-two surface combatants, sixteen submarines, antisubmarine aircraft and helicopters, and minesweeping helicopters. Air defenses include more than 360 combat aircraft, with six squadrons of F-15Js. Japan is codeveloping with the United States the FSX, a state-of-the-art derivation of the U.S. F-16, and intends to produce 100 of these aircraft by the late 1990s.

All this is for a nation whose constitution stipulates that "land, sea and air forces, as well as other war potential, will never be maintained." What are we to make of this apparent contradiction? More to the point, are there any bounds at all on the growth of Japan's military forces that derive from Japan's constitution? The fact is that the plain meaning of the Japanese constitution is contradicted by the forces that Japan now maintains. Over the years, the Liberal Democratic Party has had difficulty squaring the circle of developing an indigenous defense force within the clear meaning of the constitution's article 9.

This problem emerged almost immediately. As with Germany, once Japan's new constitution came into being and a sense of trust in Japanese postwar political leadership began to develop, the U.S. looked to cease its occupation status. There was clearly no intention that America should retain a massive and permanent occupation force in the nations it had conquered. In Japan, this process was advanced not in the first instance by a direct Soviet threat, but by the Korean War. At that time, the U.S. pressed Japan to create a "reserve" national police force—beyond the local law enforcement establishment that had been turned back to Japan—of 75,000 men. As U.S. servicemen left Japan in April 1952, this force was a military organization in all but name. It shortly afterward became the Self-Defense Force (SDF), a step that was justified under the U.N. charter, article 51, that every nation has the right of self-defense. That every nation has the right of self-defense is fair enough, and that this right is spelled out in the U.N. charter, is unambiguous. How this squares with never maintaining military forces as specified in the Japanese constitution is less clear.

It was not at all clear to opposition political parties in Japan, who vociferously denounced this step as a violation of the constitution and a step in the wrong direction for Japanese postwar policies. In part, this opposition derived from an attachment to the Marxist policies of China and the Soviet Union, masquerading as a detached concern for the sanctity of the Japanese constitution. However, it could be said in fairness that this was the first serious proof that the new constitution was working, for it is the essence of constitutional government that the constitution stand unassailably at the beginning and end of every political argument, and that all such arguments be justified in constitutional terms.

In 1954, Japan set up the Japan Defense Agency, and ground, maritime, and air forces were patterned after the U.S. military organization. The agency was not created at the ministerial level, and despite the size of current expenditures on defense, the defense organization still does not enjoy ministry status. The failure of Japan's defense organization to achieve ministry status is one of a series of political compromises the LDP has made throughout its past thirty-five years of rule. Another compromise is the parameter that Japan shall spend no more than roughly 1 percent of its GNP on defense. This number is rooted in nothing but political expediency. So, too, is the policy that Japan shall not produce, store, or allow the transit of nuclear weapons on its territory. And so too is the argument that self-defense does not permit Japan to sign collective security agreements to defend other nations, but only security agreements with other nations for the defense of Japan. This latter is precisely the outline of the Treaty of Mutual Cooperation and Security that Japan and the United States signed in 1960.

But the essential compromise of Japan's constitution occurred with the creation of the self-defense forces and the concept that these are consistent with no maintenance of armed forces at all.[1] From that point, the rest is only a matter of degree and can change as quickly or as slowly as political realities and the ingenuity of statesmen permit.

The LDP has tried from time to time to face the constitutional issue squarely, with some LDP members urging an amendment to bring the constitution into line with the creation of the self-defense forces. There is no doubt that a constitutional amendment would correct the "patent obfuscation" of the current situation.[2] However, it seems equally clear that there is no pressing need to amend the constitution: recent extensions of Japanese defense doctrine have made clear that the Japanese constitution will encompass virtually any military program Japan wishes to undertake so long as it can be called "defense."[3] In that regard, the United States provides a good model. Possessing a Department of Defense—as opposed to the former Department of War—the U.S. has forward-deployed the largest offensive force in history under the rubric of defense. Without any offensive intent, the U.S. military possesses substantial offensive force-projection capability throughout the world.

This is precisely the crux of the question. While it is fair to say that some deployments are manifestly offensive in nature, it is virtually impossible to draw a meaningful distinction between offensive and defensive manpower and weapons systems. The difference between offense and defense is, in the end, more a difference of intention and doctrine than one of capability.

Japan's current capabilities are substantial, even though now deployed in a thoroughgoing defensive mode in accord with its military doctrine. Some statistics will help to put the size of Japan's military establishment in perspective. First, largely under U.S. pressure to do more, Japan increased its defense budget at a rate of between 5 and 8 percent each year throughout the 1980s:

Defense Expenditures in Japan (in billions of U.S. dollars)

FISCAL YEAR	DEFENSE BUDGET	GROWTH RATE	PERCENTAGE OF GNP	PERCENTAGE OF GENERAL BUDGET
1980	9.82	6.5	0.90	5.24
1981	10.80	7.6	0.91	5.13
1982	10.38	7.8	0.93	5.21
1983	11.57	6.5	0.98	5.47
1984	12.33	6.6	0.99	5.80
1985	13.12	6.9	0.997	5.98
1986	19.78	6.6	0.993	6.18
1987	24.25	5.2	1.004	6.50
1988	29.60	5.2	1.013	6.53
1989	30.87	5.9	1.006	6.49

*Dollar figures are converted based on the average exchange rate for each year.

Source: *Defense of Japan 1988*, p. 313.

As this table makes clear, Japanese defense spending has grown both as a share of the government budget and as a share of the overall economy. At approximately $31 billion, Japan's defense budget is far smaller than that of the U.S. or the Soviet Union. But it is now—at an official calculation only 1 percent of Japan's GNP—the third largest defense budget in the world. If one calculates defense expenditures in the fashion of NATO countries—whose motive has been the opposite of Japan's, namely, to make them appear larger—Japanese military expenditures are closer to 1.5 percent of GNP.[4]

Figures for the Western Pacific region are even more revealing. Japan's defense spending is clearly the largest of any nation in the area (except, of course, the Soviet Union).[5] Japan spends nearly one and one-half times more than its nearest competitor, the People's Republic of China, which maintains a standing army of nearly 3 million men. Leaving China aside, Japan spends more on its military than North Korea, Vietnam, Taiwan, South Korea, Australia, the six ASEAN countries, and all smaller nations in the region combined.

The case of South Korea is instructive. Korea spends 7 percent

Asian, Pacific Defense Expenditures
1987 figures in billions of dollars

COUNTRY	AMOUNT SPENT
Australia	$ 5
China*	$20.7
Japan	$24.3
N. Korea*	$ 5.8
S. Korea	$ 5.6
Taiwan	$ 4.7
Vietnam*	$ 3
ASEAN†	$ 5.6
All Other	$ 1.1

*Trade restricted

†Association of South East Asian Nations (ASEAN) includes Brunei, Indonesia, Malaysia, the Philippines, Singapore, and Thailand

Source: Arms Control and Disarmament Agency/Electronic Industries Association

of its government budget on defense, making it among the highest proportional defense spenders of any nation in the free world. Yet Japan's defense budget alone is 1.3 times the size of the entire South Korean government budget.

For all of these reasons, leaders in other Western Pacific nations have expressed private and not so private concerns about Japan's growing military capabilities. Some of these concerns are reflected in the classified country-by-country reports that accompany the U.S. Defense Science Board's October 1989 report on Pacific Rim nations. Malcolm Currie, the chairman of the task force that prepared the report, said, "When you are frank about some of these countries, you are reaching into some very sensitive areas. They all perceive the threat in a different way. Some of them perceive [other Pacific Rim countries] as the threat."[6]

Indeed, one can observe a subtle shift in public Pentagon documents as well. In about 1987 the annual Pentagon publication *Soviet Military Power* began to identify Japan as a critical issue. By 1989, Japan's military and technological capabilities figure very strongly and explicitly in the report.[7]

Of course, the Pentagon is careful, even judicious, in its choice of words in unclassified documents. In the most recent and thoroughgoing Department of Defense review of Pacific strategy, "A Strategic Framework for the Asian Pacific Rim: Looking Toward the 21st Century," it is said that blocking Soviet expansion has never been the sole and exclusive purpose of U.S. forward-deployed forces in the region. Speaking of the U.S. role as a "balancing wheel," the report says, "A diminution of U.S. commitment to regional stability, whether perceived or real, would create a vacuum that other major players would be tempted or compelled to fill."[8] In case this is not clear enough, the report later says, "The Japan Self-Defense Force will be encouraged to improve the quality, but not necessarily the quantity, of its force structure."[9]

The Japanese Defense Industry

Despite the size of Japan's current military establishment and of its budget, no serious observer believes that Japan currently constitutes a threat to any of its neighbors. The question regarding Japan has less to do with its current force than with its obvious capability for rapid military growth, which exceeds that of any other nation in the world today.

What are the prospects for the growth of Japan's military capabilities? This is in part a political question, but it is also an economic one driven by Japan's own military industry. This is a highly consolidated industry. Roughly twenty firms in Japan account for 75 percent of all Japanese defense contracts; of these, the top six firms are responsible for nearly 60 percent of all Japanese defense contracts.[10] The leading firms are not exclusively or primarily engaged in defense work, however, in the manner of leading American defense contractors. In fact, no large contractor in Japan does more than about 20 percent of its total business in defense work; the remainder is commercial work, a configuration much desired by some of America's leading defense contractors in a time of shrinking U.S. military budgets. Japanese firms that perform defense work are a virtual who's who in world industry—Mitsubishi, Kawasaki, Toshiba, NEC, and the like—and are an integral part of the Japanese elite industrial/governmental circle. Several consequences flow from this.

First, as a matter of policy, Japan seeks a high degree of self-sufficiency in the production of military items. It produces 99 percent of its own naval vessels, 89 percent of its own aircraft, 87 percent of its ammunition, and 83 percent of its firearms.[11] Big-ticket items, especially aircraft, are produced from U.S. designs and under U.S. license. Given the fact that Japanese laws currently prevent the export of military hardware, this means that Japan must produce for its own limited domestic military market. The first consequence of this is that Japan spends a great deal more per item than does the U.S. for the capability to produce its own military equipment. For example, it spends about $64 million to manufacture under license essentially the same F-15 that the United States produces for half the price. This high unit cost tends to exaggerate the importance of the size of the Japanese defense budget.

The second consequence is that Japan must essentially handpick defense contractors to whom to award contracts, because the defense base for specific domestically designed military programs is too small. Almost all of Japan's defense contracts (86 percent in 1986) are offered on a noncompetitive basis. As large U.S. defense contractors are discovering, the possibility of foreign sales is often required to help defray research and development costs and to make defense production competitive on a per unit basis. This is far truer for Japan, whose military budget is currently about 11 percent of the U.S. defense budget.

Nevertheless, the Japanese defense budget, which has nearly tripled in the past decade, has attracted the interest of the largest Japanese companies. The high-value content of many defense articles fits neatly into corporate strategies to move upscale. Trends in Japanese firms that do defense work are clearly and unambiguously toward a greater share of total sales going to military production. This is especially true of Mitsubishi Heavy Industries, Japan's leader, but it is also the case with all of the leading firms.[12] Tomohisa Sakanaka of Aoyama Gakuin University says, "Such a shift toward the defense business seems to be the common tendency."[13]

This process is creating its own internal dynamic for increased defense business. Even in a far less traditional society like America's, the tendency to perpetuate existing levels of budgetary commitments is notorious. It is all the more true in Japan, where the defense program has now created a number of large firms whose economic success is increasingly dependent upon military contracts.

This leads to one result: extraordinary pressure on the government to lift the ban on the export of weapons. This hope has been present among Japanese business circles for decades. Even prior to the defense buildup of the 1980s, a majority of Japanese businessmen favored increasing defense spending above the 1 percent level, and urged both greater self-sufficiency in weapons production and lifting the prohibition on arms exports.[14] This view is more widely held now than a decade ago. Advances in Japanese technology and the prospects of converting that technology into profitable military items are apparent. The Defense Science Board's 1989 report *Defense Industrial Cooperation with Pacific Rim Nations* says, "For Japan, we reiterate the real potential for export of defense-related equipment as incremental relaxations of current government policy may occur with time."[15] In speaking about this report, Malcolm Currie says that Japan has "a tremendous overcapacity in the defense field. . . . This is creating industrial pressures in Japan for growth of that business and to find an outlet for it. . . . When you talk to [Japanese] industrialists on a one-on-one basis, they feel they are going to be exporting."[16] The pathway for these exports will likely be the export of "dual-use" items, which have both civilian and military application, and where legal prohibitions against exports are vague.

Military exports will be one means by which Japan helps to finance its own growing interest in indigenous research and development. Japanese expenditures on military research and development have been extremely low in the past. Instead of indigenous military research and development, Japan has been content to utilize technology transferred by the United States under licensing arrangements. Japanese military research and development investment has been little more than 1 percent of comparable American spending.

This is changing, however. Japanese capabilities in technologies with defense applications are substantial, as the following table makes clear:

Comparison of Technology Programs with Military Applications

	WARSAW PACT	NON-U.S. NATO	JAPAN	OTHERS
Microelectronic Circuits and Their Fabrication	6	4	2	4 Israel, Switzerland 6 South Korea
Preparation of Gases and Other Compound Semiconductors	6	4	1	
Software Producibility	6	4	4	5 Many Nations
Parallel Computer Architectures	6	2	2	
Machine Intelligence/ Robotics	6	2	2	5 Finland, Sweden
Simulation and Modeling	6	5	5	

	WARSAW PACT	NON-U.S. NATO	JAPAN	OTHERS
Integrated Optics	2	2	2	6 China, Israel, South Korea
Fiber Optics	6	5	2	6 Various Sources
Sensitive Radars	6	5	5	5 Sweden
Passive Sensors	5	5	5	5 Israel
Automatic Target Recognition	6	5	5	5 Israel, Sweden
Phased Arrays	6	4	6	6 Israel
Data Fusion	6	5	2	
Signature Control	6	5		
Computational Fluid Dynamics	6	4	4	4 Sweden
Air-Breathing Propulsion	4	2	4	
High-Power Microwaves	2	4		
Pulsed Power	2	5	4	
Hypervelocity Projectiles	3	5	5	6 Australia, Israel
Advanced Structural Composites	5	5	4	
Superconductivity	5	5	2	
Biotechnology	3	3	3	5 Many Nations

1 National program is clearly ahead of the U.S. in advancing the state of the art in technology.

2 Major national program overall on par with the U.S. with significant leads over the U.S. in specific important aspects of the technology.

3 Major national program on par with the U.S. overall and capable of making significant contributions to the state of the art.

4 Significant national effort generally lagging the state of the art except in certain niches wherein the country enjoys a significant world-wide lead.

5 Significant national effort generally lagging the state of the art except in certain niches wherein the nation is capable of contributing to advances.

6 Significant national effort generally trailing the world in all important aspects of the technology.

Source: Department of Defense

Japanese business leaders have been pressing for more indigenous research and development funds. In May of 1989, the leading business association, the Keidanren, called for an increase of military research and development funding to 5 percent of the Japanese defense budget in the next five-year plan, from 1991 to 1995. This would virtually double the 2.5 percent in the 1990 budget and, when overall growth of the defense budget is figured in, would approximately triple military research and development spending by 1995.

This increase is likely to be the minimum figure achieved by 1995. First, Japanese military research and development has risen from 1.49 percent of the defense budget to 2.5 percent, a two-thirds increase over the past six years. A simple extrapolation of the current growth rate (12.1 percent from 1989 to 1990 alone) would take Japanese research and development well past the 2.5 percent figure. Second, it is likely that Japanese firms will find increasing military research and development spending complementary as they continue to expand research and development spending across the board.

The FSX fighter plane episode will undoubtedly strengthen the hand of forces in Japan who favor intensifying domestic development capabilities. Japan's initial intention was to produce an advanced fighter aircraft of its own design. What occurred subsequently, in plain words, is that political pressure from the United States dissuaded Japan from this course. The U.S. choice, naturally, would have been outright purchase of U.S. aircraft and strong arguments relating to proven technology, cost, and trade balances were made on behalf of this course. The outcome was a compromise design that has come to be known as FSX, a hybrid Japanese-American plane based on the F-16. Japan currently intends to purchase 100 such aircraft.

The compromise was bitterly attacked on Capitol Hill, and even a modified proposal escaped a veto override by only a one-vote margin in the Senate. The result of this experience is clear: it has served to confirm the views of those in Japan—sometimes disparagingly called "techno-nationalists"—that Japan can and should develop its own military forces more independently of Washington.[17] Original proponents of an independent Japanese fighter plane have seen their hand strengthened immeasurably, and it is doubtful that Japan will again step up to a major project involving joint technology development.[18] Indeed, Japan has already declined to cooperate on the AMRAAM, the advanced air-to-air missile.

Indeed, it is not certain at this point that the complexities of the FSX arrangement will work themselves out satisfactorily in practice. Given a solid pretext, it is still possible that Japan will find good and sufficient reasons to propose major alterations in the FSX project. Whatever the outcome, the overall effect of the FSX experience has been to strengthen the tendency toward the development of an indigenous high-tech aircraft capability in Japan.[19] It has also thrown into doubt whatever uncertain fruits there might have been from Japan's commitment to share militarily relevant technology with the United States.

The Best Defense . . .

In 1988, Japanese Prime Minister Noburu Takeshita created a stir in East Asia when he spoke on several occasions of his country's intent to expand its defense capabilities to a level "commensurate with its national economic power." These statements raised concerns that Japan would soon embark on a course designed to expand its military power in the region. In some quarters, these statements were seen as a shift in Japanese defense policy. They were not, for it has been the LDP's policy for thirty-five years to do just what Prime Minister Takeshita suggested. When the Liberal Democratic Party was created in 1955, it called for "establishment of self-defense power appropriate to the national power and national conditions."[20] This policy has never changed. What *has* changed, of course, is the relative strength of Japan's national economic power, which makes a defense force "commensurate" with this power a force to be reckoned with.

Indeed, Japan's defense capabilities have expanded over the years right along with its growing economic strength. This has been a slow and difficult process, given the constitutional and political restraints already discussed. Japan's options have been constrained over the past forty-five years in large measure by its dependence upon the United States and the concern of its neighbors and a portion of its own populace about remilitarization. One could almost palpably feel these constraints with a prime minister like Nakasone, whose personal preference would have been to move more quickly to expand Japan's defense capabilities. This growth, of course, was no more—and indeed, far less—than Americans expected from a nation of growing economic power. Congressional demands in 1987 for Japan to achieve the NATO norm of 3 percent of GNP for defense would, for example, have brought about a tripling of Japan's defense budget and required a new set of missions and activities at which one could only guess.

What should be noted here, however, is not so much the dollar value of Japan's defense expenditures over time, but the evolution of Japan's defense missions. Two main phases can be distinguished in Japan's gradually evolving defense capabilities. The first, running from the creation of the Self-Defense Force to the late 1970s or 1980, encompassed essentially a local defense of the Japanese islands, and a general dependence on the United States for strategic, *but also conventional*, defense. This began to change around 1980. At this time, Japan quietly moved away from local self-defense into an integrated role in overall U.S. defense plans against the Soviet Union in the Western Pacific. This transition was gradual and never prominently announced. It required Japan to go beyond local defense to assume roles and missions far outside its own territory. All this was of course done in the name of self-defense.

And legitimately so, for Japan had good reasons to be concerned about the growing Soviet threat in the Pacific. Soviet air and naval power in the region grew rapidly in the 1970s, a buildup that did not slacken until the late 1980s. The Soviet Pacific fleet is the largest of the four Soviet armadas. It possesses two aircraft carriers, about seventy surface combat ships, long-range bombers, and 1,200 tactical aircraft. This power was augmented by the conversion of Cam Ranh Bay in Vietnam into the Soviet Union's largest naval base outside the Warsaw Pact.

In short, there were solid reasons for Japan not only to increase its defense spending in the 1980s, but to adopt new roles in an integrated effort aimed at countering Soviet war capability in the Pacific. Calls for changes in mission to a more forward-looking, outward-oriented defense role fell on receptive ears in Tokyo. With its aggressive military growth in the Far East, the Soviet Union brought its own problems upon itself. Just as in Europe, Soviet military power and the intervention into Afghanistan prompted a vigorous response in the Pacific.

New Japanese roles in the 1980s included the defense of a sea zone extending 1,000 miles beyond the territory of Japan, air defense over Japan, and the blockade of the Sea of Japan to bottle up Soviet naval and air power. To carry out these roles, Japan would not simply attempt to keep open shipping in the Pacific by the defensive use of convoys; it would assist the United States in trapping the "Soviet Pacific fleet behind the choke points that close off the Soviets' Far East bases. Unable to disperse, the Soviet fleet would not be able to threaten shipping on the high seas."[21] Japan's defense expenditures in the 1980s have permitted the creation of the forces necessary to achieve these goals.

At the same time, these new roles and expenditures have manifestly moved Japan beyond local self-defense:

> Japan's military objectives are thus no longer targeted solely at defending Japanese territory and territorial air and sea space, but to role-sharing with the United States targeted at fighting the Soviet Union in the northwest Pacific. This amounts to a significant but unannounced shift in Japan's fundamental defense orientation.[22]

The second phase of Japan's postwar defense system has become in effect what has been called "an offensive posture by association."[23]

Under this circumstance, it is even harder to draw a meaningful distinction between offense and defense. As has been said, "The more Japanese forces are tied to the missions of U.S. forces, the more the distinction between defensive and offensive forces breaks down. . . . Many weapons now underused by Japanese forces can be easily modified from defensive to offensive systems and used in conjunction with U.S. forces."[24] This has resulted in ingenious and creative mental gymnastics to distinguish between "defensive defense" and "offensive defense," the latter presumably to be distinguished from offense altogether. What is clear enough, though, is that a doctrine of self-defense that can encompass not only Japan's home territory but seas 1,000 miles away, and even protection of shipping in the Persian Gulf, is a very expansive doctrine of self-defense. In the coming years the evaluation of Japan's military power will increasingly include reference to its intentions as well as its capabilities. Once a nation has achieved the capability to create a strong military power, the intentions of that nation become significant. For military planners and farsighted political leaders, intentions should be treated as subject to rapid change, and capabilities as a lodestar.

What then are Japan's intentions? Japanese leaders—and commentators who echo their pronouncements—repeat almost as a mantra, "Japan has no interest in a military buildup." A proper judgment, however, will be based less on these statements than on the realities of military programs and budgets. This is all the more true for a nation like Japan, whose debate about military goals and missions is not likely to be as open and direct as in, say, the United States. The critical evidence in this assessment will be the level of defense spending in the coming years. Japan's military planners submitted a request for 1991–1995 of ¥23.5 trillion, or about $180 billion. The Japanese cabinet approved a five-year budget of ¥22.8 trillion, or about $175 billion, which required the elimination of several proposed new procurement items. The cabinet also built in some flexibility in light of changes in the Soviet Union and the possibility of improved relations between North and South Korea, and called for a review after three years. From a growth rate of 5.4 percent in 1990, the 1991 budget limited growth to about 3 percent, a step which one author said was taken so as not "to give a negative impression to other nations by steeply increasing the country's defense budget at a time when the rest of the world is working for peace."[25] The reduction from the original request by the defense agency results in the lowest level of growth for Japanese defense spending in more than a decade. Nevertheless, at a time when U.S. defense spending is being cut by 2 to 3 percent, an increase of "only" 3 percent would look good to American military planners.

Given that it has been the Soviet threat that has prompted and justified the buildup of the 1980s, why should further increases be necessary in a period of a declining menace in the 1990s? Japanese defense planners offer several different answers to this question. First, they argue that the Soviet threat in Asia has not diminished. Foreign Minister Taro Nakayama, speaking to the foreign affairs committee of Japan's upper house of parliament, expressed this line of thinking after the U.S.–U.S.S.R. summit meeting in Malta, in December 1989: "Unlike Europe, there is no essential change of the military situation in Asia."[26] Indeed, it is true that at this time Soviet deployments in the region have been undiminished in the past several years. Further, the Japanese defense white paper of September 1989 makes the case that even quantitative reductions would not tell the whole story, and that improvements in the quality of Soviet arms more than offset current reductions in overall Soviet force levels.

A second argument suggests that even if the Soviet threat—which most Japanese have never taken too seriously—is declining, current Soviet policies are easily reversible. A further Japanese military buildup is thus a form of insurance in the face of uncertainty about future Soviet policy. This, it should be noted, is precisely the same argument used by U.S. officials to limit the extent of *cuts* in U.S. military spending.

Third, Japanese military officials point to real and legitimate gaps in Japan's current defense posture. The principal gap occurs at the edge of Japan's 1,000-mile sea lane defense zone. At the margin of the zone, Japan cannot defend itself. Captain Makoto Yamazaki of the Maritime Self-Defense Force says, "At our 1,000-mile limit we have no air support. That is a big problem."[27] For this reason, Japanese military planners would like to find a way to provide air defense at the edge of the 1,000-mile zone. Either means of doing this—midair refueling capability or the construction of small aircraft carriers—would extend the range of Japanese fighter planes far beyond their current limits, and create the capacity for distant power projection.

Such a situation illustrates the difficulty of drawing limits around a defense-oriented force. There is simply no way to solve legitimate defense problems of the sort described above without creating at the same time an offensive force that raises concern among other nations in the region.

The Maturation of Japanese Military Power

To date, the gaps in Japan's military power have not been significant for its security. This is so for only one reason: Japan depends ultimately upon the United States for its protection. At this time, Japan does not intend to possess an organic and comprehensive capacity to defend itself against all possible threats. It intends to play only a limited, though important, role within a broader security system.

At this time, Japanese security doctrine consists of several tenets. First, Japan should be prepared to defend itself for a brief time against a conventional invasion of its islands. This is to be accomplished through early warning and through interception and antiship capabilities against both surface ships and submarines; through interception of attack aircraft and bombers; and through the maintenance of a small ground force concentrated particularly on Hokkaido. Japan's intent is not to be able to repel a massive force all by itself. Estimates suggest that Japan could defend itself against a conventional Soviet attack with current supplies of ammunition only for a matter of days. Japan clearly depends upon the fact that an attack on Japan would trigger a combined response from U.S. and Japanese forces, and the possibility of escalation to nuclear conflict.

Second, Japan relies upon the United States for a nuclear umbrella that not only provides deterrence but is also a hedge against nuclear blackmail by another power. In terms of available land forces and air and sea power, the Soviet Union possesses a larger quantitative force in the region than do the U.S. and Japan combined. The potential of nuclear war is part and parcel of deterrence in Asia just as it is in Europe, although in a somewhat less visible, tangible way, given the geography of the region. But there is no doubt that Japan, like every other major industrialized nation today, is under the protection of a nuclear umbrella.

Not all Japanese subscribe to the view that the U.S. nuclear umbrella is important. Indeed, opinion polls in Japan suggest that a majority of Japanese do not believe that the U.S. would offer massive assistance in the event of an attack on Japan, particularly if there were a strong prospect of retaliation against the United States.[28] This, of course, has little to do with the fact that such an umbrella has existed and continues to exist today. But it does point to the crux of the reason why Japan will continue to develop its military power into the 1990s. Japan is concerned by what it sees as declining American power and a loss of competitiveness in the world. If this process is not arrested, Japan will have to look more to its own resources to provide a long-term security policy. This is not something that might happen in the future; it has already happened. Japan's leaders came to the conclusion more than a decade ago that Japan's security would require Japan's participation. That is in part why the defense buildup was accepted in Japan so willingly.

In 1978 the U.S. contemplated withdrawing U.S. troops from Korea. This move, which was not supported in Japan, offered an early warning to Japanese leaders that the U.S. would not maintain forever all of its then-current forces in the Pacific.[29] This was a particularly troubling moment for the U.S. to have proposed such a move, coming as it did at a time of significant Soviet military buildup in the region. South Korea in 1978 was far less ready to defend itself without substantial U.S. participation than it would be today.

Although the proposed withdrawal did not occur, there have been what are for Japan ominous signs beneath the surface of the Reagan military buildup about U.S. staying power in the region. Certainly the repeated calls in Congress for massive increases in Japanese defense spending—amounting to a tripling of expenditures—were an indicator of a desire to shift the burden of defense in the Western Pacific increasingly to Japan. So, too, were the threats in the fall of 1990 to remove U.S. troops from Japan in response to Japanese hesitation in funding a significant portion of the costs of the Persian Gulf coalition force. Above all, the obvious decline in America's willingness and ability to pay for a defense budget of 6 percent or more of GNP suggested to any reasonable Japanese leader that in the long run the U.S. presence in the Western Pacific would be diminished.

All of this has been hastened, not retarded, by the apparent decline of the Soviet threat. Americans are now prepared to reduce defense spending over the coming years. This will inevitably result in a diminution of the American presence not only in Europe, but in the Western Pacific as well. Unless one postulates an extraordinarily high ratio of forward-deployed to home-based troops, aircraft, and ships, proportional reductions in U.S. forces will result in deep cuts in the U.S. presence in Asia. Japan contemplates the possibility of U.S. withdrawal from the Clark Air Force and Subic naval bases in the Philippines; removal of all but a token force in South Korea; reductions of at least one, and maybe two, carrier task forces and attendant aircraft in the Pacific; and the prospect of reductions in the 49,000 U.S. military personnel stationed in Japan itself.

In short, Japan contemplates, as it must, the final termination of the postwar security system that arose in 1945. It does so without seeing at the same time a radical reduction in the kinds of strategic or conventional Soviet forces that could threaten Japan. Nor does it see a diminution in military forces anywhere else in the region, including China, North or South Korea, or India. Under these circumstances, it would be irresponsible, if not altogether irrational, for Japanese leaders to turn away from efforts to expand Japan's own defense capabilities. At the very time Japan is developing deep economic interests throughout East Asia, it cannot afford to see its long-term potential security erode at a rate faster than potential threats to that security. Virtually every serious observer of Japanese military policy agrees that a substantial U.S. reduction of its commitment in the Western Pacific would be a sufficient cause for Japan to vastly expand its security role in the region and its independence from the United States.[30] What has been less widely noted is that this process is already well under way.

What are Japan's options as it moves toward a greater role in guaranteeing its own security? First, it should be expected that Japan will move only incrementally so long as the Liberal Democratic Party governs the country. Neither popular sentiment nor the concerns of Japan's neighbors would be answered by more radical changes. But in an economy as large as Japan's, the impact of steady military growth over the next decade would result in a substantially strengthened Japanese defence force vis-a-vis those of its neighbors.

Japanese defense expenditures will be likely to focus increasingly on high-tech items. This is so for two reasons. First, Japanese difficulties in recruiting personnel in sufficient numbers and of sufficient quality puts a premium on force-multiplying high-tech weapons. Second, these items are largely consistent with the principal needs for Japan's defense—early warning and interdiction of air and naval forces.

For these reasons, and because of Japan's generally defensive orientation, Japan will be in the vanguard of strategic defense research and development. Japan has already become, along with Germany and Israel, one of the leading cooperating nations on strategic defense initiative (SDI) or "Star Wars" research. Strategic defense will rely upon precisely the kinds of technology and skills at which Japan excels. Japan is deeply interested in staying at the forefront of technological innovations that could have commercial utility. For a high-tech nation with small geographical territory, no nuclear weapons, and the need to preserve a strong defensive character for its security program, strategic defense is a natural priority.

This is a minimum expectation for Japan's development of military power in the next decade. Should the opposition Japan Socialist Party take power, its antidefense bearing is ironically likely to lead to a far quicker military buildup. This happened in the United States when the Carter interlude was followed by the Reagan buildup of the 1980s. Such a dynamic would work even more forcefully in Japan. For the JSP would be little likely to be able to achieve deep cuts in defense. It might, at best, be capable of slowing the growth of military spending for several years. The casualty of such governance would be the U.S.–Japan relationship. The JSP, finding that real cuts in defense were difficult to achieve, would direct its energy against the security relationship with the United States. This might or might not result in the termination of the security treaty, but it *would* result in a change in the quality of the U.S.–Japan security relationship. This would inevitably produce a negative effect in the United States. Why, it would be asked, ought the United States to defend a rich and ungrateful nation like Japan, particularly when Japan was turning away from its own past commitments to joint defense?

The JSP could not have it both ways: to reduce Japan's own military spending and also to reduce reliance upon the United States. The inevitable reaction would come in a reversion to LDP rule with a much diminished security relationship with the United States. The result would be a rapid escalation of Japanese defense spending.

A buildup of Japanese forces to the extent that they were able to defeat Soviet conventional force aggression by themselves would have to include a strategy of striking at targets on Soviet soil, including ports and air bases near the Sea of Japan from which Soviet forces could attack. This would require the production of offensive weapons such as cruise missiles, ballistic missiles, and attack aircraft. It would require years of development into the 1990s to achieve reasonable force levels. It would also be highly risky against a nation armed with nuclear weapons.

The prospect of deterring conventional force aggression by the Soviet Union, or by any other power, would be vastly enhanced if Japan were to possess nuclear weapons. As long as Japan lies unambiguously under the protection of the American nuclear umbrella, this will suffice. But if there is any doubt on the part of any government—Japan's, America's, or any other's—about the credibility of the U.S. nuclear umbrella, then Japan must find that protection elsewhere. There is only one place to seek that protection, and that is from its own resources, namely, its own production of nuclear weapons.

Much has been made of Japan's opposition to nuclear weapons. Indeed, there is some substance to descriptions of Japan's so-called nuclear allergy. But too much can easily be made of this. For the government of Japan has nowhere near the allergy to nuclear weapons that might be supposed. During World War II, Japan was busily engaged in efforts to produce an atomic bomb, with each of its armed forces conducting its own research program in this area.[31] These research facilities were apparently destroyed in a May 1943 air raid.

Efforts were renewed in the latter years of the war. In 1944 Japan imported uranium oxide from Germany, a move that supplemented its ongoing efforts to find uranium in Manchuria and Korea.[32] Following the Hiroshima and Nagasaki explosions, a Japanese Navy researcher was instructed to produce an atomic bomb within six months.[33] The war's prompt end terminated this effort.

Since the end of the war, Japan has followed a consistent policy against nuclear armament. This policy was given expression in 1976 by Prime Minister Sato, who offered the three renunciations—Japan would not produce, store, or allow the transfer of nuclear weapons within its territory. The fact is, however, that Japan has made no effort to prohibit the U.S. possession of nuclear weapons in Japanese territory.

Japanese military planners have long considered the benefits of nuclear weapons. In the 1970s, the Director General of the Japan Defense Agency, Yasuhiro Nakasone, produced a report recommending that Japan possess tactical nuclear bombs.[34] Certainly it is United States doctrine that, despite forswearing a "no first use" pledge, American nuclear weapons are essentially defensive in nature. This rationale is fully consistent with Japan's commitment to a defense-only rearmament.

Given that nuclear weapons already are allowed into Japan for its own defense, the central question about Japan's potential nuclear armament is this: Can it be reasonably supposed that the Japanese government trusts *itself* less with nuclear weapons than it does a foreign power? And a foreign power which, although it has Japan's interests at heart now, is the same nation that used the only two atomic weapons ever employed—on Japan? The current antinuclear sentiment in Japan derives from the postwar situation, not from an inherent aversion to nuclear weapons. Suppose that Japan had invested more heavily in its atomic bomb program during World War II and had developed a bomb before the United States. Is there any doubt that Japan's attitude about nuclear weapons would be different than it is now? Japan's situation is analogous to Germany's. Possessing no nuclear weapons, and unable for forty-five years to pursue a fully independent policy, why should there be positive sentiment about nuclear weapons in Japan?

Japan's capacity to produce nuclear weapons quickly is not in doubt. It presently has more than thirty nuclear power plants in operation, with a goal of fifty-three to be in service by 1994. Japan possesses a stockpile of plutonium sufficient to make several hundred atomic weapons. Harold Brown, former Secretary of Defense, summarizes Japan's capacity by speaking of "the relative ease of acquiring a nuclear weapons capability, which Japan could accomplish within a few years of making the decision to do so."[35] Japan also possesses the capability to produce ballistic missiles to deliver nuclear weapons. It has long been interested in missiles and missile technology, having first committed government funds for missile development in 1955. In addition to the potential commercial benefits of the technology, missiles hold several obvious military advantages for a nation like Japan. First, they are not manpower-intensive. Second, and more importantly, they are most useful where there is no chance of a layered, in-depth defense replete with early warning of attack.

From its initial program focusing on short-range antitank, surface-to-air and air-to-air missiles, Japan has moved into development of larger missiles capable of launching satellites into space. The H-I, which is capable of launching a 550 kg payload, is being superseded by the totally domestically produced H-II, which can launch a payload of nine tons or more. The N-II, developed by Nissan, can put a 1.6-ton payload into an orbit at 1,000 km altitude.

In 1989, the Japanese government will spend $1.1 billion on space-related activities. Plans are underway for an unmanned and subsequently a manned space shuttle. A 1987 study by Japan's Consultative Committee on Long-Term Policy for the Space Activities Committee predicts that private sector and government expenditures on space technology research and development will total $72 billion between 1986 and 2000, an amount exceeding $4.5 billion each year.[36]

No single step would propel Japan so quickly and so inexpensively into the first rank of political and military powers as the production of ballistic missiles armed with nuclear weapons. But for the moment, there is no reason for it to proceed on this course. The development of even a second-strike, counterforce capability—which is how nuclear weapons will first emerge in Japan—will alarm its neighbors far beyond what Japan could hope to achieve by taking this step.

Japan *will* have a nuclear umbrella extended over it; the only question is whose umbrella it will be. If U.S. retrenchment in the Pacific proceeds far enough to call into question the credibility of the U.S. nuclear umbrella, Japan will certainly develop its own. How could it do otherwise? For not only the United States, the Soviet Union, and China will possess a nuclear capability in the region. In addition to those three long-standing nuclear powers, India, Taiwan, Korea, and perhaps other nations could possess nuclear weapons before the end of the decade. Reports of North Korean efforts to produce a bomb are illustrative of the problem Japan faces in a region in which nuclear capability is rapidly proliferating.[37] Under these circumstances, Japan cannot and will not remain unsheltered by a nuclear umbrella.

The government of Japan must inevitably contemplate the full scope of changes set into motion by the end of the bipolar world. In that world, in which a handful of nations possessed nuclear weapons, and in which only two had overwhelming nuclear force, nuclear weapons seem to have helped to deter even conventional conflict between nations. Whether one can count on this stabilizing effect in a world full of nuclear powers is less clear; whether one would bet one's entire nation on the deterrent effect of a third party's nuclear umbrella under these circumstances is altogether doubtful.

The nuclear balance of the bipolar world helped produce a stable climate within which huge new economic entities like Japan could grow. Their very growth, however, has changed the world. How new world powers like Japan will themselves deal with these military technologies remains to be seen. What is certain, though, is that Japan's gradual rearmament has positioned it to become within a very brief span a major military power.

CONCLUSION

The Year 2000: Germany, Japan, and America

Are these the shadows of the things that Will be, or are
they shadows of things that May be, only?

—*Charles Dickens*

Beyond Containment: A Tripolar World

WITHIN THE NEXT SEVERAL YEARS the trend toward a tripolar world
will be essentially completed. Japan's dominance over Asia's markets, coupled with a new independence from America and an impressive military capability, will assure its leadership in East Asia.
Germany's dominance of the European continent will be less pronounced, because its neighbors are closer in size and proportionally
more powerful than Japan's neighbors. But it will be no less real.
Germany will be first, not among equals but among less-than-equals,
on the European continent. Its strength in finance, industry, and
military power will ensure its leadership in every sphere of European
decision making.

Together with the United States, Germany and Japan will account
for half of the economic activity of the entire world. And this is
significant because it is unlikely to change for the foreseeable future.
After all, the United States was responsible for 52 percent of the

world's economic activity all by itself in the first year after World War II. But this was an artificial high that was bound to change as nations recovered from the devastation of the war. There is, however, no reason to expect that American–German–Japanese dominance will erode. To the contrary, it is more likely that for some time the relative weight of these economies will grow, not shrink, vis-a-vis the remainder of the world. As the financial and technological capabilities of these nations extend the force of their human capital into their regions and throughout the world, their power will grow.

This may seem strangest of all to the leaders and the peoples of Germany and Japan themselves. For so long accustomed to a supporting role that stressed their dependence upon America, the idea of genuine independence of action is difficult to grasp. These two nations, so long in the habit of understating their strength, do not yet know their own true ability to shape events. This ability is instinctively better understood by their neighbors than by themselves, for the moment.

What does this mean? As recently as 1985 Secretary of State George Shultz could write:

> The international order at the end of this century is certain to be far different from the pattern of world politics when the century began.[1]

What strikes one today, however, are more the similarities than the differences with the beginning of the twentieth century. Once again, Germany, Japan, and the United States will dominate world politics, and once again the United States will return to a historically more normal mode in which it competes with its friends for influence.

But are there really not substantial differences between the situation now and that at the beginning of the twentieth century? Some have said that nationalism has ceased to be meaningful, and that national boundaries no longer matter. Are relationships between peoples so far advanced as to render national boundaries anachronistic? Are the cosmopolitan youth of today's industrial societies the guarantee of harmony? It is well to remember pre-1914 Europe. It is doubtful that the Europe of today surpasses the level of interchange of that era. The elites of all European nations traveled freely among countries. They studied at one another's universities. They spoke each other's languages. They traded with one another. They required no passports or other documents to travel between nations. And they were governed by men and women who were in many cases blood relatives.

In Europe, new institutions are emerging which offer hope that national differences can be subordinated to larger goals. But there should be no mistake: at this time, decisions are made just as they have always been, in the respective capital cities of Europe's leading nation-states. The principal states of Europe still watch one another closely and guard their prerogatives jealously. The lesser states of Europe, some of which have just emerged from a suffocating sub-servience to the Soviet Union, are in a mode of relishing, not expunging, their national identities.

In Asia, there is no such movement away from the nation-state. There, despite transnational investments by Japan, national bound-aries remain very much in force. National rivalries and fears are not very far beneath the surface in East Asia; in some cases, they are not beneath the surface at all.

Does the widespread existence of democratic governments dis-tinguish our time from the beginning of the twentieth century? It would be well to remember that both Germany and Japan have had experience with democratic government on other occasions in their modern histories. Now it could be said that earlier democratic ten-dencies had not taken very deep root and that they were therefore susceptible to decay when challenged. Perhaps this is so. But it is also true that the postwar democracies of Germany and Japan have not yet been challenged. They have remained steadfast in the face of the Soviet military threat, to be sure. But they have not expe-rienced economic reversal or loss; their course has been straight upward economically and thoroughly constrained geopolitically. At the very least, we should seek the benefit of a greater, more nuanced universe of experience before we assert a liberal version of the Brezhnev doctrine—once a democracy, always a democracy.

Finally, prior to Iraq's invasion of Kuwait in August 1990 an intellectual fashion arose which asserted that political and military force was becoming irrelevant in the modern world. True power, it was said, is economic power. The decisive military victory over

Iraq has served to temper this view somewhat. But the argument that military power was growing irrelevant had all along overlooked a fundamental fact: economic power has *always* been important in world affairs. Those nations with wealth and technological advantages have always been important. Those who argue the novelty of the current world suffer from a decided myopia. Have not trade, investment, and technological interchange always been important in world history? And have not wars begun in political capitals still been regularly waged? There has never been a perfect congruity between economic life and political/military life.[2] Economic interchange has always reached across political boundaries. At times, economic relations have compelled changes in political boundaries; at other times, political boundaries have reasserted themselves and temporarily wiped out economic interchange. Are there any grounds at all to say with certainty that this cannot happen again?

Current times are good times. We are living at a moment in which the importance of national boundaries is diminished; in which the world's leading democracies live and work in harmony; and in which political and military relations between the world's most successful nations are less salient than are economic relations. But the fact is that these happy circumstances are all the result of one common, overriding cause that defined the postwar world: containment of the Soviet Union. This period is now over. For the foreseeable future, the Soviet Union will be in a mode of self-containment. This is not to say that the strategic or conventional power of the Soviet Union can safely be ignored. The Soviet Union remains a significant military power. Yet the Soviet Union will not be expanding; it will be contracting. Its threat will not be growing; it will be receding. The remainder of the world will no longer have to organize to contain it.

America's most critical relationships during the next decade will not be with the Soviet Union but with Germany and Japan. Unlike the Soviet Union, these two countries will strongly affect nations outside their own territories. As great powers, they will shape and limit opportunities for many other nations. Their decisions will matter far beyond their borders.

But why must America care? Why can we not allow the new power centers of Europe and East Asia to develop on their own?

The view that new regional power centers are emerging in Europe and Asia is both true and misleading. It is true in a general statistical way; but this general truth masks the fact that within these new power centers reside the core powers of Germany and Japan, and that also within these regional power centers lurk the historical seeds for many conflicts. To ignore these facts suggests that absolutely nothing has been learned from the tragic conflicts of the twentieth century. For the United States to leave these regions to develop as they will and to focus instead on North America or on the Western Hemisphere would be a terrible mistake. Internal conflicts in Europe and East Asia have drawn the United States into the vortex of diplomacy and full-scale war twice in this century alone. Are these not lessons enough?

It is not the extraterritorial problems of narcotics, or terrorism, or the environment that compel American involvement in Europe and East Asia. These are significant international concerns, but a continental power could choose to solve many of them by closing itself off from the rest of the world. It is also not the sheer economic competition that Europe and East Asia offer which compels American involvement in their regions. After all, individual American states are not threatened by the economic successes of their neighbors. Similarly, the United States as a whole is not threatened by foreign economic competition that creates new wealth and new employment—unless the ownership of assets leads to noneconomic forms of control by the owners.

World politics have not kept pace with the integrating tendencies of economic interchange. The crux of the matter is this: United States involvement in Europe and East Asia remains necessary to insure that economic competition does not once again descend into the barbarism of political and military competition. The world can and will have many pressing problems to address in the coming decade. But as long as the United States, Germany, and Japan remain on a common course, these problems will be soluble.

All of this argues for a continuing American involvement—economic, political, and military—in both Europe and East Asia. The United States must help to foster new organizations in both Europe and East Asia in which the U.S. is an integral part. The United States is genuinely both an Atlantic and a Pacific power. If one leaves aside Soviet air and naval deployments in Siberia, no other nation approximates this role.

At the same time, the United States generally has displayed a benevolent and disinterested quality in its exercise of power abroad. At bottom, neither Germany nor Japan inspires the same degree of trust among other nations as does the U.S. It will take some time, perhaps as long as a generation, before their neighbors will fully trust these two increasingly powerful nations.

The guiding premise of United States policy over the next decade should be this: *America should be the unique Atlantic/Pacific swing power, fully integrated into both Europe and East Asia.* This is a large task, but it is essential to the further development of a world in which national and regional power are tempered by a broader perspective.

Europe

The principal force in the creation of a new Europe will inevitably be Germany. No other European nation can compel any specific outcome without Germany's agreement. And no other nation can bring about the range of different outcomes that it can. Whether Europe will revert again to a shifting balance of power between nation-states; whether Western Europe will grow together without the East; or whether Europe will draw together in some form of pancontinental institutions—all of these outcomes, as well as the pace at which they will be decided, rest above all in Germany's hands. This is an understandably difficult, but nevertheless unavoidable, outcome for Germany's neighbors. Having defeated Germany militarily twice in this century only to see it return to an axial role cannot be a satisfying experience for those neighbors.

Although Germany will set the parameters for their decisions, France, England, Italy, and the Soviet Union all will retain a broad capacity to respond to Germany's decisions. France and Italy appear to have decided conclusively that their best course lies in embracing Germany and bringing it into the fold of a Western European union of a sort yet to be defined. England has clearly *not* made that choice, and remains, as it always has been, tempted by a thin channel of

water to think of itself as somewhat distinct from Europe. This is
an illusion as easy to understand as it is difficult to defend. One
could make a strong and credible argument that England above all
ought to press for European unification. Finally, the Soviet Union
has too recently entered into the politics of Western Europe to know
its own hopes and interests. One could suspect that, as a huge
continental power buffered by the weaker states of east-central Europe, the Soviet Union will find only limited forms of political
participation in a West European-dominated union. At all events,
the Soviet Union is likely to be preoccupied by its internal problems
for some time, and this will prevent its active participation in a new
political structure for Europe.

But the Soviet Union (or Russia, if it reverts again to that form)
is one of two nations outside of Western Europe that it is vital to
include in the new Europe's institutions of unity. European political
and security arrangements cannot possibly become stable without
the participation of the Soviet Union. This will be true even if the
U.S.S.R. continues its descent to a status as a far weaker power.
For the Soviet Union, even in the worst of circumstances, will
remain a large, resource-rich, and relatively powerful nation. Its
exclusion from pan-European institutions will tempt Germany as
well as France and England to look for increased security and influence through unique special relationships with the Soviet Union.

The full inclusion of the Soviet Union into the politics of Europe
will be a difficult psychological transition for Americans. For more
than forty years it has very correctly been the thrust of American
policy to keep the Soviet Union out of Western Europe, the Middle
East, Latin America, Southeast Asia, and Africa. The Soviet
Union's current weakness will dictate that it will not be much involved in most of these regions. But the time has come to welcome
the Soviet Union into the politics of Europe and to compel it to play
a responsible role.

The other nation that is critical to a strong and stable pan-European
organization is the United States. The United States is, among other
things, a European nation. Its language is European, and so are its
political ideals. Its population is predominantly descended from
European peoples. It has strong and legitimate interests in Europe.
Without active American involvement, England will tend naturally

to hedge its bets on participating in a pan-European organization. Without the United States, a pan-European entity will be predictably a polite regime of power balancing. With the United States, all nations of Europe will have another strong pole around which to orient themselves.

It is inconceivable how a successful European security system could exist without the United States. Twice in the twentieth century Germany has misjudged the level and the intensity of American interest in Europe. It is incumbent upon the United States to leave not a scintilla of doubt about that interest and that commitment now and for the future.

The Europe of today is nowhere near achieving an outcome that is satisfactory to insure the maintenance of peace and prosperity. Currently, there are only two trans-European institutions of any real consequence. The first of these is the European Community of twelve West European nations. This organization has made rapid strides in recent years. It has grown in breadth and depth, and it has achieved a dynamism that would have seemed improbable a decade ago. The process of integration will go forward briskly, one hopes. Yet neither the United States nor the Soviet Union is a member of this organization, and there is no clear way for them to become members in the future. There is certainly no reason to include the Soviet Union at the present time, since an economic union like the EC does not need to find a way to integrate a nonmarket economy with a nonconvertible currency into its plans. Yet it is important to point out the intrinsic limits of the EC as a unifying institution. If it does not radically alter its structure, it will end as a glorified customs union, perhaps with a common currency, among only some of the important European powers.

The other institution of consequence is the North Atlantic Treaty Organization. NATO has the virtue of including the United States. But NATO was founded entirely for the containment of Soviet communism, and that rationale has now disappeared. The new issues of European security have very little to do with the reason for which NATO was established or the purpose that it has served for forty years.

In short, Europe now possesses two meaningful integrating organizations. Neither has the same members as the other. One excludes both of the two continental powers that are required for a stable organization. The other contains one of those two powers, but has lost its reason for existence. Such is the Europe of today.

The task of the present is to create an institution that can shape the economic, political, and security relationships of Europe in a genuinely inclusive way. Economically, this argues in the short term for some way of integrating the EC with the United States. American participation in such an entity will offer assurances to each European nation that there will be several poles around which it will be organized. This structure must grow out of a strong partnership with Germany which, like America, may have to give up some independence of action in order to achieve it.

The Conference on Security and Cooperation in Europe (CSCE) is the only current entity that has the necessary major powers to succeed over the long term. As a body of thirty-five nations, it is burdened by too large a membership to make rapid progress. But some entity will be required, and whether it is the CSCE or another smaller group that grows out of the North Atlantic partners of the seven leading industrial nations (G-7) is less important than that it come into existence quickly as the one body to which each nation looks for its part in the whole.

It is even more important that security arrangements be addressed. For the economic cohesion of the last twenty years has developed within the security framework of containment, and that framework cannot be removed without serious impact on cohesion on every other front.[3] Specifically, it is vital that the United States keep a significant military presence in Europe until a successor to NATO and the structures of the cold war are fully in place. This could take a decade or more. The United States need not maintain a massive force of men and arms in Europe. It could cut down to a well-defined and carefully configured presence of no more than one-fourth to one-third of current U.S. forces deployed in Europe—say, 75,000 to 100,000. This would not be onerously expensive or intrusive; it would be possible to maintain this force level and to do everything else required within an affordable defense budget.

The idea that the United States could retain a significant force in Europe composed wholly of naval and air force units is simply not credible. As the world saw in Iraq's August 1990 invasion of Kuwait, a strong U.S. naval force does not in and of itself deter aggression over land. Ground forces are required for credibility.

It is especially important that U.S. ground forces continue to be stationed, even at small levels, on German soil. This is not so much because of a Soviet threat as because of the general assurance it would provide of the American interest in maintaining peace in central Europe, regardless of the origin of threats to that peace. European nations understand that Germany possesses the greatest potential military power (though not the intent to create such a force). U.S. forces stationed in several nations in Europe, but not in Germany, would take on the appearance of being in Europe *because* of Germany. Such an appearance would be very unwise.

Will Germany continue to permit a U.S. presence after Soviet forces in the east return home? Much depends upon how Germany develops its national identity in the next several years. But it should be possible to find ways and means to accommodate Germany's national identity and still retain U.S. forces there. One recent proposal suggests the creation of a pan-European army.[4] This is certainly a rubric in which U.S. forces could participate alongside other European forces, just as they do now in NATO. If even fuller symmetry is required, the United States should, if requested, permit Germany and other European nations to station troops in the United States for the purpose of joint training and exercises.[5] Budget constraints and the lack of missions in the U.S. that European countries would find attractive would undoubtedly limit the forces that nations might choose to deploy. But if the point of national equivalency needs to be made, then it should be accepted.

In the final consideration, much will turn on the U.S. nuclear guarantee in Europe. It has already been argued that the disappearance of the U.S. nuclear umbrella from Western Europe will inevitably force Germany to renounce its current pledges that it will not become a nuclear power. This in turn will compel further developments toward nuclear weapons by other European nations that do not wish to rely on third-party nuclear guarantees.

Here we must consider the other side of the question. Could the U.S. offer a credible nuclear deterrent without ground forces in Europe? And conversely, could the United States reasonably be expected to deploy significant forces in Europe without extending over them a nuclear umbrella? Despite much wishful thinking on the part of both European and American policymakers, for whom this would be the route of least political resistance, the answer to both these questions is no. The stakes are too high to try to achieve European security with smoke and mirrors. A Europe without American ground troops will be a Europe in which all parties, including the United States, have grounds to doubt the American commitment to its security. Much has been made of the U.S.-led coalition response to Iraq's invasion of Kuwait. Here, it is said, is proof that the United States can and *will* intervene successfully in a region where it has no ground troops. But this has never really been in doubt. After all, the United States intervened successfully twice on the European continent. But this is hardly the point. The point is deterrence, and deterrence has not been achieved—as Iraq's invasion of Kuwait proves—where U.S. ground troops are not present.

There is thus no middle way. The United States cannot meaningfully be involved in European security if it remains on the fringes, standing offshore with carrier battle groups and cruise missiles. Either the United States is in or it is out. This should not in principle be a difficult choice, either for America or, more pointedly, for nations in Europe itself. European culture has espoused universal ideals throughout the entire world. It has been the motor for universality in the modern period. But its chaotic national system of states has so far prevented it from exercising these ideals successfully. Its first and only political effort to do so was the system of imperialism, which broke down when European states turned upon one another in two savage wars. The United States has served as a better exemplar of universal ideals in this century than has any European power. As Europe gropes to transcend the limits of its nation-state system, there is every reason for the United States to contribute, if only as an insurance policy, to this extraordinary undertaking.

East Asia

What is true in Europe is truer yet in East Asia. The so-called Pacific community simply does not exist. In place of a community, there is instead: a long and heavily militarized border between the Soviet Union and China; an active Soviet nuclear fleet; a 2-million-man armed border between North and South Korea; a difficult relationship between the People's Republic of China and Taiwan; the six ASEAN nations of Southeast Asia banded together against Vietnam and against far more powerful regional and military economic forces; a newly assertive India; and the nation of whom all its neighbors remain fundamentally suspicious—Japan. This is not the kind of neighborhood that one could properly describe as a community.

The lack of community is reflected in the absence of integrating institutions in the region. There is nothing in Asia that begins to approximate the role the European Community plays in Europe. To be sure, there have been frequent economic conferences and ministerial meetings among Pacific Rim leaders in recent years. The process of consultation has been regularized in the Asia-Pacific Economic Cooperation Council's (APEC) yearly ministerials. But these consultative sessions are a far cry from the kind of institutions that reflect and create cohesion among the region's many power centers.

Nor is there any security institution in East Asia that resembles NATO. The old U.S. system of anticommunist alliances included the Australia–New Zealand–U.S. (ANZUS) pact, the Southeast Asia Treaty Organization (SEATO), and the U.S.–Republic of China mutual security treaty. These have long since lapsed. In their place is a shifting pattern of bilateral relations which are precisely predictable according to the logic of power politics.

The fact is that at the present time there is but one institution which offers the breadth of influence to affect the entire region: that is the cooperation between the United States and Japan.

This cooperation is the foundation on which must be built the transitional institutions that can help to bring lasting peace to a region with many signs of trouble below the surface. Japan must and inevitably will assert a leadership role in the region. Its power and its interests are simply too great to permit any other possibility. The choice is not whether, but how, Japan will undertake this task in the coming decade. Without American leadership, much of the Pacific Rim will fall increasingly under Japanese economic dominance. But Japan will be unable by itself to create a set of political relations that match the region's economic relations. There is too much mistrust of Japan by other nations of the region to allow meaningful political or security institutions to come into place. Without the United States, the nations of the region will fear that Japan's economic dominance will be extended to political and military dominance as well.

It is thus not only for the smaller nations of the region that the United States must remain deeply involved; it is for Japan's interests as well. For in the last analysis, the United States could not permit the entire Pacific Rim to come under a single nation's dominance. Three wars in Asia have been fought in the last fifty years to make this point. Surely it would not be too much to hope that both the American and the Japanese people understand something of their common interests by now.

Just as with Germany in Europe, Japan must grow into America's strongest partner in Asia. America and Japan must forge new institutions to help draw together the nations of the Pacific Rim—not only as trading partners, but as political and security partners as well. This will be no easy task. Japan's insular tendencies alone will make it difficult to draw that nation into regional arrangements based on anything resembling equality with other nations. Indeed, the entire region operates at a grave disadvantage compared with Europe. In Asia, none of the leading powers subscribes fully to the abstract universalism of the equal worth of all individual human beings. Where democratic forms are in place in Asia, they function slightly differently than in Europe. They place far more value on consensus within the nation. They draw less sharp demarcations than do even the Europeans between the people, the nation, and the state. The value to a Japanese of an institution that imputes equal worth to a Japanese and, say, an Indonesian or a Filipino must surely be in doubt.

If the United States fails to understand its stake in Asia and significantly reduces its military presence, the consequences are predictable. First, the pace of military growth by the region's major powers will rapidly increase as each nation competes in a vain hope to gain influence over or security against its neighbors. Second, this will cause Japan to redouble its own military growth. Japan will quickly outstrip all the other Asian powers. Third, these trends will drive apart the nations of the region, create new antagonisms, and exacerbate old ones. Fourth, the United States–Japan relationship will descend into deep difficulties. Fifth, Japan will look again to China as its potential subservient partner to offset its fear that it will lose access to raw materials and markets for its products. Finally, Japan will join all of the other major, and perhaps minor, nations of the region in developing a powerful nuclear capacity.

This is not a course the United States should wish to encourage. Japan is simply too serious a nation to misconstrue by examining only the surface of current Japanese opinion polls about rearmament. In retrospect, the Pacific War of 1941–1945 looks like a Japanese national kamikaze project. There was no imaginable way in which Japan could have defeated the United States in that war. Japanese manufacturing output was only 13 percent of America's, and its war-making potential was only 8 percent.[6] Yet that war occurred. By the year 2000, Japan's manufacturing capacity will be six times more powerful vis-a-vis the United States than it was in December 1941. This is a nation with whom our policies should be thoughtfully pursued.

The task of creating new institutions in the Pacific Rim can be achieved only if the United States and Japan work together. This cooperation is not a sufficient condition, but it is certainly a necessary one. What ought the United States to do in the region to promote these goals? First, it is vitally important that it be able to state with precision exactly what it expects from Japan. The United States was vague and imprecise about what it hoped for from Japan in the 1930s.[7] It wanted a Japan that was not so deeply involved in China, to be sure. But beyond this generalized desire there was very little clarity about American expectations or vital requirements.

In the immediate postwar years of U.S. occupation, American expectations were clearer. The United States expected a fully pacified, disarmed Japan to create a parliamentary democracy and to rebuild its society based on democratic values. As we have already discussed, this clarity gave way to conflicting expectations when the Cold War in Asia broke out. To some extent, these conflicting expectations have continued right up to the present time. America has wanted Japan to continue to rely for its security upon the United States, yet also to spend more on defense. As recently as three years ago, the United States Congress was regularly urging Japan to spend as much as 3 percent of its GNP on defense. This would have resulted in a *tripling* of Japan's defense budget. A Harris poll taken in mid-1990 showed that while 40 percent of Japanese thought that Japan should build its own independent military defense system (instead of accepting continued dependence on the United States), fully 71 percent of Americans believed Japan should do so.[8] This kind of mixed message should be replaced with a clear-cut, unambiguous set of expectations. The crux of that message should be that Japan ought to continue to spend just about what it now does on defense.[9]

On the economic side, the United States should also aim for greater clarity about what it expects from Japan. The United States harbors deeply conflicting feelings about trade and investment between the two countries. On the one hand, the U.S. subscribes to the ideal of free trade and investment, and welcomes the goods, the services, and the employment that this generates. On the other hand, Japanese successes have bred considerable resentment. In those cases where Japanese practices are clearly at odds with reciprocal treatment in the United States, these resentments are well-founded. The United States should think through carefully what are its minimal, fair expectations of Japan. These should include, at their core, total reciprocity between both countries. The U.S. should state these expectations clearly and should make equally clear the consequences of failing to achieve them. Journalist James Fallows has rightly said that such a policy would be far preferable to incessant American nagging at Japan for all failures great and small.[10] Nagging and scolding has been masquerading as trade policy for many years now, and it is hardly becoming of a great nation to reduce itself to the kind of petulance that has been occasionally in evidence on the floor of both houses of Congress.

Finally, the United States should be prepared to maintain sizable military forces in the Pacific for at least another decade.[11] This is the obvious corollary to Japan's continuing its current course on military spending. It would be precisely the wrong step to reduce the U.S. presence in East Asia and the Pacific much below its current levels.

It is possible, of course, to entertain specific limited military reductions. U.S. forces in Korea, for example, are present in order to deter a North Korean attack on the South. So long as such an attack remains a significant possibility, it would be an error to reduce these forces to a level that might invite miscalculation by the North. But if the threat from the North recedes, or if the two Koreas move toward reunification in such a way that the threat disappears altogether, then U.S. forces there could well be dispensable.

Overall, however, deep reductions in the U.S. presence in Korea, the Philippines, and Japan would surely lead nations in the Pacific to conclude that they were only marginally and very tenuously within the protection of the United States. Last year, U.S. Secretary of Defense Richard Cheney announced troop reductions of about 10 percent in U.S. Pacific forces stationed in Japan, Korea, and the Philippines. This step was in part an effort to prevent even further reductions that the Congress might have mandated in the absence of proposals by the administration. In order to cushion this step, Secretary Cheney also announced that while the U.S. was reducing, it was not withdrawing. Such assurances will count for little when measured against a trend of ongoing reductions. As one reporter said in Tokyo during Secretary Cheney's February 1990 Far Eastern tour, "Signs of a diminishing U.S. role were obvious at every stop."[12] U.S. actions will be watched very carefully by Asian nations, because they are predisposed to see signs of American disengagement. This is summed up by Hudson Institute analyst Perry Wood:

> The widespread belief that the military presence of the United States and the Soviet Union will decline in the future already appears to be encouraging some regional states to assert themselves more actively in order to take advantage of the *anticipated* power vacuum [italics added].[13]

Above all, it is important that U.S. forces remain in Japan. This is so for the same reasons that they should stay in Germany. U.S. forces in Japan are the tangible sign of U.S.–Japan defense cooperation. Stationing U.S. military throughout the region, but not in Japan, would offer the unhappy appearance that U.S. forces were in Asia *because* of Japan. For the foreseeable future, Japan would undoubtedly decline an American offer to send its troops to the

United States on joint training and exercise missions. After all, Japan continues to insist on the asymmetry of the U.S.–Japan security treaty, which commits the U.S. to help Japan but does not commit Japan to help the U.S. But the time might come when an offer to bring Japanese troops to the U.S. might find favor in that proud nation.

The most compelling reason to remain in Japan is the nuclear one. A United States administration that had no U.S. forces in Japan could still assert that Japan remained under the American nuclear umbrella. But what would this assertion mean? At best, its validity would be doubtful, raising the possibility of dreadful miscalculations in a time of crisis. More likely, such an assertion would be heavily discounted by everyone, including the government of Japan, which would have no alternative but to press forward with its own nuclear weapons program.

Japan is likely to continue on its current course over the next several years. It will continue to grow stronger economically, and it will gradually expand its military power right along with its economy. This process alone will take Japan to new levels of military capability by the turn of the century. American policies can hasten this process or retard it. Given the infancy of political integration in the region, the course of wisdom is to retard this process and gain as much time as possible with which to promote the growth of democratic institutions and regional cooperation.

Tasks at Home

The past forty-five years have required vigilance, courage, expense, and a degree of creativity as the United States sought to contain the Soviet Union. But without for a moment wishing to demean the fine efforts of American leadership since World War II, one must observe that the national energy and sacrifice required for this enterprise were limited. In no year during this period did the military budget ever consume more than 11.9 percent of the American GNP. During the height of the Vietnam War the military budget never rose above 9.1 percent of the economy.

Defense Budget's Share of Gross National Product

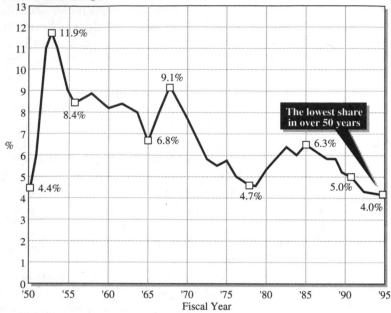

11.9%

9.1%

8.4%

6.8%

The lowest share in over 50 years

6.3%

4.4%

4.7%

5.0%

4.0%

Fiscal Year

Defense News

Including the years of the Korean and Vietnam wars, the U.S. military budget averaged approximately 6 percent of the U.S. economy between 1945 and 1990.

The United States committed a sizable force to combat in Korea and Vietnam, and substantial forces have been deployed in Europe for forty years. The United States has maintained a far-flung military, intelligence, and diplomatic network to contain the Soviet Union and its proxies. But it is also true that on no occasion did the United States ever directly confront the troops of its principal adversary in combat.[14] Since the Nixon administration, the U.S. has not had to rely on conscription to maintain its armed forces at required levels. On only two occasions—the Berlin blockade and the Cuban missile crisis—did the threat of direct conflict between the superpowers approach a serious possibility. U.S. officials acted with great resolve in both instances, but in retrospect, two flashpoints in forty-five years suggests a relatively stable form of tension.

Moreover, despite occasional bursts of concern such as the post-Sputnik educational reforms in 1957, competition with the Soviet Union never prompted any internal, domestic policy reform. We were not required to produce cars differently and better to compete with Moscow. We did not, obviously, reform our school systems to produce brighter, more innovative, or more disciplined students to compete with the Soviet Union. We did not ration goods or stockpile necessary consumer items to compete. Sporadic efforts at civil defense were never taken seriously and years ago were abandoned altogether. In short, competition with the U.S.S.R. never really challenged American life at all except in the military sphere. And this challenge could be met successfully with a military budget averaging 6 percent of GNP and a foreign military and economic assistance budget averaging less than 1 percent of GNP.

Foreign Aid
Including grants for military assistance as % of GNP

Source: Bureau of Economic Analysis

Germany and Japan already present more of an economic challenge to American technology, trade, finance, and education than the Soviet Union ever did. Meeting these challenges will not be possible by paying a 6 percent military insurance policy and expressing occasional bursts of resolve. It will demand genuine improvements in American competitiveness, and it will call for creativity, reeducation, and discipline. For Germany and Japan present organic challenges across their entire social/political/economic orders. They have not impoverished all other aspects of their societies to compete along one dimension with the United States. *Germany and Japan will offer far more thoroughgoing competition than the Soviet Union ever did.* Meeting this competition will not be easy. It will require the best efforts of Americans at all levels of life. It will require particular ingenuity from America's leaders to grasp the implications of what is occurring, and to craft domestic and foreign policies that secure the interests of America and the genuine interests of mankind.

To achieve these purposes, the United States will require two things in good measure: resources and the political will to use them. It has been the lesson of the Soviet Union's decline as a world force that a strong economic foundation is necessary for long-term competitiveness. Without this economic foundation, a nation will not in turn have the resources to compete in the international arena. In recent years the relationship between economic growth and defense spending has been questioned. The origin of this question, of course, has been Japan's economic success. Is there an inverse relationship between high defense spending and economic growth? Can nations spend themselves into failure, overemphasizing defense? At what level does this occur?

These are difficult questions to answer. At a certain level of precision, it is hard to point to decisive evidence that there is any relationship between higher defense spending and lower economic growth.[15] Those who argue that there is no negative correlation between defense spending and economic growth seem to have had the better of the argument. At some level of defense spending (perhaps that of Soviets) there will be depressing effects on economic growth. But at the levels of the U.S. military budget, it appears that American decisions about consumption vis-a-vis investment, rather than defense vis-a-vis investment, are far more significant.

Consumption is a far larger portion of the U.S. economy, and therefore proportional changes in consumption patterns have a far larger effect on the economy than proportional changes in defense spending.[16] As Harvard professor Samuel Huntington concludes, "If the United States is to increase its investment ratio significantly, that increase will have to come primarily from the 75 percent or more of the GNP devoted to consumption, not from the less than 7 percent committed to defense."[17]

This conclusion is reinforced by other anecdotal evidence. First, one can reach different conclusions depending on which countries are compared. But if the most successful economies of the modern world are included, it is impossible to find a negative correlation between defense spending and economic growth. West Germany spends three times the proportion on defense as does Japan, and this does not seem to have harmed its investment, its productivity, or its economic growth in any apparent way. The Republic of Korea and Taiwan have both spent a larger proportional share of their economies on defense than has the United States, and theirs have been among the most rapidly growing economies in the entire world.[18]

Moreover, the trend within the United States does not seem to bear out a negative relationship between economic growth and defense spending. Looked at over the years since 1950, there has been a downward trend for U.S. defense spending as a proportion of the total economy. Yet this is precisely the same period in which productivity rates, savings rates, and investment rates have declined. One cannot help but be tempted to Huntington's conclusion:

> Consumerism, not militarism, is the threat to American strength. The declinists have it wrong; Montesquieu got it right: "Republics end with luxury; monarchies with poverty."[19]

As defense spending declines as a share of the U.S. economy, which it is certain to do, the question is not how shall we use this inherently productive windfall? Rather, will we choose also to consume, rather than invest, the savings that come from defense? If we decide to consume the additional 2 percent of our economy as defense spending declines from 6 to 4 percent, we will not advantage our competitive position one whit. It cannot be said too often: it does not matter as much that we run deficits abroad or at home as it matters what we do with them. If we continue to consume too much and to invest too little, this cannot but result over time in a diminution of America's competitive position.

In short, it should remain fully possible for the United States to pay the costs of world leadership without reducing its defense spending below necessary levels—*if* the United States makes correct economic choices about consumption and investment that are unrelated to defense.

The need for strategic deterrence will continue. Indeed, as defense spending declines in real terms, this will put a premium on strategic offensive forces, which are relatively inexpensive compared with conventional forces. Deterrence will be required not only because of the maintenance of nuclear weapons and sophisticated delivery systems by the Soviet Union (which, as has been discussed, will necessarily place an even higher value on these weapons than does the United States); it also will be required by the proliferation of nuclear weapons and delivery technologies to many additional nations. It has been estimated that no fewer than fifteen countries will have the capability to produce and launch ballistic missiles by the year 2000.[20] Many of these nations will also possess chemical and/ or nuclear weapons.

Nowhere is the problem of proliferation so keen as in the Middle East. This is a highly volatile region, and one in which the United States has traditionally deployed very limited forces.[21] The Iraqi invasion of Kuwait placed the importance of the Middle East into stark relief. This is an area in which the advanced nations of the world will compete for natural resources, for markets, and for influence. It is also one populated with people who, at rock bottom, have no special fondness for European and American civilization.[22] Perhaps the oldest peoples of the world, blessed from time to time throughout history with highly cultured and developed nations, the region has seen itself fall sway to Western military domination and the imposition of Western political and social ideals. The specific European ideal of Marxism was most disliked, and as long as the Soviet Union threatened, dislike of *it* carried the day against the lesser evils embodied above all by America. Without the Soviet threat, the more generic dislike of European-based values is likely to resurface, as it began to do in the 1980s.

No nation faces more daunting prospects than Israel. In a region dominated by internecine strife,[23] there is virtually only one item of political consensus, and that is dislike of Israel. Faced by several nations with the potential to develop nuclear, chemical, and biological weapons that can be delivered at great distances, Israel faces extreme security problems over time. These problems will undoubtedly cause Israel to become overt about its own nuclear deterrent. Further, for this deterrent to be fully credible Israel must develop a variety of delivery systems, as well as locations for these systems outside its borders, most likely at sea. Even those steps, however, may not avail. For the concept of deterrence requires an opponent who is moved by fear of his own death and his own nation's devastation. In short, deterrence supposes rational, calculating opponents. Whether deterrence will function with leaders waging holy wars in which death brings eternal glory remains to be seen.

It would be wise for the stronger nations that currently possess ballistic missile and nuclear technologies to band together to prevent further proliferation. This will not be easy. For both technological and financial reasons, possession of such weapons and delivery systems is not among the most difficult objectives for developing nations to achieve. Further, trade competition between developed nations has fostered the proliferation of these technologies to interested nations. Development of a genuinely effective nonproliferation regime would require severe sanctions against offenders by *all* the strongest nations. These sanctions will have to include the possibility of military attacks against proliferation facilities if lesser sanctions like ostracism and trade embargoes fail to be persuasive.

Whether the industrialized nations of the world are prepared to adopt such a course is doubtful. The newly industrialized nations are genuinely protective of their own national prerogatives, and the threat probably does not now seem so severe as to require breaching usual diplomatic niceties. It should be a task of the present and future U.S. administrations to press hard for a genuinely aggressive nuclear nonproliferation regime, and to be prepared to accept such intrusions upon and limitations of U.S. programs as are sensibly required to achieve this end.

In the meantime, the United States should retain the best possible strategic deterrent. Because of the dangers of nuclear proliferation, and because of the greater uncertainty of deterrence in a multipolar nuclear world, the concept of strategic defense will not be, as some critics have supposed, a temporary flight of fancy. It will be an urgent security need of many nations, including especially those with a limited territory and many neighbors.[24] Indeed, it is precisely Germany, Japan, and Israel who have expressed the most interest in strategic defense and who have begun to contribute to the extraordinarily complex technologies necessary to create it.

It would be folly for the United States to turn away from research and development on strategic defense. The principal argument against it—that it would be viewed by the Soviet Union to be destabilizing—has vanished. Its need is manifest. And it is plain that other nations, particularly Germany, Japan, and Israel, will press forward with its development. Finally, it should be noted that the technologies for strategic defense—requiring rapid information processing, extreme accuracy, and lightweight, miniaturized materials—will be high-end, state-of-the-art technologies with numerous overlaps between commercial and military applications. These are precisely the kinds of technologies in which the United States must be most competitive.

Directing 4 percent of a healthy, growing economy toward defense would provide the resources necessary for the United States to serve as a strong, integrating power in Europe and East Asia; to provide a substantial force of deployable combat troops for crises elsewhere in the world; to maintain a survivable strategic offensive deterrent; and to press forward with strategic defense.

There is, however, a second question beyond resources, and that is will. Do the American people have the will to do all these things, even if it is fully within their power to do so?[25] This question has not yet been answered. During the Cold War, there was an unspoken alliance between the Left and Right to keep America involved in the world. The motives were not always the same, but the result was a working consensus in favor of the strategic triad, conventional armed forces in Europe, conventional naval and air forces in the Pacific, and even, to a point, U.S. military involvement in third world nations. This working coalition extended beyond the defense budget to foreign assistance, where each year a political alliance supporting, respectively, military assistance and economic development assistance, provided the votes for foreign aid.

It is not yet clear whether long-term support for U.S. activism abroad will be a casualty along with the Cold War. As with Germany and Japan, this is a question that will be answered in the first instance by the political party to the left of center. If the Democratic party sees in the Soviet decline only a chance to redirect defense spending into social spending, then the consensus for continuing U.S. activism abroad is in jeopardy. The temptations of isolation and protectionism are present on both the American left and the right, but they are currently stronger on the left.

For the American people to continue to support a global, political, economic, and security role, there must be a strong rationale for that involvement.[26] If Americans understand why they must remain involved, then they will most likely support that involvement. This is a task, above all, for American leaders. Leaders must define clearly and precisely the reasons for U.S. economic and political and military involvement abroad, as well as the costs of shrinking from that involvement. This has been one of the purposes of this book.

Fortune and Reason in World Affairs

Is it possible to address underlying competitive trends? Can a nation turn the course of history to its own advantage, or are underlying trends irreversible? Are we fated to dabble on the margins of the life of the world? What are the limits of human reason and human contrivance in world affairs?

Surely it is within the power of the United States to balance its budget within the next several years, and reverse the relentless growth of interest payments as a proportion of federal spending. Surely it is within the power of the United States to make marginal improvements in its balance of trade. Surely it is within the power of the United States to be able to achieve these goals while spending the 4 percent of GNP necessary to play a constructive military role in Europe and East Asia.

But even if the United States can accomplish these modest goals, some of which have been insuperable to date, can America address underlying trends and learn to compete better? The trends are not now favorable. As long as the United States continues to consume foreign goods and services far in excess of those it sends abroad, wealth will continue to slip away to Germany and Japan, opening many options for these two nations. As long as U.S. productivity and the quality of its goods and services do not improve, these trends will continue.

Democracies are often said to be poor at long-term planning. But one must look with wonder at the way in which the West German democracy suppressed its natural tendencies to unification for forty-five years in order to achieve that goal in an acceptable form. So, too, must one admire the way in which Japan has patiently suppressed and channeled its natural energy into a course that has brought it at last to the verge of true power. The United States succeeded in facing down the Soviet threat in the postwar world. But as we know now, the underlying trends were all positive, and the United States never was required to make a full-scale national effort to succeed.

Changes in the world have returned Germany and Japan to their previous status as America's principal competitors. And they are fully qualified to compete successfully in all realms of modern life, including those requiring the highest forms of training, education, and discipline. This is a matter about which no mistake should be made: *The United States cannot possibly succeed if it cedes competition in the most advanced technologies to others.* It is a formula for failure to try to carve out narrow sector-specific areas in which to compete. Competition at the margins will not produce positive results. The United States has no alternative but to accept the challenge of Germany and Japan directly and produce high-end, high-quality, competitive goods and services across the board. In some areas we will succeed better than others; it is the nature of competition that one party does not always win every event. In light of today's globally integrated trading system, no one nation can or should expect to be self-sufficient. Nevertheless, the U.S. position is slipping in virtually all of today's cutting-edge technologies. There is no escaping the fact that in Germany and Japan the United States will have highly capable and worthy competitors, and the challenges they present must be met directly.

It is frequently observed that the problems of American competitiveness derive from the fact that the time horizon of American business is too short. Business decisions, it is said, are too often made on the basis of the next fiscal quarter's profitability, not upon longer-term considerations of corporate health. This may be true, but it is no truer of American business than it is of every other sector of American life. Indeed, it is ironic that this charge against American business is most frequently made by the true perfecter of the short time horizon, the American politician. There is today no area of American life that operates upon so brief a period for gratification as does the political sector. Institutions that are supposed to draw men and women out of their narrow calculations are now serving precisely the opposite end. Contemporary American politics puts an irresistible premium on short-term calculations of success and failure. The moment-to-moment approach is the American way. But as George Kennan said so wisely nearly a half-century ago:

> A nation which excuses its own failures by the sacred untouchableness of its own habits can excuse itself into complete disaster.[27]

Can the United States retain its relative strength in the world, or is it destined to lose ground to its principal competitors? Despite the rhetoric of politicians, it is not possible to answer this question in theory until it has been answered in practice. Germany and Japan will grow stronger and more competitive, that much seems clear. We have no way to prevent that, even if we wished to do so. But there is no reason to wish to do so. Germany and Japan have been the greatest success stories of postwar American foreign policy. Nowhere else has American guidance and American assistance so fully succeeded, either before or since, as it did in these two instances.

We cannot know for certain what Germany and Japan will intend to accomplish with their newfound power. It is one thesis of this book that Germany and Japan do not themselves know this yet either. But it is the course of wisdom always to distinguish between capability, which one can measure, and intent, which, like all matters of the heart, is difficult to read. Prudence requires one to remember that great powers like Germany and Japan have many options.

Germany, Japan, and America each have unique tasks and roles to play in bringing a new, stable, and peaceful order into being. Much nonsense has been written over the years about Germany's so-called special way. Germany's role is emphatically *not* to create a "third way" between capitalism and socialism, as so many of its left-leaning thinkers have urged. It has atonement enough to do for exporting the distinctly German philosophical system of Karl Marx, which has both caused and rationalized so much human suffering. Nor is Germany's role to criticize the modern industrial economy from the standpoint of a simpler, more pastoral life. This is a re-packaged version of something that has been seen before in German history, and it has never produced good politics.

Germany's role is to prove that it is possible to transcend the nation-state system in Europe in a way that does full justice and respect to its neighbors. The words of one of Germany's philosophers, Friedrich Nietzsche, remain apt a century after they were written: "The only way to use the present kind of German power correctly is to comprehend the tremendous obligation which lies in it."

So, too, with Japan. As the target of the only two nuclear weapons ever used in anger, Japan sometimes has been held up as a nation that has a special role to play in nuclear disarmament. To be polite, it is hard to follow the logic of this view. Like Germany, modern Japan has expressed strong integrating tendencies in its region. Its task is not to prove its superior suitability for that mission. That much could be granted.

Japan's task is to genuinely overcome its own insular tendencies and to learn at last how to reconcile being Japanese with being citizens of the world.

These are large tasks that run directly up against strong elements of the national character of Germany and Japan as that character has been displayed to date. The American task is no less at odds with its character. It is to undertake a long and difficult assignment that requires both foreign involvement and domestic sacrifice, and for which there is no immediate payoff. Twice in the twentieth century the United States paid for its insularity in world wars. When it chose to lead, as it did throughout the Cold War, conflict was prevented. Now when the United States is tempted to lay down the burdens of leadership, it must instead pick itself up and press its friends and itself into creating new institutions.

The stakes today are as high as they have ever been. Shall there be no more war among the great nations of the world because weapons of mass destruction have made war unthinkable? Perhaps. But it is well to recall the many treatises prior to 1914 which argued that the new weapons of the time were so terrifying and so destructive that war was no longer possible.[28] As the first among equals of the new great powers that arose in the twentieth century, the United States has a special responsibility to transcend wishful thinking and to help bring into existence a new international order that offers the prospect of lasting peace.

Each generation finds a different world than that of its parents. But it is the tendency of new generations to see only the differences and never the similarities. It is a dangerous seduction that we live in an altogether new and different world. The question is not how to comport ourselves in a wholly new world. It is, rather, as this long and often difficult century draws to a close, have we learned anything at all?

SELECTED READINGS

What follows is a list of selected books and articles for further reading on the topics of this book. No effort has been made at completeness. Many of the sources are very recent, reflecting the great changes that have taken place in the last several years.

SOVIET UNION

Aganbegyan, Abel. *The Economic Challenge of Perestroika*. Bloomington: Indiana University Press, 1988.

Aslund, Anders. *Gorbachev's Struggle for Economic Reform*. Ithaca: Cornell University Press, 1989.

Baker, James. "Imperatives of Economic Reform: Change in Soviet and East European Economies." Testimony to the Ways and Means Committee, House of Representatives. Washington, D.C.: 18 Apr. 1990.

Bialer, Seweryn. *Stalin's Successors: Leadership, Stability, and Change in the Soviet Union*. Cambridge: Cambridge University Press, 1980.

Boskin, Michael. "Problems in Measuring the Size of the Soviet Economy." Testimony to the Committee on Foreign Relations, United States Senate. Washington, D.C.: 16 July 1990.

Brzezinski, Zbigniew. "Post-Communist Nationalism." *Foreign Affairs*, 68(5) (Winter 1989–1990): 1–25.

The Central Intelligence Agency and Defense Intelligence Agency. "The Soviet Economy Stumbles Badly in 1989." Report presented to the Technology and National Security Subcommittee, Joint Economic Committee of the Congress. Washington, D.C.: 20 Apr. 1990.

Cobb, Tyrus, ed., *Whither Gorbachev?* Alexandria, Va.: Center for Naval Analyses, 1989.

Crook, Clive. "A Survey of Perestroika." *The Economist*, 28 Apr. 1990, pp. 1–22.

Dukes, Paul. *The Last Great Game: USA Versus USSR*. New York: St. Martin's, 1989.

Eberstadt, Nicholas, and Jonathan Tombes. "The Soviet Economy: How Big?" *The American Enterprise*, July–Aug., 1990, pp. 76–80.

The Fading Threat: Soviet Conventional Military Power in Decline. Report of the Defense Policy Panel of the Committee on Armed Services, House of Representatives. Washington, D.C.: 9 July 1990.

Gaddis, John Lewis. *The Long Peace*. Oxford: Oxford University Press, 1988.

General Secretary Mikhail Gorbachev and the Soviet Military: Assessing His Impact and the Potential for Future Changes. Report of the Defense Policy Panel of the Committee on Armed Services, House of Representatives. Washington, D.C.: 13 Sept. 1988.

Glynn, Patrick, ed. *Unrest in the Soviet Union*. Washington, D.C.: American Institute, 1989.

Goldman, Marshall I. "Gorbachev the Economist." *Foreign Affairs*, 69(2) (Spring 1990): 28–44.

Goldman, Marshall I. *The U.S.S.R. in Crisis: The Failure of an Economic System*. New York: Norton, 1983.

Hough, Jerry F. "Gorbachev's Politics." *Foreign Affairs*, 68(5) (Winter 1989–1990): 26–41.

Kaiser, Robert G. "The U.S.S.R. in Decline." *Foreign Affairs*, 67(2) (Winter 1988–1989): 97–113.

Larrabee, F. Stephen. "Gorbachev and the Soviet Military," *Foreign Affairs*, 66(5) (Summer 1988): 1002–1026.

Lee, William T. Testimony on the Soviet Economy to the Committee on Foreign Relations, United States Senate. Washington, D.C.: 16 July 1990.

Newhouse, John. *War and Peace in the Nuclear Age*. New York: Random House, 1990.

1989 Joint Military Net Assessment. Washington, D.C.: Department of Defense, 1989.

Odom, William E. "Soviet Military Doctrine." *Foreign Affairs*, 67(2) (Winter 1988–1989): 114–134.

Rowen, Henry, and Charles Wolf, Jr., eds. *The Future of the Soviet Empire*. New York: St. Martin's, 1988.

Soviet Military Power. Prospects for Change. 1989. Washington, D.C.: Department of Defense, 1989.

Soviet Readiness for War: Assessing One of the Major Sources of East–West Instability. Report of the Defense Policy Panel of the Committee on Armed Services, House of Representatives. Washington, D.C.: 5 Dec. 1988.

"The Soviet Union." *Financial Times Survey*. 12 Mar. 1990, sec. 3, pp. 1–20.

"Soviet Views on National Security Issues in the 1990's." Hearing before the Committee on Armed Services, House of Representatives. Washington, D.C., 1989.

GERMANY

General

Backer, John H. *Winds of History: The German Years of Lucius DuBignon Clay*. New York: Van Nostrand, 1983.

Baring, Arnulf. *Unser neuer Grössenwahn: Deutschland zwischen Ost und West*. Stuttgart: Deutsche Verlags-Anstalt, 1989.

Bark, Dennis L., and David R Gress. *A History of West Germany*. 2 vols. London: Basil Blackwell, 1989.

Barzini, Luigi. *The Europeans*. New York: Simon and Schuster, 1983.

Bertram, Christoph. "The German Question," *Foreign Affairs*, 69(2) (Spring 1990): 45–62.

Calleo, David P. *The German Problem Reconsidered: Germany and the World Order, 1970 to the Present*. Cambridge: Cambridge University Press, 1978.

Craig, Gordon A. *Germany, 1866–1945*. Oxford: Clarendon Press, 1978.

Grant, Charles. "A Survey of the European Community." *The Economist*, 7 July 1990, pp. 1–40.

Hanrieder, Wolfram F. *Germany, America, Europe: Forty Years of German Foreign Policy*. New Haven: Yale University Press, 1989.

Hanrieder, Wolfram F. *West German Foreign Policy: 1949–1963*. Stanford: Stanford University Press, 1967.

James, Harold. *A German Identity, 1770–1990*. New York: Routledge, 1989.

Kennan, George F. *The German Problem: A Personal View*. Washington, D.C.: Institute for Contemporary German Studies, 1989.

Langguth, Gerd. "German Unification and European Integration." Washington, D.C.: Konrad Adenauer Foundation, June 1990.

Larrabee, F. Stephen, ed. *The Two German States and European Security*. New York: St. Martin's, 1989.

Marsh, David. *The Germans: Rich, Bothered and Divided*. London: Century, 1989.

Merkl, Peter H. *The Federal Republic of Germany at Forty*. New York: New York University Press, 1989.

Nawrocki, Joachim. *Relations Between the Two States in Germany*. Bonn: Press and Information Office of the Federal Republic of Germany.

Stern, Fritz. *The German–American Century*. New York: The German Forum, 1988.

Turner, Henry Ashby, Jr. *The Two Germanies Since 1945*. New Haven: Yale University Press, 1987.

Economics

"Federal Republic of Germany," *Foreign Economic Trends and Their Implications for the United States*. Washington, D.C.: Department of Commerce, February 1990.

"German Democratic Republic," *Foreign Economic Trends and Their Implications for the United States*. Washington, D.C.: Department of Commerce, February 1989.

Grant, Charles. "A Survey of the European Community." *The Economist*, 7 July 1990, pp. 1–40.

Holliday, George. "Eastern Europe: International Implications of Economic Reforms." Washington, D.C.: Congressional Research Service, 27 Dec. 1989.

Jeffries, Ian, and Manfred Melzer, eds. *The East German Economy*. London: Croom Helm, 1987.

Katzenstein, Peter J., ed. *Industry and Politics in West Germany: Toward the Third Republic*. Cornell: Cornell University Press, 1989.

Miko, Francis T. "East European Reform and U.S. Policy." Washington, D.C.: Congressional Research Service, 29 Dec. 1989.

Politics

Buckley, Anne-Marie. "The Once and Future German Question." *Foreign Affairs*, 68(5) (Winter 1989–1990): 65–83.

Craig, Gordon A. *From Bismarck to Adenauer: Aspects of German Statecraft*. Baltimore: Johns Hopkins Press, 1958.

Democracy in Germany: History and Perspectives. Bonn: Press and Information Office of the Federal Republic of Germany, 1985.

Edinger, Lewis Joachim. *Politics in West Germany*. Boston: Little, Brown, 1977.

Hamilton, Daniel. *After the Revolution: The New Political Landscape in East Germany*. Washington, D.C.: American Institute for Contemporary German Studies, 1990.

Herf, Jeffrey. "A Political Culture in Crisis: The Case for Kohl." *The National Interest*, no. 17 (Fall 1989): 55–62.

Hunter, Robert E. "Berlin: Forty Years On." *Foreign Affairs*, 68(3) (Summer 1989): 41–52.

Katzenstein, Peter J. *Policy and Politics in West Germany: The Growth of a Semisovereign State*. Philadelphia: Temple University Press, 1987.

Langguth, Gerd. *Berlin and the "German Question:" The Berlin Policy of the German Democratic Republic*. Boulder, Colorado: Westview, 1990.

Livingston, Robert G., ed. *West German Political Parties*. Washington, D.C.: American Institute for Contemporary German Studies, 1986.

Luuk, Ernst. *East Berlin*. Berlin: Berlin Information Center, 1988.

Noelle-Neumann, Elizabeth. "Main Currents of Opinion in the Federal Republic of Germany," paper delivered to a Conference on the Future of Germany. Indianapolis: Hudson Institute, June 18–19, 1990.

Smith, Gordon, William E. Peterson, and Peter H. Merkl, eds. *Developments in West German Politics*. Durham, N.C.: Duke University Press, 1989.

Stern, Fritz. *The Failure of Illiberalism: Essays on the Political Culture of Modern Germany*. New York: Knopf, 1972.

Vogel, Bernhard, and Hans-Joachim Veen. "Extremism on the Rise? The New Challenges Facing the Major Parties in the Federal Republic of Germany." Bonn: Konrad Adenauer Stiftung, 1989.

Military

Abenheim, Donald. *Reforging the Iron Cross*. Princeton: Princeton University Press, 1988.

Asmus, Ronald D. "A United Germany." *Foreign Affairs*, 69(2) (Spring 1990): 63–76.

Calleo, David P. *Beyond American Hegemony: The Future of the Western Alliance*. New York: Basic Books, 1987.

Gordon, Lincoln, and Timothy W. Stanley. *Integrating Economic and Security Factors in East–West Relations*. Washington, D.C.: The Atlantic Council, 1988.

Joffe, Josef. "The Revisionists: Moscow, Bonn, and the European Balance." *The National Interest*, no. 17 (Fall 1989): 41–54.

Kelleher, Catherine McArdle. *Germany and the Politics of Nuclear Weapons*. New York: Columbia University Press, 1975.

Layne, Christopher. "Atlanticism Without NATO." *Foreign Policy*, no. 67 (Summer 1987): 22–45.

Lind, Michael. "German Fate and Allied Fears." *The National Interest*, no. 19 (Spring 1990): 34–44.

Odom, William E., "Germany, America, and Europe in the 1990's: The Strategic Connections." Alexandria, Virginia: Hudson Institute, May, 1990.

Owen, Henry, and Edward C. Meyer. "Central European Security." *Foreign Affairs*, 68(3) (Summer 1989): 22–40.

Schmidt, Helmut. *A Grand Strategy for the West: The Anachronism of National Strategies in an Interdependent World*. New Haven: Yale University Press, 1985.

Scholz, Rupert. "Deutsche Frage und europaische Sicherheit. Sicherheitspolitik in einem sich einigenden Deutschland und Europa." *Europa Archiv: Zeitschrift für Internationale Politik*, no. 7 (10 Apr. 1990): 239–246.

Weinberg, Gerhard L. "The Nazi–Soviet Pacts: A Half-Century Later." *Foreign Affairs*, 68(4) (Fall 1989): 175–189.

JAPAN

General

Brock, David. "The Theory and Practice of Japan-Bashing." *The National Interest*, no. 17 (Fall 1989): 29–40.

Buruma, Ian. *God's Dust: A Modern Asian Journey*. New York: Farrar, Strauss, Giroux, 1989.

Christopher, Robert C. *The Japanese Mind*. New York: Fawcett Columbine, 1983.

Emmerson, John K., and Harrison M. Holland. *The Eagle and the Rising Sun*. Reading, Mass.: Addison-Wesley, 1988.

Glaubitz, Joachim. "Die Sowjetunion und Japan." *Europa Archiv: Zeitschrift für Internationale Politik*, no. 20 (10 Oct. 1989): 611–618.

Holbrooke, Richard. "East Asia: The Next Challenge." *Foreign Affairs*, no. 64 (Spring 1986): 732–751.

Iriye, Akira, and Warren I. Cohen. *The United States and Japan in the Postwar World*. Lexington: University Press of Kentucky, 1989.

Ito, Kan. "Trans-Pacific Anger." *Foreign Policy*, no. 78 (Spring 1990): 131–152.

Johnson, Chalmers. "Their Behavior, Our Policy." *The National Interest*, no. 17 (Fall 1989): 17–27.

Kahn, Herman. *The Emerging Japanese Superstate: Challenge and Response*. Englewood Cliffs, N.J.: Prentice-Hall, 1970.

Makin, John H., and Donald C. Hellman, eds. *Sharing World Leadership? A New Era for America and Japan*. Washington, D.C.: American Enterprise Institute, 1989.

Mansfield, Mike. "The U.S. and Japan: Sharing our Destinies." *Foreign Affairs*, 68(2) (Spring 1989): 3–15.

Niksch, Larry A. *Japan–U.S. Relations in the 1990's*. Congressional Research Service Report for Congress. Washington, D.C.: Library of Congress, 7 Apr. 1989.

Okimoto, Daniel I., and Thomas P. Rohlen, eds. *Inside the Japanese System: Readings on Contemporary Society and Political Economy*. Stanford: Stanford University Press, 1988.

Reischauer, Edwin. *The Japanese*. Cambridge: The Belknap Press, 1977.

Scalapino, Robert A. "Asia's Future." *Foreign Affairs*, 66(1) (Fall 1987): 77–108.

Scalapino, Robert A. *The Politics of Development: Perspectives on Twentieth Century Asia*. Cambridge: Harvard University Press, 1989.

Schaller, Michael. *The American Occupation of Japan: The Origins of the Cold War in Asia*. New York: Oxford University Press, 1985.

van Wolferen, Karel G. "The Japan Problem." *Foreign Affairs*, 65(2) (Winter 1986–1987): 288–303.

Vogel, Ezra. *Japan as Number One*. Cambridge: Harvard University Press, 1979.

Economics

Burstein, Daniel. *Yen! Japan's New Financial Empire and Its Threat to America.* New York: Fawcett Columbine, 1990.

Drucker, Peter F. "Japan's Choices." *Foreign Affairs*, 65(5) (Summer 1987): 923–941.

"Japan." *Foreign Labor Trends.* Washington, D.C.: Department of Labor, 1988–1989.

Johnson, Chalmers. *MITI and the Japanese Miracle: The Growth of Industrial Policy, 1925–1975.* Stanford: Stanford University Press, 1982.

Johnson, Chalmers, Laura D'Andrea Tyson, and John, Zysman, eds. *Politics and Productivity: How Japan's Development Strategy Works.* Cambridge: Ballinger, 1989.

Linder, Staffan Burenstam. *The Pacific Century: Economic and Political Consequences of Asian-Pacific Dynamism.* Stanford: Stanford University Press, 1986.

May, Bernhard. *Japans neue Entwicklungspolitik: Entwicklungshilfe und japanische Aussenpolitik.* Munich: R. Oldenbourg, 1989.

Nester, William R. *Japan's Growing Power over East Asia and the World Economy.* New York: St. Martin's, 1990.

Packard, George R. "The Coming U.S.–Japan Crisis." *Foreign Affairs*, 66(2) (1987): 348–367.

Pepper, Thomas, Merit E. Janow, and Jimmy W. Wheeler. *The Competition: Dealing with Japan.* New York: Praeger, 1985.

Prestowitz, Clyde V., Jr. *Trading Places: How We Allowed Japan to Take the Lead.* New York: Basic Books, 1988.

Spencer, Edson W. "Japan as Competitor." *Foreign Policy*, no. 78 (Spring 1990): 153–171.

United States International Trade Commission. *Pros and Cons of Initiating Negotiations With Japan to Explore the Possibilities of a U.S.–Japan Free Trade Area Agreement.* Report to the Senate Committee on Finance. Washington, D.C.: September, 1988.

Valery, Nicholas. "Thinking Ahead. A Survey of Japanese Technology." *The Economist*, 2 Dec. 1989, pp. 1–18.

Vogel, Ezra F. "Pax Nipponica." *Foreign Affairs*, 64(4) (Spring 1986): 752–767.

Politics

Berger, Gordon M. *Parties Out of Power in Japan, 1931–1941.* Princeton: Princeton University Press, 1977.

Bingman, Charles F. *Japanese Government Leadership and Management.* New York: St. Martin's, 1989.

Calder, Kent E. *Crisis and Compensation: Public Policy and Political Stability in Japan, 1949–1986.* Princeton: Princeton University Press, 1988.

Crowley, James B. *Japan's Quest for Autonomy: National Security and Foreign Policy, 1930–1938.* Princeton: Princeton University Press, 1966.

Curtis, Gerald L. *The Japanese Way of Politics.* New York: Columbia University Press, 1988.

Hall, J.W. *Government and Local Power in Japan.* Princeton: Princeton University Press, 1966.

Iriye, Akira. *Power and Culture: The Japanese American War, 1941–1945.* Cambridge: Harvard University Press, 1981.

McNelly, Theodore. *Politics and Government in Japan.* Lanham, Maryland: University Press of America, 1984.

Pempel, T.J. *Policy and Politics in Japan: Creative Conservatism.* Philadelphia: Temple University Press, 1982.

Scalapino, Robert A. *Democracy and the Party Movement in Prewar Japan, The Failure of the First Attempt.* Berkeley: University of California Press, 1962.

Scalapino, Robert A. "Elections and Political Modernization in Prewar Japan," in *Political Development in Modern Japan*, ed. Robert E. Ward. Princeton: Princeton University Press, 1968, pp. 249–291.

van Wolferen, Karel G. *The Enigma of Japanese Power.* New York: Alfred A. Knopf, 1989.

Military

Barnhart, Michael A. *Japan Prepares for Total War: The Search for Economic Security, 1919–1941.* Ithaca, N.Y.: Cornell University Press, 1987.

Brown, Harold. *U.S.–Japan Relations: Technology, Economics, and Security.* U.S./Japan Economic Agenda. New York: Carnegie Council on Ethics and International Affairs, 1987.

Defense Industrial Cooperation with Pacific Rim Nations. Report of the Defense Science Board of the Department of Defense. Washington, D.C.: October 1989.

Defense of Japan, 1989. Tokyo: Japan Defense Agency, 1989.

Drifte, Reinhard. *Arms Production in Japan: The Military Applications of Civilian Technology.* Boulder, Colo.: Westview Press, 1986.

Ezell, Virginia H. "Japan's Space Program Takes Off." *Journal of Defense and Diplomacy*, Sept. 1988, pp. 16–19.

Freudenstein, Roland. "Die FSX-Kontroverse zwischen den USA und Japan." *Europa Archiv: Zeitschrift für Internationale Politik*, no. 18 (25 Sept. 1989): 553–560.

George, Aurelia. *The Nakasone Challenge: Historical Constraints and New Initiatives in Japan's Defense Policy*. Commonwealth of Australia, Department of the Parliamentary Library: Legislative Research Service, Discussion Paper No. 2, 1986–1987.

Iklé, Fred, and Terumasa Nakanishi. "Japan's Grand Strategy." *Foreign Affairs*, 69(3) (Summer 1990): 81–95.

Kataoka, Tetsuya, and Ramon H. Myers. *Defending an Economic Superpower: Reassessing the U.S.–Japan Security Alliance*. Boulder, Colo.: Westview Press, 1989.

McIntosh, Malcolm. *Japan Re-armed*. New York: St. Martin's, 1986.

Moteff, John D. *FSX Technology: Its Relative Utility to the United States and Japanese Aerospace Industries*. Congressional Research Service Report for Congress. Washington, D.C.: Library of Congress, 12 Apr. 1989.

Olsen, Edward A. *U.S.–Japan Strategic Reciprocity: A Neo-Internationalist View*. Stanford: Hoover Institution Press, 1985.

Reynolds, Gary K. *Japan's Military Buildup: Goals and Accomplishments*. Congressional Research Service Report for Congress. Washington, D.C.: Library of Congress, 27 Jan. 1989.

Samuels, Richard, and Benjamin Whipple. *Defense Production and Industrial Development: The Case of Japanese Aircraft*. MIT-Japan Science and Technology Program. Cambridge, Mass.: Massachusetts Institute of Technology, 1988.

"United States–Japanese Security Cooperation and the FSX Agreement." Washington, D.C.: House of Representatives, Committee on Foreign Affairs, 13 Apr., 3, 9, 10, 18, 23 May, 1989.

Wheeler, Jimmy W., and Perry L. Wood. *ASEAN and Southeast Asian Security in the 1990's: Implications for U.S. Interests*. Indianapolis, Indiana: Hudson Institute, 1989.

Wolfowitz, Paul. Statement presented to the Armed Services Committee, United States Senate. Washington, D.C., 19 Apr. 1990.

GENERAL READING

Bator, Francis M. "Must We Retrench?" *Foreign Affairs*, 68(2) (Spring 1989): 93–123.

Brown, Seyom. *New Forces, Old Forces and the Future of World Politics*. Glenview, Illinois: Scott Foresman, 1988.

Brzezinski, Zbigniew. "Beyond Chaos: A Policy for the West." *The National Interest*, no. 19 (Spring 1990): 3–12.

Costello, Robert B. *Bolstering Defense Industrial Competitiveness*. A Report to the Secretary of Defense. Washington, D.C.: Department of Defense, July, 1988.

Drucker, Peter F. *The New Realities*. New York: Harper and Row, 1989.

Fallows, James. *More Like Us: Making America Great Again*. Boston: Houghton-Mifflin, 1989.

Fukuyama, Francis. "The End of History?" *The National Interest*, no. 16 (Summer 1989): 3–18.

Garten, Jeffery E. "Japan and Germany: American Concerns." *Foreign Affairs*, 68(5) (Winter 1989–1990): 84–101.

Hart, Gary. "Enlightened Engagement: A Foreign Policy for the 21st Century." Lectures to Georgetown School of Foreign Service, 11, 12, 13 June, 1986.

Huntington, Samuel P. "The U.S.—Decline or Renewal?" *Foreign Affairs*, 67(2) (Winter 1988–1989): 76–96.

Hyland, William G. "America's New Course." *Foreign Affairs*, 69(2) (Spring 1990): 1–12.

Iklé, Fred. "The Ghost in the Pentagon: Rethinking America's Defense." *The National Interest*, no. 19 (Spring 1990): 13–20.

Kennan, George F. *American Diplomacy: 1900–1950*. Chicago: University of Chicago Press, 1951.

Kennedy, Paul. *The Rise and Fall of the Great Powers*. New York: Random House, 1987.

Kissinger, Henry, and Cyrus Vance. "Bipartisan Objectives for Foreign Policy." *Foreign Affairs*, 66(5) (Summer 1988): 899–921.

Luttwak, Edward N. "From Geopolitics to Geo-Economics," *The National Interest*, no. 20 (Summer, 1990): 17–23.

Maynes, Charles William. "America Without the Cold War." *Foreign Policy*, no. 78 (Spring 1990): 3–25.

McNamara, Robert S. *Out of the Cold: New Thinking for American Foreign and Defense Policy in the 21st Century*. New York: Simon and Schuster, 1989.

Mearsheimer, John J. "Why We Will Soon Miss the Cold War." *The Atlantic*, August 1990, pp. 35–50.

Nau, Henry R. *The Myth of America's Decline. Leading the World Economy into the 1990's*. New York: Oxford University Press, 1990.

Nunn, Sam. *Nunn 1990: A New Military Strategy*. Washington, D.C.: Center for Strategic and International Studies, 1990.

Nye, Joseph S., Jr. *Bound to Lead: The Changing Nature of American Power*. New York: Basic Books, 1989.

Samuelson, Paul A. "America's True Decline, without Exaggeration or False Optimism." Testimony presented to the Committee on Banking, Housing, and Urban Affairs, United States Senate. Washington, D.C., 15 Nov. 1989.

Schlesinger, James. *America at Century's End*. New York: Columbia University Press, 1989.

Shultz, George. "New Realities and New Ways of Thinking." *Foreign Affairs*, 64(4) (Spring 1985): 705–721.

Sorensen, Theodore C. "Rethinking National Security." *Foreign Affairs*, 69(3) (Summer 1990): 1–18.

Steinbrenner, John D., ed. *Restructuring American Foreign Policy*. Washington, D.C.: Brookings Institution, 1988.

Tarnoff, Peter. "America's New Special Relationships." *Foreign Affairs*, 69(3) (Summer 1990): 67–80.

Tonelson, Alan. "A Manifesto for Democrats." *The National Interest*, no. 16 (Summer 1989): 36–48.

Vlahos, Michael. "The End of America's Postwar Ethos." *Foreign Affairs*, 66(5) (Summer 1988): 1091–1107.

von Laue, Theodore H. *The World Revolution of Westernization*. Oxford: Oxford University Press, 1988.

NOTES

PREFACE

1. Consider, for example, what sense it would make to refer to Kaiser Wilhelm's Germany or the Germany of the 1930s as "neutral." It has been well said that "a big power claiming neutrality is like a lorry pretending to be a hedgehog" ("Neutrality's Identity Crisis," *Economist*, 3 Feb. 1990, p. 18).

2. *Trade and Development Report, 1989*. Part 2: *The Least Developed Countries* (New York: United Nations, 1990), p. 2. According to this report, gross domestic production (GDP) per capita in developed nations grew from $9,838 to $11,080 (in constant 1986 dollars) between 1980 and 1986. In that same period GDP in the least developed countries declined from $227 to $221.

INTRODUCTION

1. Secretary of War Henry Stimson stated: "I felt it was of great importance to get the homeland into our hands before the Russians could put in any substantial claim to occupy and help rule it." Quoted in John Newhouse, *War and Peace in the Nuclear Age* (New York: Alfred A. Knopf, 1988), p. 49.

2. Paul Kennedy, *The Rise and Fall of the Great Powers* (New York: Random House, 1987), p. 325.

3. Ibid., pp. 332–333: "An increase in the defense-spending share of the American GNP to bring it close to the proportions devoted to armaments by the fascist states would automatically make the United States the most powerful military state in the world. There are, moreover, many indications that Berlin and Tokyo realized how such a development would constrict their opportunities for future expansion. . . . [Hitler] sensed that he dared not wait until the mid-1940s to resume his conquests, since the military balance would by then have decisively swung to the Anglo-French-American camp. On the Japanese side, because the United States was taken more seriously, the calculations were more precise: thus the Japanese Navy estimated that whereas its warship strength would be a respectable 70 percent of the American navy in 1941, 'this would fall to 65 percent in 1942, to 50 percent in 1943, and to a disastrous 30 percent in 1944.' "

4. George Shultz, "New Realities and New Ways of Thinking," *Foreign Affairs*, 64(4) (Spring 1985): 709.

5. See *1989 Joint Military Net Assessment* (Washington, D.C.: Department of Defense, 1989); see also William E. Odom, "Soviet Military Doctrine," *Foreign Affairs*, 67(2) (Winter 1988–1989): 114–134.

6. See, for example, Stephen F. Larrabee, "Gorbachev and the Soviet Military," *Foreign Affairs*, 66(5) (Summer 1988): 1002–1026.

7. Clive Crook, "A Survey of Perestroika," *Economist*, 28 Apr. 1990, p. 5.

8. See the summary in "The Soviet Union," *Financial Times Survey*, 12 Mar. 1990, sec. 3, p. IX.

9. William T. Lee, Testimony on the Soviet Economy to the Committee on Foreign Relations, United States Senate, 16 July 1990, pp. 2–3.

10. Ibid, p. 3. Lee estimates, for example, that Soviet military spending increased from 10–11 percent of GNP in 1970 to 11–18 percent in 1985–1988.

11. See Tyrus Cobb, ed., *Whither Gorbachev?* (Alexandria, Va.: Center for Naval Analysis, 1989), pp. 1–5, and William T. Lee, Testimony on Soviet Economy, p. 3.

12. U.S. Central Intelligence Agency and U.S. Defense Intelligence Agency, *The Soviet Economy Stumbles Badly in 1989*, report to Technology and National Security Subcommittee, Joint Economic Committee of the Congress, 20 April 1990. See also Lee, Testimony on Soviet Economy, p. 5. The Soviet government itself reported a 2 percent decline in gross national product in 1990.

13. CIA/DIA, *Soviet Economy Stumbles*.

14. Ibid, p. 13.

15. See an interesting article, "Oil Decline Fueled the Rise of Gorbachev's 'New Thinking,' " *Washington Post*, 28 May 1990, p. A1. The article develops the theme that "the Soviet oil boom, fueled by rapidly rising oil prices after the 1973 Arab-Israeli war, coincided with the start of a much more activist Soviet policy toward the Third World" (p. A18).

16. CIA/DIA, *Soviet Economy Stumbles*, p. 14.

17. Ibid., p. 14.

18. See, for example, Robert Kaiser, "The U.S.S.R. in Decline," *Foreign Affairs*, 67(2) (Winter 1988–1989): 103: "Soviet economists make no attempt to disguise the severity of the problems the country faces. One could scour the institutes in Moscow and not find an economist who thinks that perestroika or any other imaginable reform will give the Soviet Union a world-class industrial capability in this century, or in the next generation. Structural shortcomings are compounded by technological ones. The Soviet Union did not keep up with the rapid technological change of the last generation—it has missed out almost entirely on the computer revolution—and has no infrastructure to enable it to catch up now. For example, the primitive telephone system, which still only reaches a fraction of the population, is incapable of transmitting computer data. There is no reason to expect that at any time in the foreseeable future the Russians will be able to match the industrial culture of the Taiwanese, let alone the Japanese or the Germans."

19. Lee, Testimony on Soviet Economy, p. 6, concludes it was flat; CIA/DIA, *Soviet Economy Stumbles*, p. 11, concludes that a 4 percent reduction occurred.

20. Measuring the Soviet economy is a notoriously difficult task. Estimates have judged it to be 51 percent the size of the American economy (CIA), 57 percent (Robert Summers and Alan Heston), 33.6 percent (Yuri Dikhanov), and 14 percent (Victor Belkin). See: George Kolt, *Estimates of the Soviet Economy*, testimony of the Central Intelligence Agency to the Committee on Foreign Relations, United States Senate, 16 July 1990; William T. Lee, Testimony on Soviet Economy; Michael Boskin, *Problems in Measuring the Size of the Soviet Economy*, testimony to the Committee on Foreign Relations, United States Senate, 16 July 1990; and Nicholas Eberstadt and Jonathan Tombes, "The Soviet Economy: How Big?" *American Enterprise*, July/August 1990, pp. 77–80. For present purposes we will adopt Michael Boskin's general conclusion: "Soviet GNP is probably about one-third of U.S. GNP."

21. This issue has been considered in detail by many knowledgeable authors. For a good brief commentary, see Zbigniew Brzezinski, "Post-Communist Nationalism," *Foreign Affairs*, 68(5) (Winter 1989–1990): 1–25.

CHAPTER 1

1. Michael Stürmer, "The Ambivalence of a United Allied Presence in a Divided Germany," *Frankfurter Allgemeine Zeitung für Deutschland*, 16 June 1988.

2. Ibid., p. 4.

3. Quoted in Klaus Gotto, "A Realist and Visionary: Konrad Adenauer's Reunification Policy," *German Comments*, June 1990, p. 30.

4. John Backer, *Winds of History: The German Years of Lucius DuBignon Clay* (New York: Van Nostrand, 1983), p. 34.

5. Quoted in "Texts," in Joachim Nawrocki, *Relations Between the Two States in Germany* (Bonn: Press and Information Office of the Federal Republic of Germany), p. 100.

6. Ibid, pp. 100, 101.

7. Ibid., p. 102

8. Ibid., p. 99.

9. Quoted in Backer, *Winds of History*, p. 35.

10. "Texts," in Nawrocki, *Relations*, p. 106.

11. See U.S. Department of State, "German Democratic Republic," *Background Notes* (Washington, D.C., June 1987), p. 6. See also Henry Ashby Turner, Jr., *The Two Germanies Since 1945* (New Haven: Yale University Press, 1987), p. 13.

12. Backer, *Winds of History*, p. 40.

13. George Kennan still thought in 1949 that there was good sense in a further effort to secure a unified, but neutral and demilitarized Germany. See his lecture *The German Problem: A Personal View* (Washington, D.C.: American Institute for Contemporary German Studies, 1989).

14. This pledge was reaffirmed when the Federal Republic of Germany signed the Nuclear Nonproliferation Treaty.

15. David Morrison, "Germany's Future," *National Journal*, 5 Dec. 1987, p. 3118.

16. In response to the question whether "within a foreseeable time span a reunification of the Federal Republic and the G.D.R. will come about," 13 percent of West Germans answered affirmatively in 1972, 5 percent in 1984, and 3 percent in 1987. This declining confidence in reunification was not matched by a decline in the *desire* for reunification, which remained steady at 78 to 80 percent of the West German population. *Economist*, 28 Oct. 1989, p. 9.

17. Laszlo Kovacs, Deputy Foreign Minister of Hungary, said about his informal contacts with the Soviet Union, "We didn't specify, but we hinted. I was one of the men involved. We put it in such a way, that if things would go like they did, finally there would be no other choice for Hungary but just to let the East Germans go." Quoted in Blaine Harden, "Refugees Force a Fateful Choice," *Washington Post*, 14 Jan. 1990, p. A35.

18. Theo Sommer, "German Identity Faces a Double Dilemma Over the Wish for Reunification," *German Tribune*, 5 July 1987, p. 5.

CHAPTER 2

1. John Backer, *Winds of History: The German Years of Lucius DuBignon Clay* (New York: Van Nostrand, 1983), p. 256.

2. U.S. Department of Commerce, "Federal Republic of Germany," *Foreign*

Economic Trends and Their Implications for the United States (Washington, D.C., 1990).

3. U.S. Department of State cable (unclassified), November 1989.

4. *Economist*, 18 Aug. 1990, p. 41.

5. U.S. Department of State, "Federal Republic of Germany," *Background Notes* (Washington, D.C., May 1989), p. 7.

6. Dept. of Commerce, "Federal Republic of Germany," p. 10.

7. Ibid., p. 11.

8. Cf. Birger Ziebell, quoted in *German Tribune*, 12 Aug. 1990: "In comparison with the total figure of $47 billion for Japanese investments abroad, however, the share of 0.9 percent is minute. The U.S.A. accounted for the lion's share (46 percent). Of the total of 2,000 takeovers carried out by Japanese firms worldwide last year, 20 took place in the Federal Republic of Germany."

9. Cf. Reinhard Fischer of Banque Paribas Capital Markets, quoted in *Wall Street Journal*, 1 Aug. 1988, p. 8: "The others are doing a lot of strategic planning and less talking than their French and Italian counterparts. They will wait and wait and wait and when they come they will come massively."

10. U.S. Department of State, "German Democratic Republic," *Background Notes* (Washington, D.C., June 1987), p. 1.

11. Quoted in *Washington Post*, 26 Nov. 1989, p. A45.

12. Quoted in U.S. Department of Commerce, "German Democratic Republic," *Foreign Economic Trends and Their Implications for the United States* (Washington, D.C., February 1989), p. 8.

13. *Economist*, 29 July 1990, p. 54.

14. Quoted in *Der Spiegel*, no. 26, 1990, p. 25.

15. Robert J. Samuelson, "Of Deutsche Marks . . . ," *Washington Post*, 21 Feb. 1990, p. A21.

16. Quoted in Gary L. Geipel, *The Political Implications of German Economic Unification*, paper presented at a conference on the Future of Germany, 18–19 June 1990 (Indianapolis: Hudson Institute, 1990), p. 6. Geipel offers a very useful summary of the types of costs associated with reunification.

17. *The Week in Germany*, 27 July 1990 (New York: German Information Center), p. 5.

18. The 1981 and 1988 figures are not precisely parallel, and tend to overstate 1988 lending. The main pattern, however, remains clear.

19. The differences between German and Japanese lending to Eastern Europe are slightly more pronounced when one subtracts $1.8 billion German lending to China in 1988 and $4.6 billion Japanese lending to China.

20. Lawrence J. Brainard, "Finance and Debt in East–West Relations: Policy Challenges in an Era of Change," in *Japan–U.S. Joint Study Group on Trade, Finance, and Technology in East–West Economic Relations* (New York: Carnegie Council on Ethics and International Affairs, 1990), p. 9.

21. Quoted in Stephen Prokesch, ''Europe Taking a Lead in Growth,'' *New York Times*, 15 Jan. 1990, p. D5.

CHAPTER 3

1. See Jeffrey Herf, ''A Political Culture in Crisis—The Case for Kohl,'' *National Interest*, no. 17 (Fall 1989): 55–62.

2. Allensbach Archives, IfD Survey 4194, Feb./Mar. 1990.

3. For a discussion of the legal status of Berlin in the G.D.R., see Ernst Luuk, *East Berlin* (Berlin: Berlin Information Center, 1988), p. 39.

4. Results of a poll by the Wickert Institute, *Berliner Morgenpost*, 24 June 1990, p. 1.

5. Consider the comment of an SPD member from West Berlin: ''After the fall of the wall, nothing better symbolizes a strong, unified Germany than the reunified world-city of Berlin.'' (Georg Leber, quoted in ''Bonn Is a Symbol of Division,'' *Berliner Morgenpost*, 24 June 1990.)

6. Economic growth has frequently been a way in which Germany sought to uncover a sense of national identity. There are many differences between the Germany of 1918 and that of 1945, the latter having made a far more thorough effort to understand its immediate past history. Nevertheless, one can still read the judgment of Rainer Maria Rilke about the Germany of 1918 with interest: ''[She was] solely concerned with saving herself in a superficial, hasty, distrustful and greedy sense; she wanted to get moving again and work her way up and not look back.'' Quoted in Wolfgang Leppman, *Rilke: A Life* (New York: Fromm, 1984), p. 325.

7. Werner Weidenfeld, *The German National Identity*, Occasional Paper No. 2-86 (Bonn: Konrad Adenauer Stiftung, 1986), pp. 7–8.

8. Ibid., p. 8.

9. Marion Gräfin Dönhoff, ''Christian Democrats Review Reunification and Rapprochement in Europe,'' *Die Zeit*, reprinted in *German Tribune*, 17 Apr. 1988, p. 4.

10. Allenbach Archives, IfD Survey 5030.

11. Reported in Michael Lind, ''German Fate and Allied Fears,'' *National Interest*, no. 19 (Spring 1990): 35.

CHAPTER 4

1. Cf. the remarks of the European Community representative in Bonn, Gerd Langguth, *German Unification and European Integration* (Washington, D.C.: Konrad Adenauer Foundation, June 1990), p. 4.

2. Christoph Bertram, "The German Question," *Foreign Affairs*, 69(2) (Spring 1990): 55.

3. Ibid., p. 55.

4. William E. Odom, *Germany, America, and Europe in the 1990s: The Strategic Connection* (Alexandria, Va.: Hudson Institute, May 1990), p. 6.

5. Cf. a 1989 poll which found that 86 percent of West Germans between the ages of 15 and 24 favored complete denuclearization of West Germany, and 78.5 percent favored a West German role in the "vanguard of disarmament." Reported in Josef Joffe, "The Revisionists: Moscow, Bonn, and the European Balance," *National Interest*, no. 17 (Fall 1989): 49.

CHAPTER 5

1. Adam Meyerson, "Atoms for Peace: Truman Was Right to Drop the Bomb," *Policy Review*, no. 33 (Summer 1985): 47.

2. See James Fallows, "Getting Along with Japan," *Atlantic*, December 1989, p. 55.

3. Cf. Paul Kennedy, *The Rise and Fall of the Great Powers* (New York: Random House, 1987) p. 365.

4. See Herman Kahn, *The Emerging Japanese Superstate: Challenge and Response* (Englewood Cliffs, N.J.: Prentice-Hall, 1970).

5. If one leaves aside U.S. corporations, 195 of the 500 largest corporations in the world are Japanese. *Forbes*, 23 July 1990.

6. Cf. Daniel Burstein, Testimony before the Committee on Banking, Housing, and Urban Affairs, United States Senate, 14 Nov. 1989.

7. Japan Economic Institute, Report No. 8A, 23 Feb. 1990, p. 4.

8. See, for example, "Japanese May Be Rich, But Are They Satisfied with Quality of Life?" *Wall Street Journal*, 9 Jan. 1990, p. A1.

9. See Ezra F. Vogel, "Pax Nipponica?" *Foreign Affairs*, 64(4) (Spring 1986): 752–767.

10. Nicholas Valery, "A Survey of Japanese Technology," *Economist*, 2 Dec. 1989, p. 4.

11. Ibid., p. 4.

12. Ibid., p. 7.

13. "Both government and private forecasters have underestimated the growth of GNP in FY 1989 because they were too pessimistic concerning plant and equipment spending. The greater-than-expected vigor with which firms have modernized and expanded capacity over the last year has led to a variety of favorable results." Japan Econ. Inst., Report 8A, p. 4.

14. Burstein, Testimony to Senate Banking Committee, p. 3.

15. "This growth [in GNP] is underpinned particularly by the high rate of domestic

investment. Companies have been pouring money into new plants and equipment to raise their efficiency—a trend which will have a big impact on Japan's external competitiveness as well. 'Japan's industrial investment will produce a surge in productivity. This is not to be underestimated,' said Dr. Paul Summerville, an economist with Jardine Fleming Securities.'' *Financial Times*, 9 July 1990, "Japan," V. Or consider Jasper Koll, chief economist for S.G. Warburg Securities in Tokyo: "The quantum leap that will happen in two or three years will be breathtaking.'' Quoted in *Washington Post*, 13 Feb., 1990, p. A15.

16. Burstein, Testimony to Senate Banking Committee, pp. 2–3.

17. Peter Drucker, "Peter Drucker's 1990s: The Futures that Have Already Happened,'' *Economist*, 21 Oct. 1989, p. 19.

18. Ibid., p. 19.

19. Cf. Jeffrey E. Garten, "Japan and Germany: American Concerns,'' *Foreign Affairs*, 68(5) (Winter 1989–1990): 94.

20. This is a modest supposition. Cf. Japan Econ. Inst., Report 8A, p. 9: "Many experts remain convinced that the long-run movement is toward a stronger yen, perhaps to the ¥100 = $1.00 level.''

21. Quoted in *Washington Post*, 5 Nov. 1989, p. C4.

22. Ibid., p. C4.

CHAPTER 6

1. See, for example, Henry Kissinger, "The Great Foreign Policy Divide,'' *Washington Post*, 24 Nov. 1987, p. A23: "Japan, Western Europe, China and possibly India all have the capacity to become major players by the end of the century.''

2. "Asia's New Fire-Breather,'' *Business Week*, 10 Oct., 1988, p. 55.

3. Cf. William B. Bader and Jeffrey T. Bergner, *The Taiwan Relations Act: A Decade of Implementation* (Indianapolis: Hudson Institute/SRI International, 1989), pp. 143–149.

4. Jimmy W. Wheeler and Perry L. Wood, *ASEAN and Southeast Asian Security in the 1990s: Implications for U.S. Interests* (Indianapolis: Hudson Institute, 1989), p. 305.

5. Peter Drucker, "Peter Drucker's 1990s: The Futures that Have Already Happened,'' *Economist*, 21 Oct. 1989, p. 21.

6. "Survey,'' *Economist*, 2 Dec. 1989, p. 4.

7. Cf. Japan Economic Institute, Report No. 31A, 11 Aug. 1989, pp. 17–18: "Japanese investors do not appear overly anxious to diversify their manufacturing investments in developing countries beyond Asia, except insofar as ventures in Latin America can tap into the U.S. market and investments in the Middle East can secure valuable oil supplies. Even a cursory look at investment figures shows that, despite the popular perception of Japanese businesses 'buying up' the world,

firms actually are proceeding cautiously in areas that are politically unstable or culturally different.''

8. *Report of the Development Assistance Committee*, Organization for Economic Cooperation and Development, 1990.

9. See Ernest H. Preeg, *The Tied Aid Credit Issue: U.S. Export Competitiveness in Developing Countries* (Washington, D.C.: Center for Strategic and International Studies, 9[11] 1989), p. 9: "Engineering services, for example, are key to establishing engineering specifications for equipment procurement and managing overall project design and implementation. Japan, as a consequence, ties the engineering/consultancy portion of capital project loans to Japanese engineering firms while opening much of the procurement to international competitive bidding. Once the detailed engineering specifications are drawn up by a Japanese firm, procurement of major capital equipment is awarded de facto to Japanese suppliers."

10. Cf. Jeffrey Bergner, "Foreign Assistance," in *U.S. Aid to the Developing World*, ed. Doug Bandow (Washington, D.C.: Heritage Foundation, 1985), pp. 25–41.

11. Cf., for example, John Beck, "Increasing Stake in Aircraft Industry," *Japan Times Weekly*, internatl. ed., 13–19 Aug. 1990, p. 11.

12. Cf. Preeg, *Tied Aid*, p. 19: "The Japanese development assistance strategy is thus based squarely on the trade/aid interface."

13. "Japan Becomes Asia's Main Economic Power," *Washington Post*, 14 Oct. 1988, p. 32.

14. For an exposition of the view that national boundaries no longer "matter," see Kenichi Ohmae, *The Borderless World* (New York: Harper Business, 1989).

15. *Japan Times Weekly*, internatl. ed., 16–22 July 1990, p. 22.

16. Jeffrey E. Garten, "Japan and Germany: American Concerns," *Foreign Affairs*, 68(5) (Winter 1989–1990): 95.

17. In *The Japan that Can Say "No"* (New York: Simon and Schuster, 1991), Shintaro Ishihara develops a similar point. He argues that those Asian nations that are now most successful all were at one time under Japanese domination. He argues further that nations like the Philippines, which have been dominated by the United States, are least successful.

CHAPTER 7

1. See Tetsuya Kataoka and Ramon H. Myers, *Defending an Economic Superpower: Reassessing the U.S.–Japan Security Alliance* (Boulder, Colo.: Westview Press, 1989), p. 11.

2. Quoted in Kataoka, *Economic Superpower*, pp. 13–14.

3. Quoted in Robert C. Christopher, *The Japanese Mind* (New York: Fawcett Columbine, 1983), p. 213.

4. Karel G. van Wolferen, "The Japanese Problem," *Foreign Affairs*, 65(2)

(Winter 1986–1987): 289. See also his book *The Enigma of Japanese Power* (New York: Alfred A. Knopf, 1989).

5. Wolferen, "Japanese Problem," p. 289.

6. Keiwa Okuda, quoted in *Japan Times Weekly*, internatl. ed., 28 May–3 June 1990, p. 6.

7. The fingerprinting requirement for third-generation Koreans was eliminated prior to Korean President Roh Tae Woo's 1990 state visit to Japan. The first- and second-generation requirement is being "studied" for possible abolition.

8. Quoted in "Japan's Koreans Still Struggling," *Washington Post*, 20 May 1990, p. A33.

9. Quoted in *Japan Times Weekly*, internatl. ed., 30 Apr.–6 May 1990, p. 6. One is tempted to ask what are the defining characteristics in these latter areas as well.

10. Gerald Curtis, director of Columbia University's East Asia Institute, says: "Japanese voters looked at the possibility of an opposition government and said, 'No thanks,' or, at least, 'Not yet.' This was a vote of no-confidence in the opposition." Quoted in *Washington Post*, 20 Feb. 1990, p. A12.

11. Shintaro Ishihara, *The Japan that Can Say "No": The New U.S.–Japan Relations Card* (New York: Simon and Schuster, 1991). This work, written with Akio Morita, president of Sony, has received widespread criticism, as has Ishihara. But no amount of ad hominem attacks, and no amount of deprecating his role in the Liberal Democratic Party can detract from the merit of his point of view.

12. Robert Christopher, quoted in William Raspberry, "Matter-of-Fact Racism in Japan," *Washington Post*, 5 Aug. 1988, p. A23.

13. Christopher, *The Japanese Mind*, p. 55.

14. Cf. *Washington Post*, 3 July 1988, p. A29.

15. Cf. Jeffrey E. Garten, "Japan and Germany: American Concerns," *Foreign Affairs*, 68(5) (Winter 1989–1990): 89. See also U.S. Department of State, "Japan," *Background Notes* (Washington, D.C., Feb. 1989), p. 5.

16. Christopher, *The Japanese Mind*, p. 321.

17. In asking why Japan has been so cavalier about manifest unfairness in its trade policies, James Fallows refers to "the weakness of 'universal principles' in Japan—of the view that Japanese lives run according to the same rules of human beings' lives around the world.

18. Lee Hong Koo, quoted in *Washington Post*, 15 May 1990, p. A14.

19. Cf. Christopher, *The Japanese Mind*, p. 55: "There are many institutions elsewhere in the world . . . which can accurately be described as 'un-American' and which in the ultimate philosophic sense would remain un-American even if they were somehow imposed on this country. But in the philosophic sense, it is not really possible to speak of an un-Japanese society: a truly Japanese society— like truly Japanese behavior—is whatever the Japanese consensus holds it to be at any given period."

20. Karel van Wolferen argues that Japan cannot therefore command respect that

derives from the universal validity of its ideals, but only by the accommodation that foreigners make in order to display their "understanding" of Japan. "Japan Problem," p. 300.

21. Cf. Christopher, *The Japanese Mind*, p. 31: "It would be folly to assume that another radical transformation of Japanese society is a total impossibility—particularly under the kind of outside impetus that a breach with the United States would provide."

CHAPTER 8

1. For a good discussion of Article IX, see Edward A. Olsen, *U.S.–Japan Strategic Reciprocity: A New-Internationalist View* (Stanford, Ca.: Hoover Institution, 1985), pp. 78–81.

2. Ibid., p. 79.

3. Prime Minister Nakasone suggested that sending Japan's minesweepers into the Persian Gulf would be constitutionally permissible.

4. Professor Shindo Eiichi of Tsukuba University says, "By the standardized NATO calculations of military expenditure, Japan is spending 1.7 percent of its gross national product on defense." Quoted in "Japan's Defense Plan Rattles Its Neighbors," *Washington Times*, 6 June 1988, p. A11.

5. In fact, Japan's capacities are now greater in some aspects than those of the U.S. Seventh Fleet, whose mission includes the Western Pacific and the Indian Ocean. See Gary K. Reynolds, "Japan's Military Buildup: Goals and Accomplishments," Congressional Research Service Report (Washington, D.C., 27 Jan. 1989), pp. 10–11.

6. Malcolm Currie, quoted in *Defense News*, 16 Oct. 1989, p. 3.

7. U.S. Department of Defense, *Soviet Military Power: Prospects for Change* (Washington, D.C., 1989), pp. 136–139.

8. U.S. Department of Defense, *A Strategic Framework for the Asian Pacific Rim: Looking Toward the 21st Century* (Washington, D.C.: April 1989), p. 10.

9. Ibid., p. 19.

10. "In Self-Defense," *Business Tokyo*, no.2 (Feb. 1988), pp. 50–51.

11. Cf. John Phillips, "Japan's Military Plan Stresses Cooperation with U.S.," *Armed Forces Journal International*, June 1989, p. 104.

12. "In Self-Defense," pp. 50–53.

13. Ibid., p. 52.

14. Larry A. Niksch, "Japanese Attitudes Toward Defense and Security Issues," Congressional Research Service Report (Washington, D.C., 7 July 1981): "Spokesmen for such organizations as the Federation of Employer's Associations, the Kansai Economic Federation, and the Japan Chamber of Commerce and Industry have proposed such steps as higher defense budgets, more indigenous arms production, and a lifting of the ban on export of arms."

15. U.S. Department of Defense, *Defense Industrial Cooperation with Pacific Rim Nations*, Report of the Defense Science Board (Washington, D.C., Oct. 1989).

16. Quoted in *Defense News*, 16 Oct 1989, p. 3.

17. Cf. George Packard, "The Coming U.S.-Japan Crisis," *Foreign Affairs*, 66(2) (Winter 1987–1988): 357.

18. Cf. Roland Freudenstein, "Die FSX-Kontroverse zwischen den USA und Japan," *Europa Archiv: Zeitschrift für Internationale Politik*, 18 (25 Sept. 1989), p. 560.

19. Ibid., p. 560.

20. Quoted in Aurelia George, *The Nakasone Challenge: Historical Constraints and New Initiatives in Japan's Defense Policy*, Discussion Paper 2, Legislative Research Service, Parliamentary Library, Commonwealth of Australia, 1986–1987, p. 24.

21. John Lehman, quoted in George, *Nakasone Challenge*, p. 33.

22. George, *Nakasone Challenge*, p. 33.

23. Ibid., p. 33.

24. Ibid., p. 33.

25. Quoted in "National Budget Rises Sharply," *Japan Times Weekly*, internatl. ed., 6–12 Aug. 1990, p. 5.

26. Quoted in *Defense News*, 18 Dec. 1989, p. 1.

27. Quoted in *New York Times*, 6 Mar. 1989, p. A6.

28. Even during the height of the Soviet buildup, opinion polls found large pluralities of Japanese who doubted that the U.S. would aid Japan if Japan were attacked. See Niksch, "Japanese Attitudes," p. 26.

29. George, *Nakasone Challenge*, p. 9.

30. Cf. Larry A. Niksch, "*Japan–U.S. Relations* in the 1990's," Congressional Research Service Report (Washington, D.C., 7 Apr. 1989), pp. 14, 18. Cf. also Harold Brown, *U.S.–Japan Relations: Technology, Economies, and Security*, U.S./Japan Economic Agenda (New York: Carnegie Council on Ethics and International Affairs, 1987).

31. Malcolm McIntosh, *Japan Re-armed* (New York: St. Martin's, 1986), p. 18.

32. Ibid., p. 19.

33. Ibid., p. 19.

34. Ibid., p. 64. The report was titled "Concerning Our Nation's Independent Defense and Its Potential Power."

35. Brown, *U.S.–Japan Relations*, p. 20.

36. Virginia H. Ezell, "Japan's Space Program Takes Off," *Journal of Defense and Diplomacy*, Sept. 1988, p. 18.

37. "North Korea Gaining Nuclear Capability," *Defense News*, 19 Mar. 1990, p. 16.

CONCLUSION

1. George Shultz, "New Realities and New Ways of Thinking," *Foreign Affairs*, 63(4) (Spring 1985): 705.

2. Edward N. Luttwak, "From Geopolitics to Geo-Economics," *National Interest*, no. 20 (Summer 1990): 17–23.

3. Cf. William E. Odom, *Germany, America, and Europe in the 1990s: The Strategic Connection* (Alexandria, Va.: Hudson Institute, May 1990), p. 29.

4. Jim Hershberg, "A Pan-European Military?" *Washington Post*, 17 June 1990, p. D3.

5. Senator Bill Roth of Delaware added an amendment to the 1990 Senate defense authorization bill requiring the secretary of defense to study the use of U.S. military bases for NATO training and exercises. In his judgment, this would provide additional uses for some U.S. military bases that might otherwise be closed.

7. Paul Kennedy, *The Rise and Fall of the Great Powers* (New York: Random House, 1987), pp. 330, 332.

8. George Kennan, *American Diplomacy: 1900–1950* (Chicago: University of Chicago Press, 1951), pp. 43ff.

8. Quoted in *National Journal*, 14 July 1990, p. 1742.

9. Cf. Lawrence Eagleburger and Warren Christopher, "To the President, Subject: Foreign Policy," in *American Agenda* (Camp Hill, Pa.: Book-of-the-Month Club, 1988), p. 93: "It is our view that the past efforts of the United States to push Japan to increase its percentage of GNP devoted to defense have run their course and should not be continued for reasons relating to the United States' own long-term interests." Eagleburger is the current deputy secretary of state, and Christopher former deputy secretary.

10. James Fallows, *Atlantic*, Dec. 1989, pp. 53–54.

11. Major General Henry Stackpole, commanding general of U.S. Marine forces in Japan, said publicly in March 1990 that the U.S. should stay in Japan for another decade.

12. Fred Hiatt, "Cheney's Message to Asia: Troop Cuts, But No Withdrawal," *Washington Post*, 24 Feb. 1990, p. A21.

13. Perry L. Wood, "No 'Peace Dividend' in Southeast Asia," Hudson Institute Briefing Paper No. 118, 29 Mar. 1990, p. 2.

14. Indeed, with the exception of putting down insurrections in East Berlin, Budapest, and Prague, the troops of the Soviet Union were never directly used in combat until Afghanistan. That conflict provided a good corrective to overestimations of their capabilities. In Afghanistan, Soviet forces revealed what should have been suspected—that they had many weaknesses.

15. This issue is well summarized in John H. Makin, "American Economic and Military Leadership in the Postwar Period," in *Sharing World Leadership? A New Era for America and Japan*, ed. John H. Makin and Donald C. Hellman (Washington, D.C.: American Enterprise Institute, 1989), pp. 11–18.

16. Cf. Francis M. Bator, "Must We Retrench?" *Foreign Affairs*, 68(2) (Spring 1989): 107: "The level of defense spending is of secondary importance. Because consumption has at present a share of GNP ten times that of defense, large relative changes in the defense budget give rise to small relative changes in consumption. For example, increasing defense spending in step with potential output, from $295 billion in 1987 to $345 billion in 1993, would reduce the consumption of the representative family in 1993 by only $625 below the nearly $40,000 that it otherwise could be. Conversely, were we to reduce the share of defense in potential output to its 30-year low of 4.8 percent, the resulting $39-billion saving in defense spending would allow the representative family to increase its consumption by only $488."

17. Samuel P. Huntington, "The U.S.—Decline or Renewal?" *Foreign Affairs*, 67(2) (Winter 1988–1989): 87. See also Murray Weidenbaum, "Why Defense Spending Doesn't Matter," *National Interest*, no. 16 (Summer 1989): 91–96.

18. Tetsuya Kataoka and Ramon H. Myers, *Defending an Economic Superpower: Reassessing the U.S.–Japan Security Alliance* (Boulder, Colo.: Westview Press, 1989), p. 21.

19. Huntington, "Decline or Renewal?" p. 88.

20. Cf. General John Robinson, quoted in *Defense News*, 29 Jan. 1990, p. 35.

21. U.S. forces in Africa, the Near East, and South Asia totaled only 6, 457 men in 1989. U.S. Department of Defense, *Defense 89* (Washington, D.C., 1989), p. 26.

22. Cf. Bernard Lewis, "The Roots of Muslim Rage," *Atlantic*, Sept. 1990, pp. 47–60.

23. Recent wars or hostilities in the region have included those between: Morocco and the Polisario; Libya and virtually all her neighbors; Ethiopia and Eritrea; Iran and Iraq; Iraq and Kuwait; India and Pakistan; and the Soviet Union and Afghanistan.

24. Cf. Zbigniew Brzezinski, "Entering the Age of Defense," *Washington Post*, 2 Oct. 1988, p. C2.

25. Cf. Paul Volcker, "Who Says We Can't Pay the Costs of Leadership?" *Washington Post*, 17 Dec. 1989, p. B1.

26. Several recent articles have discussed this problem. See William G. Hyland, "America's New Course," *Foreign Affairs*, 69(2) (Spring 1990): 1–12, and Charles William Maynes, "America Without the Cold War," *Foreign Policy*, no. 78 (Spring 1990): 3–25.

27. Kennan, *American Diplomacy*, p. 65.

28. Luigi Barzini, *The Europeans* (New York: Simon and Schuster, 1983), p. 200.

Index

Australia–New Zealand–U.S.
(ANZUS) pact, 206
Austria, 42, 87, 88

Bad Godesberg Program, 68, 157
Bangkok, 150
Banks, 60, 63, 84
Barzini, Luigi, 25, 104
"Basic Law" of West Germany,
37, 98
Basic Treaty (1972), 39, 40, 41
Bator, Francis M., 250*n16*
Belgium, 90
Berlin, 242*nn*; blockade, 5, 7,
36–37, 76, 212; as capital of
unified Germany, 74–78;
division of, 31; politics in, 68;
Soviets and, 67; voting in, 74;
Wall, 39, 41, 79, 81, 242*n5*
Bertram, Christoph, 86–87
Bipolar world, 1–24, 193
Boeing, 145
Brazil, xix
Brezhnev, Leonid, 12, 17, 22,
197
Britain, xiv, 14, 46, 49, 90, 157,
162, 200, 201–2; and division
of Germany, 31, 33, 35, 41;
and EC, 84, 85–86; and
nuclear weapons, 97, 98
Brown, Harold, 191
Bundeswehr, xiv, 92, 93
Burma, 146
Bush, George, xiv
Business: and government, in
Japan, 158; largest, 115,
243*n5*; new, in East Germany,
58, 98

Cam Ranh Bay, 182
Capital investment, 119, 120
Carter, Jimmy, 13–14
Central America, 9, 11
Cheney, Richard, 210
Chernenko, Konstantin, 17, 22
China, People's Republic, xiv,
xix, 109, 118, 126, 129,
241*n19*; and Japan, 132–36,
146, 171; military, 134, 174,
188; and nuclear weapons, 98;
and Soviet Union, 10, 13, 16,
206
Christian Democratic Party (CDU)
of West Germany, 67, 68, 69,
70, 72, 73, 74; and Christian
Social Union (CDU/CSU)
alliance, 14, 163
Christopher, Robert, 166, 167,
168, 246*n19*, 247*n21*
Christopher, Warren, 249*n9*
Churchill, Winston, 20, 37, 105
Clay, Gen. Lucius, 35
Cold War, 35, 37, 86, 90, 155,
208, 218, 223
Commercial aircraft production,
145
Communism, 11, 23, 153, 154
Communist Party of East
Germany, 75
Communist Party of Japan, 163
Communist Party of West
Germany, 67, 68, 75
Community, 150–51
Competitiveness, 214, 219–21
Conference on Security and
Cooperation in Europe
(CSCE), 203
Conservatives, Japanese, 154